THE ENTREPRENEUR AND SMALL BUSINESS MARKETING PROBLEM SOLVER

OTHER BOOKS BY WILLIAM A. COHEN

THE EXECUTIVE'S GUIDE TO FINDING A SUPERIOR JOB (Amacom)

BUILDING A MAIL ORDER BUSINESS (John Wiley & Sons)

TOP EXECUTIVE PERFORMANCE (*with Nurit Cohen*) (John Wiley & Sons)

MAKING IT BIG AS A CONSULTANT (Amacom)

WINNING ON THE MARKETING FRONT (John Wiley & Sons)

DEVELOPING A WINNING MARKETING PLAN (John Wiley & Sons)

THE STUDENT'S GUIDE TO FINDING A SUPERIOR JOB (Avant Books)

THE PRACTICE OF MARKETING MANAGEMENT (Macmillan Publishing Co.)

THE ENTREPRENEUR AND SMALL BUSINESS FINANCIAL PROBLEM SOLVER
(John Wiley & Sons)

THE ART OF THE LEADER (Prentice-Hall)

THE ENTREPRENEUR AND SMALL BUSINESS PROBLEM SOLVER (John Wiley & Sons)

THE ENTREPRENEUR AND SMALL BUSINESS MARKETING PROBLEM SOLVER

William A. Cohen

John Wiley & Sons Inc.

New York • Chichester • Brisbane • Toronto • Singapore

Library of Congress Cataloging-in-Publication Data:
Cohen, William A.,
    The entrepreneur and small business marketing problem solver /
William A. Cohen.
        p. cm.
    Includes index.
    ISBN 0-471-53133-2 (paper)
        1. Marketing—Management. 2. Small business—Management.
I. Title.
HF5415.13.C634   1991
658.8—dc20   91-13562

Printed in the United States of America
10 9 8 7 6 5 4 3 2 1

This book is decicated to
the memory of my mother,
Theresa B. Cohen

═══ ACKNOWLEDGMENTS ═══

I wish to thank the U.S. Small Business Administration, especially the staff at the Los Angeles Office, the U.S. Department of Labor, the U.S. Copyright Office of the Library of Commerce, the U.S. Department of Commerce Patent and Trademark Office, and many others, through whose courtesy many of the excellent checklists, bibliographies, sources, and other information published by the U.S. Government were obtained.

W.A.C.

═ PREFACE ═══════════════════════════

When I first started my entrepreneurial activities some years ago, much of the information that I wanted to know about business simply wasn't in one place where I could get hold of it easily. As a result, in order to get the answers to my numerous questions, I spent many hours over many days at several different libraries. This was not only a waste of time; it actually cost me money. Countless opportunities were lost because I did not obtain the information until it was too late to be of use.

To save other entrepreneurs from having to go through the same trouble, I wrote *The Entrepreneur and Small Business Problem Solver*. It became a best seller, and is currently in its second edition. But the information contained in that book was massive. I couldn't put in everything that I wanted to on marketing. My editor and I put our heads together and decided to develop separate books on each of these areas. *The Entrepreneur and Small Business Marketing Problem Solver* is part of this solution. Not only is the book updated, it contains new chapters on mail order and government marketing, and a complete sample marketing plan is in the appendix.

As a marketing professor and Director of the Small Business Institute at California State University Los Angeles, as well as a management consultant for small and large businesses, I am continually amazed at the variety of information about small business and the starting of small businesses required by investors, entrepreneurs, and established small businesspeople. Most of this information is available . . . somewhere. However, it must be obtained at the cost of two of your most precious resources: time or money. Either you must spend your valuable time, or a management consultant must be hired at $100 an hour or more to provide the answer. Sometimes a consultant's expertise is needed and well worth the fee. But many times the answer is simple and easily understood—if only you knew where to look.

The purpose of this book is to place this essential information about marketing at your fingertips. In it I have gathered together the answers to the questions having to do with marketing most frequently asked of me by business clients and entrepreneurs whom I help. The book is designed to do the following things for you:

1. Save hours, days, and perhaps months of research for any marketing problem that you want answered.

2. Save the cost of hiring consultants when such consultants are not necessary to solve your problem.
3. Enable you to know when and how to get help if you do need it, and how to do so at the lowest possible cost.

In one sentence, the book's purpose is this: It was written to help you to be successful in marketing with your small business or entrepreneurial project. Each chapter was designed to stand by itself and assist you with a certain class of marketing problems. Chapter 1 covers marketing research. Marketing research is very important. It can determine how to make your business successful without a huge investment in money. Chapter 2 shows you how to find and introduce a new product. Chapter 3 tells you the right way to price your product or service. Chapter 4 gives you the complete story on advertising and publicity, and how each can be accomplished at a low cost. Chapter 5 discusses the important area of personal selling and how to develop your own sales force. Chapter 6 is all about the use of trade shows to promote your products. Trade shows can really boost your sales. Chapter 7 takes you step-by-step through the development of your own marketing plan. Chapter 8 describes important mail order secrets for selling your products or services, and many entrepreneurs have made their fortunes that way. Chapter 9 is about selling your products or services to the U.S. government. That's a multibillion dollar market buying everything from toys to weaponry.

In the appendixes you will find addresses and phone numbers of important government agencies, and trade associations and better business bureaus that can assist you in different ways with your marketing. You will also find a complete sample marketing plan. My students who have prepared marketing plans like this have sold them for $5,000 or more.

A glance at the chapter titles and subheadings will give you some idea of the concrete assistance this book can give to anyone interested in beginning a small business or anyone who has already established one. Throughout, specific examples have been used to show you step-by-step what to do, and forms and checklists are amply supplied.

If this book doesn't save you at least five times its cost the first time you use it, I will be surprised. If the use of the book enables you either to save or make at least 1,000 times its price during the years you use it, I won't be surprised at all.

Pasadena, California   WILLIAM A. COHEN
September 1991

CONTENTS

CHAPTER 1

MARKETING RESEARCH

MARKETING RESEARCH—WHAT IT IS AND HOW IT CAN MAKE MONEY FOR YOU

Marketing research is the gathering, recording, and analyzing of information about problems relating to marketing. It will help you to identify who your market is as well as which methods will best satisfy the needs of your market. But it encompasses many other aspects of marketing, including new product introductions, pricing, advertising, consumer behavior, and so on. So important is marketing research that certain basic marketing strategies, such as market segmentation, in which you identify a specific portion of the market and concentrate your resources on selling to that one segment, or product differentiation, in which you differentiate your product from that of a competitor in such a way as to best appeal to potential buyers, would be absolutely impossible without it.

Among the many things that marketing research will tell you are the following:

1. Who are your customers and who are your potential customers?
2. What kinds of people are your customers? (This includes demographic categories, such as age, income, and education, and psychographic categories, such as interests and preferences.)
3. Where do your customers live?
4. Why do your customers buy?
5. Do they have the ability to pay?
6. Are you offering the kinds of goods and services that your customers want?
7. Are you offering your products or services at the best place, at the best time, and in the correct amounts?
8. Are your prices consistent with the value your customers place on the product or service that you are selling?

9. How are your promotional programs working?
10. What do your customers think of your business and its image?
11. How do your business and your business procedures compare with those of your
    competitors?[1]

Correct use of marketing research can mean amazing profits for your business and tremendous advantages over your competitors. A famous example took place in the early 1960s. Ford, along with two other major American motor companies, had developed cars to compete with foreign cars such as the Volkswagen. Ford's entry had been the Falcon, introduced in 1959. As the years passed, the numbers of Ford Falcons that were sold began to decrease as a percentage of Ford's total sales. This was also true for the competing cars offered by the two other American companies. Ford might simply have concluded that American small cars were no longer wanted. Instead, Ford did marketing research to find out more about the falling off of Falcon sales. During this research, Ford discovered an interesting and important fact: while sales of the Falcon were declining, sales of sporty options such as bucket seats and a special interior were increasing. This was due primarily to the greater numbers of young adults who were purchasing the vehicle. Ford's careful study of the market research findings led the company to put out the Ford Mustang, introduced in 1965. This sporty vehicle demolished all previous records for sales and developed a new market after which competitors followed as best they could, some two to three years behind. The head of Ford's Mustang project was none other than a young engineer by the name of Lee Iacocca.

But successful use of marketing research is not limited to major companies such as Ford. Thousands of small firms and entrepreneurs have used marketing research successfully to carve out huge shares of their respective markets. An optical firm totally turned its company around and doubled sales within a year by identifying its customers. A mail order entrepreneur sold $10 million worth of a single product through marketing research techniques. A small computer firm successfully took on IBM for a segment of the total computer market and won through the correct application of marketing research.

In this chapter you will learn the same techniques used so successfully by these and other firms.

THREE IMPORTANT CATEGORIES OF MARKETING RESEARCH

Three categories of marketing research important to any small business are internal information, secondary research, and primary research. Let's look at each in turn.

---

[1] Adapted from J. Ford Laumer, Jr., James R. Harris, and Hugh J. Guffer, Jr., *Learning About Your Market*, Small Business Administration (1979).

Internal Information

Internal information is extremely useful because it is generally close at hand and costs you little or nothing to obtain. Therefore, before thinking about expensive field experiments or surveys, look at your own records and files. These include: sales records, receipts, complaints, all of the records noted in the record-keeping section of this book, and anything else that shows and tells about your customers, what they are interested in, and what they buy. One source of information is your customers' addresses. This alone will tell a great deal about them—not only where they live, but also their income and life-styles. This information can be of great assistance to you in determining what your customers will be interested in buying. The most successful mail order firms make millions not by selling a single product once to a customer, but by selling numerous products to their customer list again and again.

Secondary Research

Secondary research concerns information already available outside your company. The key here is its availability. It has already been put together by someone else. This information may have been collected by other firms or government agencies, and may be found in books, newspapers, and a host of other sources. But the important fact is that this information is already available. Someone else has done the work; that's why it's called "secondary" research. It costs you little or nothing to obtain. You don't have to design the survey method. You don't have to do the interviewing. And you don't have to spend time and resources collecting this information yourself. Where can you find this information? At the end of this chapter you will find over 100 sources of statistics, studies accomplished, and secondary research that you can analyze to obtain more facts regarding your customers. You can also purchase completed marketing research reports. Three firms that sell such reports are:

1. Cambridge Information Group
    Findex
    7200 Wisconsin Ave.
    Bethesda, MD 20814
2. Mediamark Research, Inc.
    708 Third Ave.
    New York, NY 10017
3. Off-the-Shelf Publications, Inc.
    2171 Jericho Turnpike
    Commack, NY 11725

Primary Research

Perhaps you have already looked at the cheaper and easier research methods—your internal records and secondary sources of information—and found that the specific information that you need simply isn't available. In this case, you must do the research yourself or hire someone else to do it for you. The means of getting this information, specifically tailored to your needs, is called primary research.

EXPLORATORY VERSUS SPECIFIC RESEARCH

There are two basic types of research that you should consider once the decision is made that primary research is necessary. One type is called *exploratory research*, and the other, *specific research*. Exploratory research is aimed at helping you to define the problem. It is typically done through in-depth interviews with a relatively small number of people. Questions are asked that invite detailed, lengthy answers from the respondents. These interviews tend to be nonstructured, freewheeling, and open-ended. One example of exploratory research was accomplished by a soup company some time ago. The basic promotion had been that a customer would receive a free pair of nylons for trying the soup. But the promotion—and thus the soup—had failed. In-depth interviews were conducted with a limited number of customers to discover the answer. From this limited research, the result was found that an image of "feet in soup" had resulted. This error in consumer behavior psychology had caused the promotion for the new product to fail.

Specific research is used when the basic problem has already been defined. It focuses on ways of solving the problem. Specific research typically uses much larger samples than exploratory research, and because of this it tends to be much more expensive. The interviews used with specific research are very structured, complete, and of formal design. Following the example of the soup, specific research would be conducted to find out what promotion to offer, that is, what premium, if any, to give to consumers for trying the new product. The respondent might be given a number of choices from which to select his or her preference.

THE MARKETING RESEARCH PROCESS

The marketing research process can be divided into certain steps:

1. Define the problem
2. Decide whether marketing research is needed
3. Identify objectives
4. State specific data to be obtained

5. Design the research instrument to be used
6. Decide on the sample
7. Collect the data
8. Tabulate and analyze
9. Draw conclusions and decide on courses of action

Define the Problem

You cannot proceed until you have a good definition of what your problem is, whether it be a new product introduction, identification of customers for a certain market, or whatever. This first step of the research process seems obvious and therefore many people tend to overlook it. Yet, experts tell us that it is the most important step. When defining the problem, look beyond symptoms: declining sales, declining profits, and so on. You must ask yourself: Why are sales declining? Why are profits down? List every possible reason. Could your customers be changing? Is there new competition? List all possibilities, but focus on those that can be measured. These are the ones that you can base your marketing research on. Problems that cannot be measured are not candidates for marketing research.

Decide Whether Marketing Research Is Needed

As noted previously, if you cannot measure the influence on the problem, you cannot do marketing research. But even if measurement is possible, before you decide to invest your time and treasure in marketing research, you should consider several factors: (1) Is internal or secondary research available? (2) What in general will it cost in money, resources, and time to do the research?

If the research has already been done and is available free, it makes little sense to do it over. If the research can be obtained, but at too high a cost, higher than the increase in sales or profits that may result, the research is clearly not worthwhile. The same thing is true if it will take so long to get the information that you will not be able to use it. Therefore, always recognize that doing marketing research may not be the answer to the problem that you have defined. However, if thinking through the situation shows that you can conduct research that will be of assistance in solving the problem, then proceed to the next step.

Identify Objectives

You should understand everything you can about the problem and the information you are seeking before proceeding. This will enable you to specify clearly the objective or objectives of the study that you are undertaking. You may have a single objective or you may have several. Either way, you must state it or them in the clearest possible terms. For example: "The objective of this study is to determine who is buying memberships in health clubs within 10 miles of my location."

State Specific Data to Be Obtained

Now, you must decide on exactly what information you want to obtain. If you want to know who is purchasing memberships in health clubs in a 10-mile area, you may wish to know them by (1) income, (2) education, (3) age, (4) sex, (5) occupation, (6) employment, (7) precise geographical location, (8) what type of media they read, see, or listen to, and so forth. All of this information should be specified in this section.

Design the Research Instrument to Be Used

Now, you must decide how you will do the research. First, you must decide whether you wish to do exploratory or specific research. Then, you must decide where and how the information is to be obtained. Your questionnaire must motivate the respondents to supply the information you want, sometimes concealing the reasons for obtaining it so as not to introduce extraneous factors into the results. It can have several different forms: it may be a set of questions designed to be asked over the telephone or in a personal interview, or a survey going through the mail. Each form has advantages and disadvantages, and which one to use depends on your situation. For example, a mail survey must be as short as possible, or people won't respond. The same is true for the telephone interview. But a personal face-to-face interview can be as long as an hour or more. You must also consider the complexity of the questions you will ask. For most complex questions, a personal interview is necessary. If you are handling a touchy subject, the telephone interview may be extremely difficult because the respondent may hang up. Also, the personal interview may be risky because the individual making the interview may bias the reply. In a mail interview, because you are not there to obtain feedback, you must strongly motivate the individual to answer. A self-addressed, stamped envelope is almost a necessity, to enable the respondent to send the survey back to you easily. But you don't use a postage stamp. You would waste your money if the person did not answer. Instead, use a special reply permit indicia, which you can obtain at your local post office. Even with this the respondents by mail will be far fewer than with other survey means. You must allow for this in the number of samples that you attempt to obtain. One survey that used all three methods had comparative responses as follows: mail, 15%; telephone survey, 70%; and personal interview, 80%. There are also tradeoffs regarding cost. Mail is probably the cheapest, followed by telephone. Personal interview is three times as costly as phone because an individual must go from place to place and must be compensated for his time. Use Figure 1.1 for a means of comparing the three methods in detail.

Once you've decided which type of questionnaire to construct, you must then begin to design it. Usually the questionnaire should be divided into several sections. The first section contains the basic classification data, including the name of the

Survey Aspect	Mail	Telephone	Personal Interview
Questionnaire			
Length of interview	The shorter the better	Short (15 minutes or less)	Longer (can be up to one hour or more; plus possible mail back) Usually maximum of 30 minutes
Complexity of questions	May be moderately complex	Must be simple	Can be more complex; can use cards or props
Flexibility	Poor (no feedback)	Fair	Excellent
Probing	Poor	Better	Best
Getting at reasons (determining "why")	Poor	Better	Best
Handling touchy subject	Relatively good	Risky: Respondent may hang up	Risky: Researcher or respondent may bias replies
Control of question order	Respondent may read ahead	Excellent	Excellent
Sample			
Sample bias	A real problem. Respondent usually higher in education and interest. Other biases uncertain	Underrepresents low income (no phone) and high income and others (not listed, especially in urban areas, but note random dialing)	Best, but occasionally a problem
Sample of nonrespondents	Often necessary	Usually not necessary	Usually not necessary
List availability	Must provide list of addresses	Free, renewed annually	Area sampling a problem Must get maps, population estimates by sub-areas

Figure 1.1. Comparison of mail, telephone, and personal interview data collection. (Adapted from William A. Cohen and Marshall E. Reddick, *Successful Marketing for Small Business*, Figure 4.1, pgs. 50–51 [AMACOM: New York, 1981]).

(*Figure continues on p. 8.*)

Survey Aspect	Mail	Telephone	Personal Interview
Geographic clustering	Can be controlled by zip code	Sometimes (but usually not dangerous number of clusters)	Often if reasonably large
Stratifying information	May have	Usually not available	May have income, race, etc., by area (from Census, etc.)
Interviewing			
Response rate	Low: Can be as low as 15% or so for a single mailing to general public, higher for special groups, especially professionals, and for several mailings	High: about 70%	High: about 80%
Interviewing bias and cheating by interviewer	None	Can occur. But supervisor can counteract to a considerable extent	Can occur—telephone a sample of respondents to check cheating
Identity of Respondent	Not certain	Known	Known
Administration and Cost			
Cost	Low, especially if response rate is high and telephone sample of nonresidents not necessary	Moderately expensive depending on area, and equipment used	High: three or more times cost of mail or telephone
Administrative load	Light	Heavier: must hire, train and supervise telephoners	Heaviest: must hire train, supervise, check and pay at a distance

Figure 1.1. (*Continued*)

respondent, the address, and so forth. Frequently this information can be filled in by the interviewer prior to the interview.

The introductory statement is usually the second section. It establishes rapport with the interviewee. Although it may be structured into the questionnaire section itself, if this is a personal or phone interview it should be put in the interviewer's own words so as not to sound stilted. Establishing this early rapport will make the difference between success or failure of the interview.

The next section may describe the product or service if the research has to do with your wares directly. Be careful of overselling the product here so as not to bias the results. The description should be complete and it should be factual. Generally, initial impression questions should appear first. They should be neither complicated nor personal. If the questionnaire is exploratory in nature, the questions should be open-ended without leading to any specific answers. If specific, the questions should give the respondent a choice of alternative answers. You may use attitude scales to determine the intensity of the respondents' feelings as in Figure 1.2.

It is important with products to determine buying intentions, because sometimes individuals will like a product but will not want to purchase it. If you can determine the reasons for this attitude, you may be able to change the product or service as necessary to make it successful. Product appeals are necessary to determine how to promote the product effectively. This information will help you to determine what is important to emphasize and what to deemphasize. Pricing is also a very important aspect, and here you should attempt to determine a selective demand curve for your products or your service. That is, by asking your potential customers

---

Nissan Attributes

1. Competitive purchase price	5. Serviceability
poor 1 2 3 4 5 6 7 8 9 excellent	poor 1 2 3 4 5 6 7 8 9 excellent
2. Fuel consumption	6. Distinctive modern styling and appearance
poor 1 2 3 4 5 6 7 8 9 excellent	poor 1 2 3 4 5 6 7 8 9 excellent
3. Durability	7. Riding comfort
poor 1 2 3 4 5 6 7 8 9 excellent	poor 1 2 3 4 5 6 7 8 9 excellent
4. Reliability	8. Handling characteristics
poor 1 2 3 4 5 6 7 8 9 excellent	poor 1 2 3 4 5 6 7 8 9 excellent

Figure 1.2. Example of measuring attitude intensity using scales.

about the likelihood of their purchase of the product at different prices, you can later tabulate the results and know at which price the product is demanded more than at any other. It may be difficult to get exact answers for this question, but it will certainly help to give you a general idea of the price range. You should also determine distribution channels by asking the consumer where he or she would expect to find the product. Determine the advertising medium in which he or she would expect to see, hear, or read about the product or service.

Certain information of a personal nature, such as age, education, income, and the like, should be left to the end of the questionnaire. You should be careful never to ask for a person's specific age or income or other information of this type but rather to indicate a range. Finally, at the end of the interview, deliver a friendly thank you. Your subjects deserve it.

Be certain that the information you want is contained in your questionnaire. As mentioned previously, in some cases it may be necessary to conceal what you are actually after in order to obtain unbiased responses. For example, if you are trying to determine which one of a number of products is favored by the consumer and your product is one of these, it may be important to conceal the fact that you are representing one of the products indicated in the survey.

Always consider:

- Whether your respondent has the information that you are asking for.
- Whether he or she has the necessary experience to provide you with an accurate answer.
- Whether it is likely that he or she will remember well enough to provide you with an accurate answer.
- Whether he or she will have to work hard to get the information.
- Whether he or she is likely to give you the information.
- Whether he or she is likely to give you the *true* information.

Of the many types of questions that you may use in your questionnaire, some which you may find useful are:

1. *Open-ended.* This is where you ask the question and allow the respondent to talk at some length. The question is not structured and there is no one specific answer.

2. *Multiple choice.* Here you give a number of different choices to your respondent. Each choice may be a different product or a different description of some information that you are trying to obtain. Or, in the case of demographics, it may simply be a different age group.

3. *Forced choice.* Forced choice means that you give two choices, one or the other. Sometimes it is very difficult for a respondent to give a specific answer, but you may wish to have him or her choose one of two. An example is, "Do you eat ice cream primarily (1) at home, or (2) at an ice cream parlor?"

4. *Semantic differential.* A semantic differential allows for an intensity of feelings about some statement. For example, if the subject is ice cream, you might ask a question such as this: "The XYZ brand of ice cream is . . . ?" You would then have an adjective scale ranging from "delicious" to "terrible." In between these two extreme points would be other adjectives such as "fair," and there would be different points on the scale such as in Figure 1.2.

By analyzing a number of responses, you can come up with an average for each question.

Sequencing of your questions is extremely important to ease your respondent into the questionnaire. In general, your opening questions should motivate and not challenge your respondents psychologically. As pointed out earlier, identification items fit easily into this classification.

Difficult questions should come in the body or at the end of the questionnaire. Why? First, your respondents are more at ease after they've answered some of the questions. Second, they are more accustomed to answering your questions and are less likely to hesitate.

Another important point is that earlier questions will influence questions that follow. For example, the mention of a product in one question may influence the answer to a following question. Consider this question: "ABC Soap has recently changed its formulation to be even more cleansing. Have you used this new formulation?" Let's say your next question is: "What do you think of the new ABC Soap?" You can see how the first question will influence the next question.

A summary of these guides to questionnaire preparation is provided in Figure 1.3. Figure 4.1 in Chapter 4 is a consumer profile questionnaire containing a number of questions you may want to ask regarding demographics, psychographics, lifestyle, social class, media use and interest, and other information. You can draw on this questionnaire when you design your own.

Decide on the Sample

Deciding on the sample means defining which and how many people you will survey. Whom you survey will depend on your objectives and on the method of selection of your sample subjects. For example, you may use random or nonrandom sampling. If you use random sampling, every individual from the population surveyed has an equal chance at being selected. If you use nonrandom sampling, you may select groups containing specific types of individuals, or you may simply obtain responses on the basis of availability.

The sample size decision depends upon how much confidence you have or wish to have in your results. For 100% confidence you would need to sample everyone. But of course this isn't always possible or desirable. If you can't sample randomly or sample everyone, you may try systematic sampling. That means you sample every nth element in the total population. Let's say that you are sampling customers. Perhaps you talk to every 25th or every 50th customer. Another way of handling

Very basic *classification* data can usually be filled in by the interviewer before the interview. Complicated or very personal classification data should go at the end of the questionnaire.

Name of respondent _____ Name of interviewer _____
Address _____ Date _____
Phone _____ Time _____
Other (nonpersonal) relevant data _____

The introductory statement establishes rapport with the interviewee. It should not be read, but rather put in the interviewer's own words. This introduction will make the difference between success and failure for the interview.

Good morning, my name is _____, and I am conducting a marketing study for a new product (service) called _____. The answers you give to the following questions will help determine whether or not to introduce this new product (service) idea, and what features to incorporate into the product. May I have a few minutes of your time?

Product description tells the interviewee about the product or service. It should be a complete description of the product. Do not try to oversell the product; that may bias the results.

The name of this product is _____. It is a _____, and its functions/ purposes are _____

The benefits of this product are _____

Initial impression questions should appear first. They should be uncomplicated, nonpersonal, closed-end questions. Attitude scales are used to determine the intensity of the respondents' feelings.

1. What is your immediate reaction to this idea?

Positive		*Negative*
		So-so _____
Great _____		I do not particularly like it _____
Like it very much _____		I do not like it at all _____
Like it somewhat _____		

Open-end questions are useful for determining why the person feels the way he or she does.

Why do you say that? Explain.

2. Which of the following best expresses your feeling about buying this product should it become available to you?

Positive	Negative
I'm absolutely sure I would buy it ___	I probably would not buy it ___
I'm almost sure I would buy it ___	I am almost sure I would not buy it ___
I probably would buy it ___	I am absolutely sure I would not buy it ___

Why do you say that? _____

_____

_____

3. Tell me, all things considered, what aspects of this product idea appeal to you most. What do you consider its most important advantages?

Most Appealing	Advantages
1. _____	1. _____
2. _____	2. _____
3. _____	3. _____

4. How much do you think such a product would cost? _____

5. Where would you expect to buy such a product? _____

Buying intentions are important to determine. A person may like the idea, but not want to buy it. If one can determine why not, perhaps the product can be revised to better meet their demands.

Product appeals must be determined for effective promotion of the product. Such information will indicate what to emphasize and what to deemphasize.

Pricing is an important aspect. Here one can determine a relative demand curve for the product. It is difficult for the consumer to answer this question precisely, but it should at least give the entrepreneur an ideal of the price range.

The retail outlet—where the product would most likely be found—is important.

Figure 1.3. Designing a questionnaire: summary of rules.

(Figure continues on p. 14.)

The advertising medium must also be determined. Sometimes consumers dislike a product for minor reasons, and when these reasons are alleviated, they will buy it. The more difficult, tiring questions should be placed at the end of the interview.

Classification data of a personal nature should be asked at the end of the interview. Never ask for a person's specific age or income; he or she may become suspicious of you or angry.

Always *close* with a friendly thank you.
You may wish to interview this respondent again.

6. Where would you expect such a product to be advertised? _____

7. Are there any suggestions you would care to make that you think might improve this product? _____

Classification data:
1. In what category does your age fall:
   - below 15 ___
   - 16–21 ___
   - 22–29 ___
   - 30–49 ___
   - 50–60 ___
   - over 60 ___

2. Please tell me where your total family income falls:
   - below $5,000 ___
   - $5,000–9,999 ___
   - 10,000–14,999 ___
   - 15,000–19,999 ___
   - 20,000 and above ___

3. Check one:
   - Female; single ___ married ___
   - Male; single ___ married ___

   Thank you for your cooperation!

Figure 1.3. (*Continued*)

this problem is to subdivide the total universe of people that you want sampled into a few groups that are mutually exclusive. You would then randomly sample these smaller groups. Or, you could divide the total number of people into many groups and randomly choose some of the groups for sampling. Determining how many responses you need in order to reflect the nature of the total universe of individuals you are sampling depends upon the standard deviation or dispersion of the responses the consumer may give. If you are going to use a random sampling, one way of determining sample size is with the following method.

Let us say you have a new product on the market and have introduced it into your area, in which there are 2,000 stores selling the product. The reports on the new product won't be in for a month, but you want to know how well this product is doing immediately in order to make investment and inventory decisions. One way, of course, is to survey all 2,000 stores. However, this would be needlessly expensive and time consuming. Another is to survey a certain number of stores at random. This would give us an answer useful for decision making.

The first step is to look at a few samples of the stores and calculate an average. Let us say we looked at five stores and they sold the following numbers of our new product: Store No. 1, 10 units; Store No. 2, 18 units; Store No. 3, 30 units; Store No. 4, 42 units; Store No. 5, 50 units. All together, 150 units were sold, divided by 5 equals an average of 30 units.

The second step is to decide how much accuracy we want. Let's say the accuracy that we're happy with is plus or minus 10%. This is an arbitrary figure; we could have decided on plus or minus 15%.

The third step is to calculate an acceptable limit based on an accuracy that we calculated in the previous step. Plus or minus 10% times 30 units equals plus or minus 3 units. Therefore, acceptable units of accuracy in our case are plus or minus 3 units.

The fourth step is to estimate the standard deviation of our sample. Of any normal distribution, 68% of the units will fall within one standard deviation. We've looked at five stores. Therefore, 68% times 5 is 3.4. Since we can't use a partial store, we will say that 68% times 5 stores equals 3 stores. Now, let's look at Figure 1.4 with the stores noted on it. Figure 1.4 shows that on the left, Store No. 1 is 10 units. The next in the line is Store 2 with 18 units. Then comes Store No. 3 with 30, Store No. 4 with 42, and Store No. 5 with 50. The 3 units we're looking

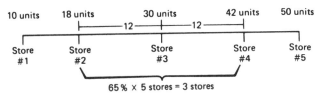

Figure 1.4. Calculating the standard deviation.

at would be stores in the center, Stores 2, 3, and 4, with 18, 30, and 42 units, respectively. We can see that the difference between 18 and 30 is 12, and the difference between 30 and 42 is 12 as well. Therefore, the standard deviation would be 12.

For the fifth step, we calculate the required sample size using the following formula, which will provide the answer at a 95% confidence level:

$$n = \left(\frac{S}{I/1.96}\right)^2 + 1$$

where: n = sample size

S = standard deviation of sample

I = acceptable limits

In our example,

$$n = \left(\frac{12}{3/1.96}\right)^2 + 1 = 64 \text{ stores}$$

What would we do if we wanted an accuracy of 15% instead of 10%? In that case, the acceptable limits would be 15% times 30 equals plus or minus 4.5 instead of plus or minus 3.

This approach is good only if our answer—64 stores divided by the total number of stores, 2,000—is less than 5%. In our case, 64 divided by 2,000 equals 0.032, or 3.2%, which is less than 5%, so we're all right. But let's say that instead of 2,000 stores there were only 200 stores. What would we do then? In this case, we adjust our answer. We do so using the following formula:

$$n^1 = \frac{n}{1 + \dfrac{n}{N}}$$

where n is our sample size, N is the total number of units surveyed, and n^1 is our adjusted sample size. In this case:

$$n^1 = \frac{n}{1 + \dfrac{n}{N}} = \frac{64}{1 + \dfrac{64}{200}} = 48.48 = \text{approx. } 48$$

If we had 200 stores selling the product instead of 2,000, we would sample 48 stores.

Collecting Data

Once the sample size has been decided upon, we can then begin to utilize the research tool that we have designed actually to collect data. Remember, if you are doing this either in person or by telephone, be neat, courteous, and professional.

Tabulation and Analysis

In this step, the data that have been collected should be tabulated according to the specific questions that we have constructed to find information. This data can then be analyzed on a percentage basis to tell us the answers to our questions. For example, our demographic analysis may show us that the majority of our customers are ages 18 to 24, and that they are single. It may also show that most of our customers have graduated from high school and taken some college courses, and that they are mostly white-collar workers. This information can be extremely important. One local record shop had been carrying large stocks of classical records for years though most of its buyers were teenagers. A dress shop that was doing poorly was offering racks of expensive dresses, which most of its customers could not afford.

Conclusions and Decisions on Courses of Action

At this point, conclusions should be drawn based on your analysis of the data as to your customers, the product, or whatever you were researching. You shouldn't stop with conclusions, but should make changes to increase your profits based on these conclusions.

Examples of Research You Can Do

The kind of marketing research you do is limited only by your imagination. Some research can be done, even of the primary type, at very little cost except for your time. Here are some examples of simple research done by small businesses which greatly increased sales. These ideas were suggested by J. Ford Laumer, Jr., James R. Harris, and Hugh J. Guffey, Jr., all professors of marketing at Auburn University of Auburn, Alabama, in their booklet *Learning About Your Market*, published by the Small Business Administration.

1. *License plate analysis.* In many states, license plates give you information about where car owners live. Therefore, simply by taking down the numbers of cars parked in your location and contacting the appropriate state agency, you can estimate the area from which you draw business. Knowing where your customers live can help you in your advertising or in targeting your approach to promotion. By the same method you can find who your competitors' customers are.

2. *Telephone number analysis.* Telephone numbers can also tell you the areas in which people live. You can obtain customers' telephone numbers from sales slips, credit card slips, or checks. Again, knowing where they live will give you excellent information about their life-styles.

3. *Coded coupons.* The effectiveness of your advertising vehicle can easily be checked by coding coupons that can be used for discounts or inquiries about products. You can find out the areas that your customers come from, as well as which vehicle brought them your message.

4. *People watching.* Simply looking at your customers can tell you a great deal about them. How are they dressed? How old are they? Are they married or single? Do they have children or not? Many owners use this method intuitively to get a feel about their customers. However, a little sophistication with a tally sheet for a week can provide much more accurate information simply, easily, and without cost. It may confirm what you've known all along, or it may completely change your picture of your typical customer.

CHECKLIST FOR APPRAISAL OF YOUR RESEARCH STUDY

Figure 1.5 is a complete checklist for appraisal of your research study. If you use it, your research should provide you with excellent results.

SOURCES OF SECONDARY RESEARCH

Following are more than 100 sources based on bibliographies but together by Lloyd M. DeBoer, Dean of the School of Business Administration at George Mason University, Fairfax, Virginia, and the Office of Management and Training of the SBA and published by the Small Business Administration as a part of two booklets, *Marketing Research Procedure*, *SBB 9*, and *National Directories for Use in Marketing*, *SBB 13*.

U.S. Government Publications

The publications in this section are books and pamphlets issued by federal agencies and listed under the issuing agency. Where availability of an individual listing is indicated by GPO (Government Printing Office), the publication may be ordered from the Superintendent of Documents, U.S. Government Printing Office, Washington, DC 20402. When ordering a GPO publication, give the title and series number of the publication, and name of agency. You may also order by phone by calling (202) 783-3238. Contact GPO for current prices.

Publications should be requested by the title and any number given from the issuing agency. Most libraries have some listings to identify currently available federal publications. Some keep a number of selected government publications for ready reference through the Federal Depository Library System.

1. Review of research objectives
   a. In relation to the problem.
   b. In relation to previous research.
   c. In relation to developments subsequent to initiation of research.

2. Overall study design
   a. Are the hypotheses relevant? Consistent?
   b. Is the terminology relevant and unambiguous?
   c. Is the design a logical bridge from problem to solution?
   d. Are there any biases in the design that may have influenced the results?
   e. Was care taken to preserve anonymity, if needed?
   f. Were proper ethical considerations taken into account?
   g. Was the study well administered?

3. Methods used
   a. Were the right sources used (populations sampled)?
   b. Do any of the data collection methods appear to be biased?
   c. What precautions were taken to avoid errors or mistakes in data collection?
   d. If sampling was used, how representative is the sample? With what margin of error?
   e. Were the data processed with due care? What precautions were taken to assure good coding?
   f. Are the categories used in tabulation meaningful?
   g. Were any pertinent tabulations or cross classifications overlooked? On the other hand, are the tabulations so detailed as to obscure some of the main points?
   h. Do the analytical (statistical) methods appear to be appropriate?
   i. Is the report well executed in terms of organization, style, appearance, etc.?

4. Review of interpretations and recommendations
   a. Do they follow from the data? Are they well supported?
   b. Are they comprehensive? Do they relate to the whole problem or only part of it?
   c. Are they consistent with the data? With existing information—other studies, executives' experiences, etc.?
   d. Were any relevant interpretations overlooked?

5. Responsibility for action and follow-up
   a. Will information receive due consideration from all those concerned?
   b. What are the implications of the results for action? Will all action possibilities be considered? (How do the results affect aspects of total operation outside the scope of the report?)
   c. Is an action program necessary? Will it be formulated?
   d. Is further information needed? If so, along what lines?
   e. Is responsibility for follow-up clearly assigned?
   f. Should a time be set for reevaluation of the action program, e.g., to reevaluate an innovation, or test a new package after introduction?

Figure 1.5. Checklist for appraisal of your research study.

American Statistics Index: A Comprehensive Guide and Index to the Statistical Publications of the United States Government. Washington, DC: Congressional Information Service, 1973– . Monthly, with annual cumulations. This is the most comprehensive index to statistical information generated by the federal agencies, committees of Congress, and special programs of the government. Approximately 7,400 titles of 500 government sources are indexed each year. The two main volumes are arranged by issuing breakdown, technical notes, and time period covered by publication. Separate index volume is arranged by subject and title and also includes the SIC code, the Standard Occupation Classification, and a list of SMSAs (standard metropolitan statistical areas).

Bureau of the Census
Department of Commerce
Washington, DC 20233

Contact the Public Information Office for a more complete listing of publications. The following is a sample.

Catalog of United States Census Publications. Published monthly with quarterly and annual cumulations. A guide to census data and reports. This catalog contains descriptive lists of publications, data files, and special tabulations.

Census of Agriculture. Performed in years ending in 4 and 9. Volumes include information on statistics of county; size of farm; characteristics of farm operations; farm income; farm sales; farm expenses; and agricultural services.

Census of Business. Compiled every five years (in years ending in 2 and 7). Organized in three units: *Census of Construction Industries.* Information from industries based on SIC codes. Included is information about number of construction firms; employees; receipts; payrolls; payments for materials; components; work supplies; payments for machinery and equipment; and depreciable assets.

Census of Governments. Done in years ending in 2 and 7. This is the most detailed source for statistics on government finance. *Census of Housing.* Provides information on plumbing facilities whether a unit is owned or rented, value of home, when built, number of bedrooms, telephones, and more.

Census of Manufacturers. Compiled every five years (in years ending in 2 and 7). Reports on 450 different classes of manufacturing industries. Data for each industry includes: information on capital expenditures, value added, number of establishments, employment data, material costs, assets, rent, and inventories. Updated yearly by the *Annual Survey of Manufacturers.*

Census of Mineral Industries. Covers areas of extraction of minerals. Information on employees; payroll; work hours; cost of materials; capital expenditures; and quantity and value of materials consumed and products shipped.

Census of Population. Compiled every ten years (in years ending in 0). Presents detailed data on population characteristics of states, counties, SMSAs, and census tracts. Demographics data reported include: age, sex, race, marital status, family composition, employment income, level of education, and occupation. Updated annually by the *Current Population Report*.

Census of Retail Trade. This report presents statistics for over one hundred different types of retail establishments by state, SMSAs, counties, and cities with populations over 2,500. It includes data on the number of outlets, total sales, employment, and payroll. Updated each month by *Monthly Retail Trade*.

Census of Selected Services. Provides statistics similar to those reported by the *Census of Retail Trade* for retail service organizations such as auto repair centers and hotels. Does not include information on real estate, insurance, or the professions. Updated monthly by *Monthly Selected Service Receipts*.

Census of Transportation. Information on four major phases of United States travel. 1) National Travel Survey, 2) Truck Inventory and Use of Survey, 3) Commodity Transportation Survey, and 4) Survey of Motor Carriers and Public Warehousing.

Census of Wholesale Trade. Statistics for over 150 types of wholesaler categories. The data detail the number of establishments, payroll, warehouse space, expenses, end-of-year inventories, legal form of organization, and payroll. Updated each month by *Monthly Wholesale Trade*.

Statistical Abstract of the United States. Published annually. This is a useful source for finding current and historical statistics about various aspects of American life. Contents include statistics on income, prices, education, population, law enforcement, environmental conditions, local government, labor force, manufacturing, and many other topics.

State and Metropolitan Area Data Book. A Statistical Abstract Supplement. Presents a variety of information on states and metropolitan areas in the U.S. on subjects such as area, population, housing, income, manufacturers, retail trade, and wholesale trade.

County and City Databook. Published every five years, this supplements the *Statistical Abstract*. Contains 144 statistical items for each county and 148 items for cities with a population of 25,000 or more. Data is organized by region, division, states, and SMSAs. Standard demographics are contained in addition to other harder-to-find data.

County Business Patterns. Annual. Contains a summary of data on number and type (by SIC number) of business establishments as well as their employment and taxable payroll. Data are presented by industry and county.

Bureau of Economic Analysis
Department of Commerce
Washington, DC 20230

Business Statistics. This is the biennial supplement to the *Survey of Current Business* and contains data on 2,500 series arranged annually for early years, quarterly for the last decade, and monthly for the most recent five years.

Bureau of Industrial Economics
Department of Commerce
Washington, DC 20230

United States Industrial Outlook. Projections of sales trends for major sectors of the United States economy including business services; consumer services; transportation; consumer goods; and distribution.

Domestic and International Business Administration
Department of Commerce
Washington, DC 20230

County and City Data Book. Published every other year, supplements the *Statistical Abstract.* Using data taken from censuses and other government publications, it provides breakdowns by city and county for income, population, education, employment, housing, banking, manufacturing, capital expenditures, retail and wholesale sales, and other factors.

Measuring Markets: A Guide to the Use of Federal and State Statistical Data. GPO. Provides federal and state government data on population, income, employment, sales, and selected taxes. Explains how to interpret the data to measure markets and evaluate opportunities.

Selected Publications to Aid Business and Industry. Listing of federal statistical sources useful to business and industry.

Statistics of Income. Annual. Published by the Internal Revenue Service of the Treasury Department. This publication consists of data collected from tax returns filed by corporations, sole proprietorships and partnerships, and individuals.

State Statistical Abstract. Every state publishes a statistical abstract, almanac, or economic data book covering statistics for the state, its counties and cities. A complete list of these abstracts is in the back of each volume of the *Statistical Abstract* and *Measuring Markets*.

International Trade Administration
Department of Commerce
Washington, DC 20230

Country Market Survey. These reports describe market sectors and the markets for producer goods, consumer goods, and industrial material.

Global Market Surveys. Provides market research to verify the existence and vitality of foreign markets for specific goods as well as Department of Commerce assistance to United States business to help in market penetration.

Foreign Economic Trends. Prepared by United States embassies abroad. Each volume has a table of "Key Economic Indicators" and other data on the current economic situation and trends for the country under discussion.

Overseas Business Reports. Analysis of trade opportunities, marketing conditions, distribution channels, industry trends, trade regulations, and market prospects are provided.

Trade Opportunity Program (TOP). On a weekly basis indexes trade opportunities by product as well as type of opportunity.

U.S. Small Business Administration
Washington, DC 20416

SBA issues a wide range of management and technical publications designed to help owner-managers and prospective owners of small business. For general information about the SBA office, its policies and assistance programs, contact your nearest SBA office.

A listing of currently available publications can be obtained free from the Small Business Administration, Office of Public Communications, 409 Third St., SW, Washington, DC 20416 or call 1-800-U-ASK—SBA toll free. The SBA offers 51 publications currently. One particular publication, *Basic Library Reference Sources*, contains a section on marketing information and guides to research. Get the lastest *Directory of Publications* by writing or calling the 800 number. You can also obtain a free booklet, *Your Business and the SBA* which gives you an overview of all SBA services and programs.

Management Aids (3- to 24-page pamphlet). This series of pamphlets is organized by a broad range of management principles. Each pamphlet in this series discusses a specific management practice to help the owner-manager of a small firm with management problems and business operations. A section on marketing covers a wide variety of topics from advertising guidelines to marketing research to pricing.

Periodicals

United States. International Trade Administration. *Business America: The Magazine of International Trade*. Biweekly. Activities relating to private sector of the Department of Commerce are covered including exports and other international business activities.

United States. Department of Commerce. Bureau of Economic Analysis. *Business Conditions Digest*. Washington, DC: Government Printing Office. Monthly. Title includes estimates on forecasts for recent months. Very useful for data not yet published elsewhere.

United States. Council of Economic Advisors. *Economic Indicators*. Washington, DC: Government Printing Office. Monthly. Statistical tables for major economics indicators are included. Section on credit is useful for marketers. Statistics quoted annually for about six years and monthly for the past year.

United States. Board of Governors of the Federal Reserve System. *Federal Reserve Bulletin*. Washington, DC: Government Printing Office. Monthly. Contains official statistics on national banking, international banking, and business.

United States. Bureau of Labor Statistics. *Monthly Labor Review*. Washington, DC: Government Printing Office. Monthly. This publication covers all aspects of labor including wages, productivity, collective bargaining, new legislation, and consumer prices.

United States. Department of Commerce. Bureau of Economic Analysis. *Survey of Current Business*. Washington, DC: Government Printing Office. Monthly, with weekly supplements. The most useful source for current business statistics. Each issue is divided into two sections. The first covers general business topics; the second, "Current Business Statistics," gives current data for 2,500 statistical series or topics. Also, indexed in *Business Periodicals Index*.

United States. Department of the Treasury. *Treasury Bulletin*. Washington, DC: Government Printing Office. Monthly. Statistical tables are provided on all aspects of fiscal operations of government as well as money-related activities of the private sector. Useful for consumer background or from a monetary view.

Directories

The selected national directories are listed under categories of specific business or general marketing areas in an alphabetical subject index.

When the type of directory is not easily found under the alphabetical listing of a general marketing category, such as "jewelry," look for a specific type of industry or outlet, for example, "department stores."

Apparel

Hat Life Year Book (Men's). Annual. Includes renovators, importers, classified list of manufacturers, and wholesalers of men's headwear. Hat Life Year Book, 551 Summit Ave., Jersey City, NJ 07306.

Knitting Times—Buyer's Guide Issue. Annual. Lists manufacturers and suppliers of knitted products, knit goods, materials, supplies, services, etc. National Knitwear and Sportswear Association, 386 Park Ave. South, New York, NY 10016.

Men's & Boys' Wear Buyers, Nation-Wide Directory of (exclusive of New York metropolitan area). Annually in August. More than 20,000 buyers and merchandise managers for 6,100 top department, family clothing, and men's and boys' wear specialty stores. Telephone number, buying office, and postal zip code given for each firm. Also available in individual state editions. The Salesman's Guide, Inc., 1140 Broadway, New York, NY 10001. Also publishes *Metropolitan New York Directory of Men's and Boys' Wear Buyers*. Semiannually in May and November. (Lists same information for the metropolitan New York area as the nationwide directory.)

Women's & Children's Wear & Accessories Buyers, Nationwide Directory of (exclusive of New York metropolitan area). Annually in October. Lists more than 25,000 buyers and divisional merchandise managers for about 6,100 leading department, family clothing, and specialty stores. Telephone number and mail zip code given for each store. Also available in individual state editions. The Salesman's Guide, Inc., 1140 Broadway, New York, NY 10001.

Appliances—Household

Appliance Dealers—Major Household Directory. Annual. Lists manufacturers and distributors in home electronics, appliances, kitchens. Gives complete addresses and phone. Compiled from Yellow Pages. American Business Directories, Inc., 5711 S. 86th Circle, Omaha, NE 68127.

Automatic Merchandising (Vending)

NAMA Directory of Members. Annually in June. Organized by state and by city, lists vending service companies who are NAMA members. Gives mailing address, telephone number, and products vended. Also includes machine manufacturers and suppliers. National Automatic Merchandising Association, 20 N. Wacker Dr., Chicago, IL 60606.

Automotive

Manufacturers' Representatives Division. Irregular. Alphageographical listing of about 300 representatives including name, address, telephone number, territories covered, and lines carried. Automotive Service Industrial Association, 444 N. Michigan Ave., Chicago, IL 60611.

Automotive Warehouse Distributors Association Membership Directory. Annually in April. Includes listing of manufacturers, warehouse distributors, their products, personnel, and territories. Automotive Warehouse Distributors Asssociation, 9140 Ward Parkway, Kansas City, MO 64114.

Automotive Consultants Directory. Annually in November. Lists 380 consultants and consulting firms in automotive engineering specialties, including safety, manufacturing, quality control, engine design, marketing, etc. Society of Automotive Engineers, 400 Commonwealth Dr., Warrendale, PA 15096-0001.

Aviation

World Aviation Directory. Published twice a year in March and September. Gives administrative and operating personnel of airlines, aircraft, and engine manufacturers and component manufacturers and distributors, organizations, and schools. Indexed by companies, activities, products, and individuals. McGraw-Hill, Inc. 1156 15th St., NW, Washington, DC 20005.

Bookstores

Book Trade Directory, American. Annually in July. Lists more than 25,000 retail and wholesale booksellers in the United States and Canada. Entries alphabetized by state (or province), and then by city and business name. Each listing gives address, telephone numbers, key personnel, types of books sold, subject specialties carried, sidelines and services offered, and general characteristics. For wholesale entries gives types of accounts, import-export information and territory limitations. R. R. Bowker Company, 245 W. 17th St., New York, NY 10011.

Building Supplies

Building Supply News Buyers Guide. Annually in May. Classified directory of manufacturers of lumber, building materials, equipment, and supplies. Cahners Publishing Co., 1350 E. Touhy Ave., Des Plaines, IL 60018.

Business Firms

Dun & Bradstreet Million Dollar Directory—Top 50,000 Companies. Annually. Lists about 50,000 top corporations. Arranged alphabetically. Gives business name, state of incorporation, address, telephone number, SIC numbers, function, sales volume, number of employees, and name of officers and directors, principal bank, accounting firm, and legal counsel. Dun's Marketing Services, Dun & Bradstreet, Inc., 3 Sylvan Way, Parsippany, NJ 07054-3896.

Dun & Bradstreet Million Dollar Directory. Annually in February. Lists about 160,000 businesses with a net worth of $500,000 or more. Arranged alphabetically. Dun's Marketing Services, Dun & Bradstreet, Inc., 3 Sylvan Way, Parsippany, NJ 07054-3896.

Buying Offices

Buying Offices and Accounts, Directory of. Annually in March. Approximately 220 New York, Chicago, Los Angeles, Dallas, and Miami resident buying offices, corporate offices, and merchandise brokers together with 7,700 accounts listed under its own buying office complete with local address and alphabetically by address and buying office. The Salesman's Guide, Inc., 1140 Broadway, New York, NY 10001.

China and Glassware

American Glass Review. Glass Factory Directory Issue. Annually in March. Issued as part of subscription (13th issue) to *American Glass Review*: Lists companies manufacturing flat glass, tableware glass and fiber glass, giving corporate and plant addresses, executives, type of equipment used. Doctorow Communications, Inc., 1115 Clifton Ave., Clifton, NJ 07013.

China Glass & Tableware Red Book Directory Issue. Annually in September. Issued as part of subscription (13th issue) to *China Glass & Tableware*. Lists about 1,000 manufacturers, importers, and national distributors of china, glass, and other table appointments, giving corporate addresses and executives. Doctorow Publications, Inc., 1115 Clifton Ave., Clifton, NJ 07013.

City Directories Catalog

Municipal Year Book. Annual. Contains a review of municipal events of the year, analyses of city operations, and a directory of city officials in all the states. International City Management Association, 777 N. Capitol St., NE, Washington, DC 20002-4201.

College Stores

College Stores, Directory of. Published every two years. Lists about 3,000 college stores, geographically with manager's name, kinds of goods sold, college name, number of students, whether men, women, or both, whether the store is college owned or privately owned. B. Klein Publications, P.O. Box 8503, Coral Springs, FL 33065.

Confectionery

Candy Buyers' Directory. Annually in January. Lists candy manufacturers; importers and United States representatives, and confectionery brokers. The Manufacturing Confectionery Publishing Co., 175 Rock Rd., Glen Rock, NJ 07452.

Construction Equipment

Construction Equipment Buyer's Guide. Annually in November. Lists 1,500 construction equipment distributors and manufacturers; includes company names, names of key personnel, addresses, telephone numbers, branch locations, and lines handled or type of equipment produced. Cahners Publishing Co., 1350 E. Touhy Ave., Des Plaines, IL 60018.

Conventions and Trade Shows

Directory of Conventions. Annually in January. Contains over 18,000 cross-indexed listings of annual events, gives dates, locations, names and addresses of executives in charge, scope, expected attendance. Bill Communications, Inc., 633 Third Ave., New York, NY 10017.

Trade Show and Exhibits Schedule. Annually in January with supplement in July. Lists over 10,000 exhibits, trade shows, expositions, and fairs held throughout the world with dates given two years in advance. Listings run according to industrial classification covering all industries and professions; full information on dates, city, sponsoring organization, number of exhibits, attendance, gives title and address of executive in charge. Bill Communications, Inc., 633 Third Ave., New York, NY 10017.

Dental Supply

Dental Supply Houses, Hayes Directory of. Annually in August. Lists wholesalers of dental supplies and equipment with addresses, telephone numbers, financial standing and credit rating. Edward N. Hayes, Publisher, 4229 Birch St., Newport Beach, CA 92660.

Department Stores

Sheldon's Retail. Annual. Lists 1,500 large independent department stores, 600 major department store chains, 150 large independent and chain home-furnishing stores, 700 large independent women's specialty stores, and 450 large women's specialty store chains alphabetically by states. Gives all department buyers with lines bought by each buyer, and addresses and telephone numbers of merchandise executives. Also gives all New York, Chicago, Dallas, Atlanta, and Los Angeles buying offices, the number and locations of branch stores, and an index of all store/chain headquarters. Phelon, Sheldon & Marsar, Inc., 15 Industrial Ave., Fairview, NJ 07022.

Discount Stores

Discount Department Stores, Directory of. Annually. Lists headquarters address, telephone number, location, square footage of each store, lines carried, leased operators, names of executives and buyers (includes Canada). Also special section on leased department operators. Chain Store Guide Publications, 425 Park Ave., New York, NY 10022.

Drug Outlets—Retail and Wholesale

Chain Drug Stores Guide, Hayes. Annually in September. Lists headquarters address, telephone numbers, number and location of units, names of executives and buyers, wholesale drug distributors. Edward N. Hayes, 4229 Birch St., Newport Beach, CA 92660.

Druggist Directory, Hayes. Annually in March. Lists about 52,900 retail and 700 wholesale druggists in the United States, giving addresses, financial standing, and credit rating. Also publishes regional editions for one or more states. Computerized mailing labels available. Edward N. Hayes, 4229 Birch St., Newport Beach, CA 92660.

Drug Topics Red Book. Annually in March. Gives information on wholesale drug companies, chain drug stores headquarters, department stores maintaining toilet goods or drug departments, manufacturers' sales agents, and discount houses operating toilet goods, cosmetic, proprietary medicine or prescription departments. Medical Economics Company, 680 Kinderkamack Rd., Oradell, NJ 07649.

National Wholesale Druggists' Association Membership and Executive Directory. Annually in January. Lists 800 American and foreign wholesalers and manufacturers of drugs and allied products. National Wholesale Druggists' Association, Box 238, Alexandria, VA 22313.

Electrical and Electronics

Electronic Industry Telephone Directory. Annually in August. Contains over 22,890 listings of manufacturers, representatives, distributors, government agencies, contracting agencies, and others. Harris Publishing Co., 2057 Aurora Rd., Twinsburg, OH 44087.

Electrical Wholesale Distributors, Directory of. Detailed information on 3,400 companies with over 7,630 locations in the U.S. and Canada, including name, address, telephone number, branch and affiliated houses, products handled, etc. McGraw-Hill, Inc., 1221 Avenue of the Americas, New York, NY 10020.

Who's Who in Electronics, Regional/National Source Directory. Annually in January. Detailed information (name, address, telephone number, products handled, territories, etc.) on 12,500 electronics manufacturers, and 4,800 industrial electronic distributors and branch outlets. Purchasing index with 1,600 product breakdowns for buyers and purchasing agents. Harris Publishing Co., 2057 Aurora Rd., Twinsburg, OH 44087.

Electrical Utilities

Electrical Utilities, Electrical World, Directory of. Annually in November. Complete listings of electric utilities (investor-owned, municipal, and government agencies in U.S. and Canada) giving their addresses and personnel, and selected data on operations. McGraw-Hill, Inc., Directory of Electric Utilities, 1221 Avenue of the Americas, New York, NY 10020.

Embroidery

Embroidery Directory. Annually in November. Alphabetical listing with addresses and telephone numbers of manufacturers, merchandisers, designers, cutters, bleacheries, yarn dealers, machine suppliers, and other suppliers to the Schiffli lace and embroidery industry. Schiffli Lace and Embroidery Manufacturers Association, Inc., 8555 Tonnelle Ave., North Bergen, NJ 07087.

Export and Import

American Export Register. Annually in September. Includes over 30,000 importers and exporters and products handled. Thomas International Publishing Co., Inc., 1 Penn Plaza, 250 West 34th St., New York, NY 10119.

Canadian Trade Directory, Fraser's. Annually in May. Contains more than 42,000 Canadian companies. Also lists over 14,000 foreign companies who have Canadian representatives. Fraser's Trade Directories, Maclean Hunter Ltd., 777 Bay St., Toronto, Ontario, Canada, M5W 1A7.

Flooring

Flooring Directory and Buying Guide Issue. Annually in October. Reference to sources of supply, giving their products and brand names, leading distributors, manufacturers' representatives, and associations. Edgell Communications, 7500 Old Oak Ave., Cleveland, OH 44130.

Food Dealers—Retail and Wholesale

Food Brokers Association, National Directory of Members. Annually in April. Arranged by states and cities, lists member food brokers in the United States and Europe, giving names and addresses, products they handle and services they perform. National Food Brokers Association, 1010 Massachusetts Ave., Washington, DC 20001.

National Frozen Food Association Directory. Annually in January. Lists packers, distributors, supplies, refrigerated warehouses, wholesalers, and brokers; includes names and addresses of each firm and their key officials. Contains statistical marketing data. National Frozen Food Association, 604 W. Derry Rd., Hershey, PA 17033.

Food Industry Register, Thomas'. Annually in May. Volume 1: Lists supermarket chains, wholesalers, brokers, frozen food brokers, exporters, warehouses. Volume 2: Contains information on products and services; manufacturers, sources of supplies, importers. Volume 3: A–Z index of 48,000 companies. Also, a brand name/trademark index. Thomas Publishing Co., One Penn Plaza, New York, NY 10119.

Tea and Coffee Buyers' Guide, Ukers' International. Annual. Includes revised and updated lists of participants in the tea and coffee and allied trades. The Tea and Coffee Trade Journal, Lockwood Trade Journal, Inc., 130 W. 42nd St., 22nd Floor, New York, NY 10036.

Gas Companies

Gas Companies, Brown's Directory of North American and International. Annually in November. Includes information on every known gas utility company and holding company worldwide. Energy Publications Division, Edgell Communications, Inc., 1 East First St., Duluth, MN 55802.

LP/Gas. Annually in March. Lists suppliers, supplies, and distributors. Energy Publications Division, Edgell Communications, Inc., 1 East First St., Duluth, MN 55802.

Gift and Art

Gift and Decorative Accessory Buyers Directory. Annually in September. Included in subscription price of monthly magazine, *Gifts and Decorative Accessories.* Alphabetical listing of manufacturers, importers, jobbers, and representatives in the gift field. Listing of trade names, trademarks, brand names, and trade associations. Geyer-McAllister Publications, 51 Madison Ave., New York, NY 10010.

Gift, Housewares and Home Textile Buyers, Nationwide Directory of. Annually with semiannual supplement. For 7,000 types of retail firms lists store name, address, type of store, number of stores, names of president, merchandise managers, and buyers, etc., for giftwares and housewares. State editions also available. The Salesman's Guide, Inc., 1140 Broadway, New York, NY 10001.

Gift & Stationery Business Directory Issue. Annually in September. Alphabetical listing by category of each (manufacturer, representative, importer, distributor, or jobber) of about 1,900. Includes identification of trade names and trademarks, and statistics for imports, manufacturing, and retail sales. Gralla Publications, 1515 Broadway, Suite 3201, New York, NY 10036.

Gift Shops Directory. 68,490 listings. American Business Directories, Inc., 5711 S. 86th Circle, Omaha, NE 68127.

Hardware

Wholesaler Directory (Hardware). Irregularly issued. Alphabetical listing of hardware wholesalers, and distributors of lumber and building materials. National Retail Hardware Association, 5822 W. 74th St., Indianapolis, IN 46278.

Home Furnishings

The Antique Dealers Directory. Annual. Lists 31,000 dealers with name, address, and phone number as well as size of advertisement and first year advertised in

Yellow Pages. American Business Directories, Inc. 5711 S. 86th Circle, Omaha, NE 68127.

Home Fashions—Buyer's Guide Issue. Annually in December. Lists names and addresses of manufacturers, importers, and regional sales representatives. Fairchild Publications, Capital Cities Media, Inc., 7 E. 12th St., New York, NY 10003.

Interior Decorator's Handbook. Semiannually in spring and fall. Published expressly for decorators and designers, interior decorating staff of department and furniture stores. Lists firms handling items used in interior decoration. Columbia Communications, Inc., 370 Lexington Ave., New York, NY 10017.

Hospitals

Hospitals, Directory of. Annually in January. Lists 7,800 hospitals, with selected data. SMG Marketing Group, Inc., 1342 N. LaSalle Dr., Chicago, IL 60610.

Hotels and Motels

Hotels and Motels Directory. Annually. Lists more than 61,040 hotels and motels. American Business Directories, Inc. 5711 S. 86th Circle, Omaha, NE 68127.

OAG Travel Planner and Hotel Red Book. Quarterly. Lists over 26,000 hotels in the United States. Also lists 14,500 destination cities, etc. Official Airline Guide Inc., 2000 Clearwater Dr., Oak Brook, IL 60521.

Hotel Systems, Directory of. Annually in March. Lists over 800 hotel systems in the Western hemisphere. American Hotel Association Directory Corporation, 1201 New York Ave., NW, Washington, DC 20005.

Housewares

NHMA Membership Directory and Buyer's Desk Top Guide to Houseware Manufacturers. Annually in March. Compilation of resources of the housewares trade, includes listing of their products, trade names, and a registry of manufacturers' representatives. National Housewares Manufacturers Association, 1324 Merchandise Mart, Chicago, IL 60654.

Jewelry

Jewelers' Circular/Keystone-Jewelers' Directory Issue. Annual in June. Lists manufacturers, importers, distributors, and retailers of jewelry; diamonds; precious, semiprecious, and imitation stones; watches, silverware; and kindred articles. Includes credit ratings. Chilton Co., Chilton Way, Radnor, PA 19098.

Liquor

Wine and Spirits Wholesalers of America—Member Roster and Industry Directory.
Annually in January. Lists names of 700 member companies; includes parent
house and branches, addresses, and names of managers. Also, has register of
1,900 suppliers, and gives state liquor control administrators, national associations,
and trade press directory. Wine and Spirits Wholesalers of America, Inc., 1023
15th St., NW, Fourth fl., Washington, DC 20005.

Mailing List Houses

Mailing List Houses, Directory of. Lists 1,800 list firms, brokers, compilers,
and firms offering their own lists for rent; includes the specialties of each firm.
Arranged geographically. Todd Publications, 18 N. Greenbush Rd., West Nyack,
NY 10994.

Mail Order Businesses

Mail Order Business Directory. Lists 10,000 names or mail order firms with
buyers' names, and lines carried. Arranged geographically. B. Klein Publications,
P.O. Box 8503, Coral Springs, FL 33065.

Manufacturers

MacRae's Blue Book. Annually in March. In three volumes: Volume 1—Corporate
Index lists company names and addresses alphabetically, with 40,000 branch
and/or sales office telephone numbers. Volumes 2 and 3—companies listed by
product classifications. MacRae's Blue Book, Business Research Publications,
817 Broadway, New York, NY, 10003.

Manufacturers, Thomas' Register of American. Annual. Volume 1–14—products
and services; suppliers of each product category grouped by state and city. Vols.
15–16 contain company profiles. Vols. 17–23—manufacturers' catalogs. More
than 150,000 firms are listed under 50,000 product headings. Thomas Publishing
Co., One Penn Plaza, New York, NY 10119.

Manufacturers' Sales Representatives

Manufacturers & Agents National Association Directory of Members. Annually
in May/June. Contains individual listings of manufacturers' agents throughout
the United States, Canada, and several foreign countries. Listings cross-referenced
by alphabetical, geographical, and product classification. Manufacturers' Agents
National Association, Box 3467, Laguna Hills, CA 92654.

Mass Merchandisers

Major Mass Market Merchandisers, Nationwide Directory of (exclusive of New York, metropolitan area). Annual. Lists men's, women's, and children's wear buyers who buy for about 257,000 units—top discount, variety, supermarket and drug chains; factory outlet stores; leased department operators. The Salesman's Guide, Inc., 1140 Broadway, New York, NY 10001.

Metalworking

Metalworking Directory, Dun & Bradstreet. Annually in June. Lists about 65,000 metalworking and metal producing plants with 20 or more production employees. Arranged geographically. Dun's Marketing Services Division, Dun & Bradstreet Corporation, 3 Sylvan Way, Parsippany, NJ 07054-3896.

Military Market

Military Market Magazine—Buyers' Guide Issue. Annually in January. Lists manufacturers and suppliers of products sold in military commissaries. Also lists manufacturers' representatives and distributors. Army Times Publishing Co., Times Journal Co., 6883 Commercial Dr., Springfield, VA 22159.

Paper Products

Sources of Supply Buyers' Guide. Lists 1,700 mills and converters of paper, film, foil, and allied products, and paper merchants in the United States alphabetically with addresses, principal personnel, and products manufactured. Also lists trade associations, brand names, and manufacturers' representatives. Advertisers and Publishers Service, Inc., 300 N. Prospect Ave., Park Ridge, IL 60068.

Physicians and Medical Supply Houses

Medical Directory, American. Volumes 1–4 give complete information about 633,000 physicians in the United States and possessions—alphabetical and geographical listings. American Medical Association, 535 North Dearborn St., Chicago, IL 60610.

Physician and Hospital Supply Houses, Hayes' Directory of. Annually in August. Listings of 1,850 U.S. wholesalers doing business in physician, hospital and surgical supplies and equipment; includes addresses, telephone numbers, financial standing, and credit ratings. Edward N. Hayes, Publisher, 4229 Birch St., Newport Beach, CA 92660.

Plumbing

Manufacturers' Representatives, Directory of. Annually in February. Lists 2,000 representatives of manufacturers selling plumbing, heating and cooling equipment, components, tools and related products to this industry through wholesaler channels, with detailed information on each. Delta Communications, 400 N. Michigan Ave., Chicago, IL 60611.

Premium Sources

Premium Suppliers and Services, Directory of. Annually in February. Lists about 1,800 suppliers with title, telephone number, address. Gralla Publications, 1515 Broadway, Suite 3201, New York, NY 10036.

Incentive Resource Guide Issue. Annually in February. Contains classified directory of suppliers, and list of manufacturers' representatives serving the premium field. Also, lists associations and clubs, and trade shows. Bill Communications, 633 Third Ave., New York, NY 10017.

Purchasing—Government

U.S. Government Purchasing and Sales Directory. Irregularly issued. Booklet designed to help small business receive an equitable share of government contracts. Lists types of purchases for both military and civilian needs, catalogs procurement offices by state. Lists SBA regional and branch offices. Order from Superintendent of Documents, U.S. Government Printing Office, Washington, DC 20402.

Refrigeration and Air Conditioning

Air Conditioning, Heating & Refrigeration News—Directory Issue. Annually in January. Lists 1,900 manufacturers and 3,000 wholesalers and factory outlets in refrigeration, heating, and air-conditioning. Business News Publishing Co., 755 W. Big Beaver Rd., 10th fl., Troy, MI 48084.

Restaurants

Chain Restaurant Operators, Directory of. Annually in May. Lists headquarters address, telephone number, number and location of units, trade names used, whether unit is company operated or franchised, executives and buyers, annual sales volume for chains of restaurants, cafeterias, drive-ins, hotel and motel food operators, industrial caterers, etc. Chain Store Information Services, 425 Park Ave., New York, NY 10022.

Roofing and Siding

RSI Trade Directory Issue. Annually in April. Has listing guide to products and equipment manufacturers, jobbers and distributors, and associations in the roofing, siding, and home improvement industries. RSI Directory, Edgell Communications, Inc., 7500 Old Oak Blvd., Cleveland, OH 44130.

Selling Direct

Direct Selling Companies, World Directory. Annually in April. About 30 direct selling associations and 750 associated member companies. Includes names of contact persons, company product line, method of distribution, etc. World Federation of Direct Selling Associations, 1776 K St., NW, Suite 600, Washington, DC 20006.

Shoes

National Directory of Footwear Companies/Footwear Buyers' Guide. Biennial. Lists about 400 New York and 300 out-of-town and foreign manufacturers. New York City Footwear Buyers' Guide, 47 W. 34th St., Suite 601, New York, NY 10001.

Shopping Centers

Shopping Center Directory. Annual. Alphabetical listing of 30,000 shopping centers, location, owner/developer, manager, physical plant (number of stores, square feet), and leasing agent. National Research Bureau, Division of Information, Product Group, Automated Marketing Systems, Inc., 310 S. Michigan Ave., Chicago, IL 60604.

Specialty Stores

Women's Apparel Stores, Phelon's. Lists over 7,000 women's apparel and accessory shops with store headquarters name and address, number of shops operated, New York City buying headquarters or representatives, lines of merchandise bought and sold, name of principal and buyers, store size, and price range. Phelon, Sheldon, & Marsar, Inc., 15 Industrial Ave., Fairview, NJ 07022.

Sporting Goods

Sporting Goods Buyers, Nationwide Directory of. Including semiannual supplements. Lists over 7,500 top retail stores with names of buyers and executives, for all types of sporting goods, athletic apparel and athletic footwear, hunting and fishing, and outdoor equipment. The Salesman's Guide, Inc., 1140 Broadway, New York, NY 10001.

Sporting Goods Business—Directory of Products, Services and Suppliers Issue. Annually in August. 3,000 suppliers of sporting goods merchandise and equipment. Gralla Publications, 1515 Broadway, Suite 3201, New York, NY 10036.

Trailer Parks

Campground Directory, Woodall's. Annual. Lists and star-rates public and private campgrounds in North American continent alphabetically by town with location and description of facilities. Also lists more than 800 RV service locations. Regional editions available. Woodall Publishing Company, 28167 North Keith Dr., Lake Forest, IL 60045.

Trucking

Trucksource: Sources of Trucking Industry Information. Annually in November. Includes over 700 sources of information on the trucking industry, classified by subject. American Trucking Association, 2200 Mill Road, Alexandria, VA 22314-4677.

Variety Stores

General Merchandise, Variety and Specialty Stores, Directory of. Annually in March. Lists headquarters address, telephone number, number of units and locations, executives and buyers. Chain Store Guide Information Services, 425 Park Ave., New York, NY 10022.

Warehouses

Public Warehousing, Guide to. Annually in July. Lists leading public warehouses in U.S. and Canada, as well as major truck lines, airlines, steamship lines, liquid and dry bulk terminals, material handling equipment suppliers, ports of the world and railroad piggyback services and routes. Chilton Co., Chilton Way, Radnor, PA 19089.

Members Associated Warehouses, Directory of. Irregularly. Listing of 90 members. Associated Warehouses, Inc., Box 471, Cedar Knolls, NJ 07927.

Stationers

Giftware and Stationery Business—Directory Issue. Annually in September. Alphabetical listing by company of over 1,900 manufacturers, importers, distributors, and representatives. Gralla Publications, 1515 Broadway, Suite 3201, New York, NY 10036.

Textiles

Textile Blue Book, Davison's. Annually in February. Contains over 8,400 separate company listings (name, address, etc.) for U.S. and Canada. Firms included are cotton, wool, synthetic mills, knitting mills, cordage, twine, and duck manufacturers, dry goods commission merchants, converters, yarn dealers, cordage manufacturers' agents, wool dealers and merchants, cotton merchants, exporter, brokers, and others. Davison Publishing Co., Box 477, Ridgewood, NJ 07451.

Toys and Novelties

Playthings—Who Makes It Issue. Annually in June. Lists manufacturers, products, trade names, suppliers to manufacturers, supplier products, licensors, manufacturers' representatives, toy trade associations, and trade show managements. Geyer–McAllister Publications, Inc., 51 Madison Ave., New York, NY 10010.

Small World—Directory Issue. Annually in December. Lists 200 wholesalers, manufacturers, manufacturers' representatives of toys, games, and hobbies for children and infants. Earnshaw Publications Inc., 225 West 34th St., Suite 1212, New York, NY 10122.

Other Important Directories

The following business directories are helpful to those persons doing marketing research. Most of these directories are available for reference at the larger libraries. For additional listings, consult the *Guide to American Directories* at local libraries.

AUBER Bibliography of Publications of University Bureaus of Business and Economic Research. Lists studies published by Bureaus of Business and Economic Research affiliated with American colleges and universities. Done for the Association for University Bureaus of Business and Economic Research. Issued annually. Previous volumes available. Association for University Business and Economic Research, c/o Indiana Business Research Center, 801 W. Michigan St., BS 4015, Indianapolis, IN 46223.

Bradford's Directory of Marketing Research Agencies and Management Consultants in the United States and the World. Gives names and addresses of over 1,600 marketing research agencies in the United States, Canada, and abroad. Lists service offered by agency, along with other pertinent data, such as date established, names of principal officers, and size of staff. Bradford's Directory of Marketing Research Agencies, P.O. Box 276, Fairfax, VA 22030.

Consultants and Consulting Organizations Directory. Contains 16,000 entries. Guides reader to appropriate organization for a given consulting assignment. Entries include names, addresses, phone numbers, and data on services performed. Gale Research Company, 835 Penobscot Bldg., Detroit, MI 48226-4094.

Research Centers Directory. Lists more than 11,000 nonprofit research organizations. Descriptive information provided for each center, including address, telephone number, name of director, data on staff, funds, publications, and a statement concerning its principal fields of research. Has special indexes. Gale Research Company, 835 Penobscot Bldg., Detroit, MI 48226-4094.

MacRae's Blue Book—Manufacturers. Annual. In three volumes: Vol. 1 is an index by corporations; Vols. 2–3 are a classification by products showing under each classification manufacturers of that item. Business Research Publications, Inc., 817 Broadway, New York, NY 10003.

Thomas' Food Industry Register. Annually in May. Lists wholesale grocers, chain store organizations, voluntary buying groups, food brokers, exporters and importers of food products, frozen food brokers, distributors and related products distributed through grocery chains in two volumes. Thomas Publishing Company, One Penn Plaza, New York, NY 10019.

Thomas' Register of American Manufacturers. Annually in February. In 23 volumes. Vols. 1–14 contain manufacturers arranged geographically under each product, and capitalization or size rating for each manufacturer, under 50,000 product headings. Vols. 15 and 16 contain company profiles and a brand or trade name section with more than 112,000 listings. Vols. 17–23 are catalogs from more than 1,500 firms. Thomas Publishing Co., One Penn Plaza, New York, NY 10019.

SOURCES OF ADDITIONAL INFORMATION

Business Competition Intelligence, by William L. Sammon, Mark A. Kurland, and Robert Spitalnic, published by John Wiley & Sons, Inc., 605 Third Avenue, New York, NY 10158.

Business Research: Concept and Practice, by Robert G. Murdick, published by Richard D. Irwin, Inc., 1818 Ridge Road, Homewood, IL 60430.

Competitor Intelligence, by Leonard M. Fuld, published by John Wiley & Sons, Inc., 605 Third Avenue, New York, NY 10158.

Do-It-Yourself Marketing Research, by George E. Breen, published by McGraw-Hill Book Co., 1221 Avenue of the Americas, New York, NY 10020.

Honomichl on Marketing Research, by Jack J. Honomichl, published by NTC Business Books, 4255 West Touhy Avenue, Lindenwood, IL 60646-1975.

A Manager's Guide to Marketing Research, by Paul E. Green and Donald E. Frank, published by John Wiley & Sons, Inc., 605 Third Avenue, New York, NY 10158.

Market and Sales Forecasting, by F. Keay, published by John Wiley & Sons, Inc., 605 Third Avenue, New York, NY 10158.

Marketing Research: A Management Overview, by Evelyn Konrad and Rod Erickson, published by AMACOM, a division of the American Management Association, 135 West 50th Street, New York, NY 10020.

Research for Marketing Decisions, by Paul E. Green and Donald S. Tull, published by Prentice-Hall, Inc., Englewood Cliffs, NJ 07632.

HOW TO FIND AND INTRODUCE A NEW PRODUCT

THE IMPORTANCE OF NEW PRODUCT INTRODUCTION

It is an unfortunate fact that eight out of ten new products fail in the marketplace. Yet, new product introduction is absolutely essential. Why is this so? Without new products your business cannot survive. You cannot continue to produce the old products that have made your company successful because of the product life cycle. The product life cycle shows that every product goes through the stages of introduction, growth, maturity, and decline. In this final phase, while sales may continue to be made, the product becomes more and more unprofitable. Now, naturally, life cycles are of different lengths for different products. Some life cycles are extremely long, such as those for the safety pin or the hairpin. Others, such as those for electronic calculators and electronic watches, are extremely short. However, no product or service can be offered in one form forever.

Of course, a company does not introduce a new product only because it is forced to do so. Below is a list of some of the possible reasons for a company's decision to offer something new.

1. Your product has become noncompetitive because improvements in competitive products have rendered yours obsolete.
2. The use for which your product was created has either disappeared or has gone into decline.
3. Your product may be related to some phase of the national or local economy. This may be war or peace; it may be heavy industry, the military, energy, agriculture, or any other facet of economic life.
4. A new product may be desirable to take up excess plant capacity.

5. You may have surplus capital that you wish to utilize.

6. You may find the opportunity to utilize by-products and materials in the manufacture of other products.

7. You may want to make maximum use of your sales organization and have additional products that will allow you to amortize these overhead costs over a broader base.

8. You may be in a business that has cycles known as "peaks and valleys," either due to seasonal fluctuations or ordering phases. Sometimes these upswings and downturns can be leveled out by the use of new products that sell during the valleys.

9. You may wish to make use of marginal or partly used manpower or other facilities.

As noted earlier, the mortality of new product ideas is extremely high. Alan A. Smith, of the consulting firm Arthur D. Little, Inc., of Cambridge, Massachusetts, researched the experience of 20 companies concerned with successful new product development:

In the idea stage there were 540 possibilities considered for research. Of these 540, 448 were eliminated during initial screening of items to be pursued. This left 92 selected for preliminary laboratory investigation. Only 8 of the 92 appeared sufficiently promising to warrant development, and 7 of the 8 were dropped as unsalable or unprofitable as determined during some process of development or introduction into the marketplace. Only 1 of these 7, or 1 out of the original 540 idea possibilities, was placed in regular production.

While many possibilities for new ideas and new products should be considered, you can see that 92 to 1 or even 8 to 1 is not a terrific success ratio, and much money was wasted finding the one product that was successful. In this chapter you will see how to increase your new products' success ratio dramatically.

THE ADVANTAGES OF NEW PRODUCT INTRODUCTION

Earlier we gave several reasons for introducing a new product. Here are some clear-cut advantages for new product development that should encourage you to look at new products and introduce them to the marketplace.

1. A new product may reduce your overhead by allowing you to amortize administrative sales and advertising and distribution costs over additional products.

2. Your new product may lead you into new markets that may be even greater than the current market you are serving.

3. New products may add substantially to your profit as well as to the stability of your company.

4. New products may lead you into using distribution channels that will benefit your old product line and working together may synergistically help both.

5. Tax laws frequently encourage you and in effect share the cost of developing new products.

PRODUCT INTEREST CHECKLIST

Before you look over my list of sources of new product ideas, you should have a
general idea of the type of product you're looking for based on factors such as your
company's strengths, market preference, the sales volume you desire, product status,
the product configuration you may be interested in, and finance. This will give you
a profile of product interest. The following checklist was developed by John B.
Lang, technology utilization officer of the Small Business Administration in Los
Angeles.[1] Use it to develop a profile of product interest.

Your Company's Strengths

	Yes	No
1. Is manufacturing your company's strength?		
2. Do you prefer a highly automated production line?		
3. Do you prefer a product with a high ratio of labor to production costs?		
4. Are your production personnel highly skilled?		
5. Are your industrial product designers exceptionally skilled?		
6. Does your present equipment have a long usable life?		
7. Is your present equipment largely underutilized?		
8. Do you have a strong sales force?		
9. Is your sales force hampered by too narrow a product?		
10. Do you have strong capability in a particular technology?		
11. Does your company have cash or credit resources not used in your present operations?		
12. Does your company have a reputation for high quality products?		
13. Does your company have a reputation for low cost production?		

Market Preference

	Yes	No
14. Do you prefer a particular industry?		
15. Do you prefer a product sold to retail consumers?		
16. Do you prefer a product sold to industrial uses?		
17. Do you prefer a product sold to the government?		
18. Do you prefer a product with long usage?		
19. Will you accept a product that may be a fad item?		
20. Do you prefer a consumable item?		
21. Is there a distribution system (trade practice) you prefer?		

[1] John B. Lang, *Finding a New Product for Your Company*, Small Business Administration (1980).

	Yes	No
22. Would you consider a product limited to a given locality? (Or a product in demand largely in overseas markets?)	___	___
23. Is a product that requires specialty selling desirable?	___	___
24. Is a product that needs mass merchandising suitable?		
25. Do you intend overseas distribution?	___	___
26. Must your present sales department be able to sell a new product?	___	___
27. Are you willing to create a new or separate marketing department to sell a new product?	___	___

Sales Volume Desired

28. Have you determined the optimum annual volume from the product over the next three years?	___	___
29. Do you have any preference for a unit price range in a product?	___	___
30. Do you have 5- and 10-year volume objectives for a new product?	___	___
31. Will this product have to support its own sales organization?	___	___
32. Will the product support its own manufacturing equipment?	___	___
33. At what volume does a product exceed your company's capability?	___	___

Product Status

34. Will you accept an idea for a product?	___	___
35. Will you accept an unpatentable product?	___	___
36. Is a nonexclusive license of a patent acceptable?	___	___
37. Are you willing to develop an idea to a patentable stage?	___	___
38. Will you develop a patent without acceptable prototype?	___	___
39. Will you accept a product that has been on the market but is not yet profitable?	___	___
40. Will you license a patent?	___	___
41. Do you insist on owning the product's patent?	___	___
42. Will you enter a joint venture for a new product with another company?	___	___
43. Would you merge with or buy a company that has good products but needs your company's strengths in manufacturing, sales, finances, or management?	___	___

The Product Configuration

44. Are there any maximum size limitations to a product you can manufacture?	___	___
45. Would weight of a product be a factor?	___	___

	Yes	No
46. Do warehousing facilities or yard space impose size limitation?	——	——
47. Does length of production time influence the desirability of a product?	——	——
48. Have you determined your equipment tolerance?	——	——
49. Do you have adequately trained personnel to do the job?	——	——
50. Would you prefer that a product be made of certain materials?	——	——
51. Are there manufacturing processes that should constitute the major portion of a new product?	——	——
52. Are there any manufacturing processes the product should not have?	——	——
53. Would a product requiring extensive quality control costs be desirable?	——	——

Finance

	Yes	No
54. Has an overall budget been established for a new product?	——	——
55. Have separate budgets been established for finding, acquisition, development, market research, manufacturing, and marketing the new product?	——	——
56. Has a time period been established by which a new product must become self-supporting, profitable, or capable of generating cash?	——	——
57. Does the new product require a certain profit margin to be compatible with your financial resources or company objectives?	——	——
58. Has external long-range financing been explored for your new product?	——	——
59. Is the length of the sales cycle for the new product known?	——	——
60. Do trade practices require you to furnish financial assistance, such as floor planning or dating plans, for distribution of your product?	——	——
61. Have you determined average inventory to sales ratio for the new product?	——	——
62. Have you determined average aging of accounts receivable for your new product?	——	——
63. Does the product have seasonal aspects?	——	——

SCREENING QUESTIONS

Other questions you should ask yourself may be grouped by your company's operations, the potential market, concept marketability, and engineering production. These are shown in Figure 2.1[2] and are known as screening questions because they act as a screen to eliminate products you should not consider.

Profile of Product Interest

Your answers to the 63 questions can lead to a well-thought-out guide as to the acceptability of any potential new product. A short, condensed profile helps communicate your needs. Such a profile also indicates a high degree of professional management, which sources of new products will welcome. For illustrative purposes a sample profile of the fictitious XYZ company follows.

The XYZ company, a defense-aerospace oriented precision metal stamping and machine shop, desires to acquire a product or product line to the following specifications:

Market—The product desired is one for use by industrial or commercial firms of a specific industry but not by the government or general public except incidentally.

Product—The product sought is one in which 60 percent of the total direct manufacturing cost consists of metal stamping and/or machining processes.

Price range—Open, but preferably the unit price to the user will be in the $100 to $400 range.

Volume—Open, but preferably a product that, when aggressively marketed, will produce $500,000 in sales the first year with an annual potential sale of 3 to 5 million dollars.

Finance—Initial resources to $150,000 in addition to present plant capacity are available for manufacturing a new product.

Type of acquisition—Prefer royalties to a patent but will consider purchase of a patent, joint venture, merger, or purchase of a company outright.

EIGHTEEN SOURCES FOR NEW PRODUCTS

Any of these sources may give you a new product idea that could make you a fortune.

1. *Currently successful products.* Look at currently successful products, but be careful not to copy them. Copy only the concept. If the idea is covered by a patent and you copy it exactly, you may be in violation of the law, copyright, or other types of protection. Even if your product is only very similar to another one, the individual who has introduced the product into the market has already captured a fair share, and you will be in the position of trying to take away that share.

2. *Inventor shows.* Many inventors are not good marketers. In fact, few inventions that are patented are ever actually produced in quantity. At inventor shows you will have the opportunity to see hundreds of new products that the inventors would like to license for

---

[2] Adapted from Tom W. White, "Use Variety of Internal, External Sources to Gather and Screen New Product Ideas," *Marketing News*, September 10, 1983, p. 12.

Company Operations

- How compatible is the concept with the current product lines?
- Does it represent an environmental hazard or threat to our production facility and to the facilities of our neighbors?
- Would it unreasonably interrupt manufacturing, engineering, or marketing activities?
- Could we meet the after-sale service requirements that would be demanded by customers?

Potential Market

- What is the size of the market?
- Where is the market located?
- What would be our potential market share?
- How diversified is the need for the product? Is it a one-industry or multi-industry product?
- How fast do we anticipate the market for the concept to grow?
- How stable would such a market be in a recession?

Concept Marketability

- Who would be our competitors?
- How good is their product?
- How well capitalized are potential competitors?
- How important is their product to the survival of their business?
- How is our product differentiated from the competition's? Will the differentiation provide a market advantage?
- Could we meet or beat the competiton's price?
- Is the product normally sold through our current distribution channels or would we have to make special arrangements?
- Do we have qualified sales personnel?
- Do we have suitable means by which to promote the product?
- What would we anticipate to be the life expectancy of the product? Is it going to move through the various life cycle stages in six months, six years, or sixty years?
- Will the product be offensive to the environment in which it will be used?

Figure 2.1. Screening questions. Adapted from Tom W. White, "Use Variety of Internal, External Sources to Gather and Screen New Product Ideas," *Marketing News* (September 16, 1983), p. 12. (*Figure continues on p. 48.*)

Engineering and Production

- What is the technical feasibility of the product?
- Do we have the technical capability to design it?
- Can it be manufactured at a marketable cost?
- Will the necessary production materials be readily available?
- Do we have the production capabilities to build it?
- Do we have adequate storage facilities for the raw materials and completed product?

Financial

- What is our required return on investment?
- What is our anticipated ROI for this product?
- Do we have the available capital?
- What would be the pay-back period?
- What is our break-even point?

Legal

- Is the product patentable?
- Can we meet legal restrictions regarding labeling, advertising, shipment, etc.?
- How significant are product warranty problems likely to be?
- Is the product vulnerable to existing or pending legislation?

Figure 2.1.   (*Continued*)

someone else to manufacture and sell for a royalty; perhaps they would like to sell the invention outright. You can find the inventor shows in your area by contacting your local chamber of commerce. Or, you can write to the Office of Inventions and Innovations, National Bureau of Standards, Washington, DC 20234, for a listing of the major inventor shows throughout the United States.

3. *Foreign products.* Foreign products are not always available in the United States, and frequently these products may be outstanding and sell quite well. Also, every country would like to see the number of its exports increased. This points to one primary source of foreign products: the commercial attachés of foreign consulates and embassies. You can find the numbers of foreign consulates or embassies in your telephone book if you happen to live in or near a large city. If you do not live close enough to these offices to make calling feasible, get a copy of the *Interntional Commerce Magazine Weekly*, published by the U.S. Department of Commerce. This magazine contains a license opportunity section in which

many foreign-made products available for licensing in the United States are listed. To get a copy, contact the Department of Commerce's local field office, which you will find in your telephone book. There are other books available that will help you if you are looking for products to import. One is the *American Register of Exporters and Importers*, published by the American Register of Exporters and Importers Corp., 38 Park Row, New York, NY 10038. Another is the *Directory of New York Importers*, published by Commerce Industry Association Institute, Inc., 65 Liberty St., New York, NY 10005. Also, in your local library, you will find at least one directory of importers and exporters published annually for almost every country in the world. Check in the reference or business section of your library. There are also overseas trade publications to help you. Some that are excellent sources of new product ideas are:

Hong Kong Enterprise, 36th-39th Fl., Office Tower, Convention Plaza, Harbour Road, Hong Kong.

Made in Europe, P.O. Box 174027, D-6, Frankfurt am Main, Germany.

Canada Commerce, Department of Industry, Trade and Commerce, Ottawa, Ontario, Canada K1A 0H5.

Commerce in France at the Chamber, 21 Avenue George V, Paris 8E, France.

Other foreign trade magazines can be found in your local library and will contain many additional products for you to manufacture or sell. Write to each and ask for a sample of the magazine.

   4. *Newspapers.* Read the business opportunity section of your local paper as well as such publications as the *Wall Street Journal*. Very frequently individuals who have a product to sell will advertise. You can contact them to negotiate the best deal possible for a product that may be very successful. In addition, you may consider advertising in these publications yourself, or in trade magazines, stating that you are interested in acquiring certain types of new products.

   5. *Local manufacturers.* Many manufacturers, at one time or another, have created a product that was not successful for his or her particular line of work or business, but that you may be able to make very successful. Simply call the president of each company and ask whether any old tooling exists for discontinued products from your line. Sometimes you can buy this tooling very cheaply, for perhaps only two or three hundred dollars, even though it may be worth $40,000 or more. This is one of Joe Cossman's secrets which helped to make him a multimillionaire. He frequently purchased old tooling from manufacturers, turned the product around, and made a fortune with it. Among the products acquired in this way were his famous Potato Spud Gun and Flippy the Frogman, both toys that sold in the millions.

   6. *NASA's Tech Briefs.* These bulletins are published periodically by the National Aviation and Space Administration. They describe new ideas, concepts, and patents for new products, all by-products of the space program. All of these are available for licensing from NASA. To get a copy of NASA's *Tech Briefs*, write to National Technical Information Service, U.S. Department of Commerce, Springfield, VA 22151.

   7. *Patent Abstracts Bibliography.* This semiannual publication lists NASA- and government-owned patents and applications for patents as a service to those seeking new licensable products for the commercial market. This may be ordered from the address above.

8. *New products from corporations.* You can write or contact major U.S. corporations. Most have research and development divisions that develop products the corporation has no interest in producing or selling. As a result, many have established special offices to market the licensing of their patents to individuals outside the company. The titles of these individuals vary; however, you can usually get in touch with them by contacting any corporation large enough to have a research and development division and asking for the director of patent licensing.

9. *Distress merchandise.* Every retailer has been in a situation where certain merchandise could not be sold. Under these circumstances, he cuts the price tremendously and then attempts to sell it at bargain rates. This material is called distress merchandise. When you see distress merchandise and think you have a market for it, check to see if there is a patent number on it. If there is, you can locate the inventor by purchasing a copy of the patent from the patent office. Or, if you live close to a depository for patents, you can look at the patent and find out the inventor's name and address at no cost at all. As I mentioned earlier, inventors are frequently poor marketers; that this is distress merchandise indicates that if the inventor still controls the patent, he or she may well be interested in licensing or outright sale. Contact the U.S. Patent Office, Washington, DC 20231.

10. *The Official Gazette of the U.S. Patent Office.* This bulletin is published weekly and lists all the patents granted by the patent office. Annual subscriptions are available from the Superintendent of Documents, Government Printing Office, Washington, DC 20402. The gazette contains a section that lists one-time-only patents available for sale or licensing. Many libraries also subscribe to the *Official Gazette* of the U.S. Patent Office. Patent attorneys in your area also may know of new products recently patented and available for licensing.

11. *Expired patents.* In the United States, a patent is good for only 17 years. The only exception is an ornamental design patent, which is good for 3½, 7, or 14 years. After that period, the patent is in the public domain and may be produced and sold by anyone. Also, you can look at the entire technology of any general product area by writing the patent office and asking for a list of all the patent numbers falling into a specified product area. The patent office will charge you for this service, but once you have the list of numbers you can go to a federal depository of patents, which is usually located in a major library, look up the patent number and get the full information. If the patent on the invention has expired, you are free to do with it what you will. If it has not expired, you may get the name and address of the inventor from the patent and approach him or her about licensing or purchasing the idea outright.

12. *Trade shows.* Like inventor shows, trade shows will have hundreds of products, some of which will be outstanding for your particular purposes. To find out about trade shows, get a copy of the *Directory of the United States Trade Shows, Expositions and Conventions.* Write to the United States Travel Service, U.S. Department of Commerce, Washington, DC 20230. Or, you may ask your local chamber of commerce about upcoming trade shows. Also, see Chapter 6.

13. *Old items from magazines.* If you look through an old Sears or Montgomery Ward catalog, you will notice how many of the products described therein are still of tremendous interest. You can also get good ideas from old magazines. Old mail order products are especially well suited for reissue. An afternoon spent in the library looking at old magazines may give you an idea to use as is or one to which you can give a new twist.

14. *Personalizing items.* People like to see items and buy items that have their names on them. This idea has been used again and again to sell products of all sorts, from brass business card cases sold through the *Wall Street Journal*, to briefcases, wallets, address labels, and paperweights. Do some research, because the field is far from exhausted. If you can find a product on which you can imprint someone's name, you probably have a winner.

15. *Commercial banks.* If you acquire all or part of another business, you may also acquire the products that business controls. Many small companies will find outstanding products that may need the strength your company can provide to become successful. This strength may have to do with personnel, facilities, equipment, know-how, marketing, or capital. Frequently, commercial banks will know of such a situation and can arrange the meeting between you and someone with a product you might be interested in. The bank does this for no charge with the expectation of receiving banking business, which might ensue from some sort of an arrangement.

16. *Small Business Investment Companies (SBICs) and investment bankers.* These companies are continually examining potential businesses, all of which have products of one sort or another. If you contact SBICs and investment bankers, they might well lead you to new products or an equity position in a business that has products desirable for your firm. You can obtain the latest list of SBICs from your local SBA office. A list of SBICs is also contained in the appendix of this book.

17. *Licensing brokers.* A licensing broker is a type of consultant having a wide range of contacts in the licensing field. They represent companies seeking licenses, that is, companies with products that they wish to license, as well as companies searching for products to license. They often have considerable experience in developing fair and reasonable licensing arrangements and can advise you or their client along these lines. You can locate licensing brokers through patent attorneys, in your local telephone book, and sometimes in your local newspapers under the Business Opportunities heading.

18. *The Thomas Register of Manufacturers.* This publication consists of several volumes listing manufacturers of all types of items in the United States. There are several such directories, and you can find them at your local library. You will find not only the names and addresses of the individuals running these companies, but also products that are available and the individuals to write about obtaining them. Every page is a source of another potential product for your business.

HOW TO DECIDE WHICH NEW PRODUCT TO DEVELOP OR INTRODUCE

As you begin to think about new product introduction and development, you will discover that there are many products among which to choose. Of course you can't develop them all; the problem then is deciding which products are best for your company. You may think this will be fairly easy—simply introduce those products that will bring the most profit. However, the choice is *not* easy. You may have limited financial resources and a more profitable product will have to be passed over in favor of one that you can afford. Or, it may be important to you to recoup your investment rapidly. Then, too, you must consider the particular background and experience you have, either with the type of product or with marketplaces. Here are 10 questions you should ask yourself about each product you are considering.[3]

1. Is the product one which fits the company's needs, interests, and abilities?
2. Is the chance of success good within the limits of reasonable time and expenditure?
3. Are the people connected with the project capable of carrying it to completion or can suitable people be hired?
4. Will a successfully completed project result in
   (a) new products?
   (b) improved products?
   (c) reduced cost?
5. Is there a market for the new or improved product?
6. Is the market substantial and profitable?
7. Can the present marketing organization really sell the product?
8. Will the product expand the base of operations of the company?
9. Will the product fill a real need or will it be only a fad?
10. Can the product be made with the present equipment? If not, can the estimated cost of tooling up be covered by increased sales?

These questions will help you screen out many products that will clearly be unsuited to your company or your particular situation.

Other factors you must consider in comparing potential new products for development and for which you must obtain factual information or forecasts include the following:

Total profit
Profitability
The cost to develop
The market for the product
The life cycle, including estimated length
The cost of research and development
The plant overcapacity or undercapacity
The synergistic effect with other products in your product line
The cost of putting the product on the market
Technical know-how required
Labor skills required
Availability of raw materials
By-products that may be sold from the manufacture of this product
Good will
Marketing know-how available

[3] Alan A. Smith, *Technology and Your New Products*, Small Business Administration (1967), p. 11.

Physical distribution facilities
Available distribution channels

You can see that deciding which product to introduce is no five-minute task. But the effort is worthwhile: you want the product you select to be a success.

Now we must get down to the serious assessment of the wisdom of spending money for one project over another. The end result is a decision as to which potential products you will introduce and which you will not. First, list those factors you think are most important for comparison: high return on investment, a proprietary position, a large market share, low risk of failure in development, low risk of failure in marketing, huge demand, and so forth. Certain quantitative methods of comparison are also recommended. For example, you can calculate the total profit of a particular project if you can estimate its life cycle by using either the present value or internal rate of return methods shown for comparison in the financial section of this book. You can compare the return for each investment, for each project, by dividing the projected return by the investment and choosing those projects that have the larger return. If time to recoup your investment is important, compare using the pay-back formula, investment divided by the return per year. All of these various quantitative and nonquantitative comparisons are placed on a rating sheet as shown in Figure 2.2.

Now, you must determine factor weighting. You do this by taking your list of important factors and deciding which of these factors are more important than others. Let us say that you have four factors you consider to be of equal importance. These four factors may be technical know-how, profitability, product synergism with other products in your product line, and marketing know-how. If these are your only factors and you consider them to be of equal importance, each would be assigned a weighting of 25%. The importance of the factors to you will be indicated by their percentages. Let's say that you consider profitability far and away the most important of the four factors. Perhaps you will assign it 50%. This then leaves 50% to be apportioned among the other three factors. You might assign 10% to technical know-how, 20% to product synergism, and 20% to marketing know-how. In all cases, the total percentages assigned to all the different factors you have listed should equal 100%.

Now, look at each product you are considering and assign points to the project for each factor you have listed. The points assigned are from 1 to 10. Those products that seem very good in relation to a particular factor receive 10 points. Those that are very poor receive only 1 point. For example, consider technical know-how. If you have the technical know-how to develop a particular product easily, give it a 10-point rating. If you do not, give it a low point score, perhaps only 1 or 2.

Now that you have completed the point assignments, you must multiply the weighting percentage by the points assigned. The result (shown in Figure 2.3) is a total point rating for this product. Those products with the highest ratings are the ones you should introduce.

Relevant Factor	Relative Factor Weighting
Demand for product	
Strength	3%
Period	3
Need	4
Market	
Size	6
Location	5
Competition	5
Product	
Compatibility with current line	1
Uniqueness of features	8
Price	4
Protection	3
Company strengths	
Marketing	6
Location	2
Special facilities	4
Production	2
Financial considerations	
Capital budgeting	8
ROI	8
Pay-back	8
Cash flow	8
Product development	
Technical Risk	5
Producibility	4
Scheduling	3
Total	100%

Figure 2.2.   Relevant factors for selecting new products for introduction.

HOW TO BEAT YOUR COMPETITION IN NEW PRODUCT INTRODUCTION AND DEVELOPMENT

You may feel that because you are a small firm you have little or no chance to beat your larger competitors, especially in introducing a new product or a new service. Actually, a small firm can often win out over its competition. Here's how.

Ability to Make Quick Decisions

A small company, where one man or a few men make decisions, has an extreme advantage in terms of time. Larger companies, when making even simple decisions, act slowly because of bureaucracy and many levels in the managerial chain of

Factor	Relative Weight	Point Value	Final Value
Demand for product			
Strength	0.03	7	0.21
Period	0.03	3	0.09
Need	0.04	1	0.04
Market			
Size	0.06	4	0.24
Location	0.05	2	0.10
Competition	0.05	7	0.35
Product			
Compatibility with current line	0.01	6	0.06
Uniqueness of features	0.08	2	0.16
Price	0.04	1	0.04
Protection	0.03	1	0.03
Company strengths			
Marketing	0.06	2	0.12
Location	0.02	8	0.16
Special facilities	0.04	1	0.04
Production	0.02	1	0.02
Financial considerations			
Capital budgeting	0.08	5	0.40
ROI	0.08	4	0.32
Pay-back	0.08	3	0.24
Cash flow	0.08	2	0.16
Product development			
Technical risk	0.05	1	0.05
Producibility	0.04	7	0.28
Scheduling	0.03	2	0.06
	1.00		
	Total point value for this product		3.17

Figure 2.3. New product selection matrix (analysis for a simulated product).

command. You can operate much more rapidly and efficiently. It is not unusual for a small firm to make a decision in one day that would take a large firm several months or even a year or more.

Lower Break-Even Point

Because a smaller firm carries a much lower overhead, the break-even point for your introduction of a new product or a new service will be much lower than that of a larger firm. Also, because as a smaller firm you can be more efficient, your break-even point can be lower than that of a larger competitor. Many large firms cannot introduce certain new products or services unless the volume is sufficiently large. You are able to introduce products or services to service a smaller market.

A volume that is tremendously profitable for you may be unprofitable for a larger company.

Regional Sales

Because of these same qualities, many small firms can serve a specific region in their locality and provide much better customer service and a far more effective and efficient promotional effort than can their larger competitors. This is the reason that many local areas have their own brands of beer and other commodities. In the local area the small company frequently outsells the larger competitor many times over.

Custom-Made Quality Products

Large firms, because of their volume requirements, frequently cannot do custom work. For the same reason, quality sometimes suffers. This leaves a niche for the smaller company that can do custom work with individuals or other companies that desire this type of product or service. In fact, some small companies absolutely monopolize the custom-made quality markets in their industries. They charge high prices and make huge profit margins because they have developed this market, which their bigger competitors cannot reach.

SOURCES OF HELP FOR DEVELOPING AND INTRODUCING NEW PRODUCTS

Much of the work necessary in order to introduce a new product or service can be purchased by you, and other help can be obtained at no or very little cost. Here are some sources that will help you with your development and introduction of new products.

Management and Marketing Consultants

Management and marketing consultants can perform a wide range of services for you in the development and introduction of a new product. These services include evaluating potential sales, creating a marketing plan, setting up pricing, locating executives to run your programs, investigating material costs and sources, checking out competitive problems the new product may face, budgets, developing financial schedules, and other tasks.

Industrial Designers and Engineers

These individuals will help you to design the new product, help you make it more efficient, or allow you to produce it more cheaply. They can improve the physical appearance of the product, making old products look new and visually appealing. They can redesign products; correct product defects; reduce noise vibration, weight and bulk, and the number of parts; eliminate hazards; solve engineering problems; and suggest new materials.

Patent Attorneys and Agents

Patent attorneys and agents can help you make patent searches and applications and help you with related patent, copyright, and trademark work.

Package Designers

Package designers will help by developing trademarks or logos, designing containers to hold the product (recommending sizes and shapes of packages, bottles, and enclosures), designing merchandise tags, advising on label requirements levied by city, state, or federal government, conducting drop tests for packaging, and so forth.

Advertising Agencies

Advertising agencies can handle your entire promotional effort, including writing copy, preparing graphics, suggesting other means of promotion, and suggesting which medium and vehicle most suitable to your product.

Marketing Research Firms

Marketing research firms can help you decide what new products to introduce. They offer preliminary consumer research, preliminary industrial research, exploratory research, and other means of determining whether it makes sense to introduce a new product at all.

All of the commercial firms above can be located either through the Yellow Pages or through engineering, marketing, or consultant trade associations. Before engaging any firm, it is wise to check their references; talk to at least three firms who have used their services. You might also check with their trade association and with your local Better Business Bureau. Remember that this book shows you how you can do many of these services yourself at a much reduced cost.

Noncommercial Sources

Some universities have centers funded by the National Science Foundation for helping inventors and innovators with their new product development and introduction into the marketplace. One of the better ones is the University of Oregon's Experimental Center for the Advancement of Invention and Innovation. Much of the information that the University of Oregon has is computerized. This allows the university to evaluate any new product idea on 33 different criteria and help you screen out bad ideas. Each submitted idea is evaluated against the following criteria: legality, safety, environmental impact, societal impact, potential market, product life cycle, usage for learning, product visibility, service, durability, new competition, functional feasibility, production feasibility, development status, investment cost, trend of demand, product line potential, need, promotion, appearance, price, protection, pay-back period, profitability, product interdependence, research and development, stability of demand, consumer, user compatibility, marketing research, distribution, perceived function, existing competition, and potential sales. The address is: Experimental Center for the Advancement of Invention and Innovation, College of Business Administration, 131 Gilbert Hall, University of Oregon, Eugene, OR 97403.

The Small Business Institute (SBI) is sponsored by the Small Business Administration and currently is located at 450 colleges and universities around the country. The assistance provided by the SBI usually addresses the business part of new product introduction, including marketing, finances, accounting, management problems, and so forth. Business students of the university supervised by professors provide this service to you free of charge. Contact your local Small Business Administration to learn more. The addresses of the SBA are listed in Appendix I. The following two organizations may also be of assistance to you with your new product development and introduction problems: (1) the American Association of Small Research Companies, 8794 West Chester Pike, Upper Darby, PA 19082, and (2) the Association for the Advancement of Invention and Innovation, Suite 605, 1735 Jefferson Davis Highway, Arlington, VA 22202.

YOUR OWN PRODUCT SURVEY

You might also consider doing some simple marketing research to help yourself. Basically, you want to ask these questions:[4]

1. What do you think of the product concept?
2. Would you buy it?
3. How much do you think it should sell for?
4. How often would you purchase it?
5. Where would you expect to purchase it?
6. What additional features should the product have?
7. What features should be eliminated?
8. How would you expect to learn about the product's availability?
9. How large should the product be?

[4] William A. Cohen, *The Practice of Marketing Management* (Macmillan Publishing Co.: New York, 1988), p. 310.

10. What color should the product be?
11. How would you use the product?
12. Are there benefits of this product over competing products or products that it might replace?
13. Would you buy this product to replace the product you are currently using?

TWENTY-ONE WARNING SIGNALS

Peter Hilton, founder of the New Product Institute and the president of Kastor, Hilton, Chesley, Clifford and Atherton, Inc., an advertising agency in New York, has documented 21 warning signals, from the consumer, the trade, or company management, that indicate something is wrong with new product or new service introduction.[5] If any of these occur as you begin new product introduction or development, take the required action.

From the consumer:

1. The price is too high.
2. I don't know how to use it—I must be educated.
3. Certainly it's a better product, but it's not quite worth the extra money.

From the trade:

4. The product will have a low rate of turnover.
5. The product will disturb our business on established items—maybe destroy more business than it creates.
6. We are afraid of the servicing problems this new item may create.
7. The product is an unwanted addition to a field already crowded.
8. There is no retail shelf space or floor space available for this product.
9. The nature of the product is such that it must be sold in an odd size or shape ill suited to shipping or display facilities.
10. This product cannot be sold without individual demonstration.

From company management:

11. It is difficult to procure or procure consistently the right raw materials for this product.
12. It is difficult to project costs because the raw material market is subject to considerable price fluctuation.

[5] Peter Hilton, *New Product Introduction* Small Business Administration, 1961.

13. Plant production would be seriously hampered if changes were made to handle the manufacture of this new product.
14. The product is good but impossible to package.
15. The patent situation is confused and we would be vulnerable.
16. The probable channel of distribution of this new product is not clearly defined.
17. To make salesmen's time available for this product would jeopardize our established line.
18. The new product does not hold promise of sufficient volume or frequency of purchase to maintain distribution.
19. The trademark situation is unsatisfactory.
20. Certain government regulations would make marketing of this product difficult.
21. With this product we would be competing in a field dominated by strong, aggressive companies with superior marketing resources.

SOURCES OF ADDITIONAL INFORMATION

Corporate Strategy and New Product Innovation, edited by Robert R. Rothberg, published by the Free Press, a division of Macmillan Publishing Co., Inc., 866 Third Avenue, New York, NY 10022.

Handbook of New Product Development, by Peter Hilton, published by Prentice-Hall, Inc., Englewood Cliffs, NJ 07632.

Innovation, by Richard Foster, published by Summit Books, a division of Simon & Schuster, Inc., 1230 Avenue of the Americas, New York, NY 10020.

Innovation, by Milton D. Rosenau, Jr., published by Lifetime Learning Publications, a division of Wadsworth, Inc., 10 Davis Drive, Belmont, CA 94002.

New Product Development Strategies, by Frederick D. Buggie, published by AMACOM, a division of the American Management Association, 135 West 50th Street, New York, NY 10020.

New Product Introduction for Small Business Owners, by Peter Hilton, published by the Small Business Administration, Washington, DC 20402.

New Products, New Profits, edited by Elibeth Marting, published by the American Management Association, 135 West 50th Street, New York, NY 10020.

Planning New Products, by Philip Marvin, published by the Penton Publishing Co., Cleveland, OH 44101.

Product Planning, edited by A. Edward Spitz, published by Auerbach Publishers, 121 North Broad Street, Philadelphia, PA 19107.

Technology and Your New Products, by Alan A. Smith, published by the Small Business Administration, Washington, DC 20402.

HOW TO PRICE YOUR PRODUCTS AND SERVICES

COST VERSUS PRICE

It is important to realize right from the start that it is the market, not your costs, that determines the price at which you can sell your product or service. Your costs only establish a floor below which you cannot sell your product or service and make money. Therefore, in determining the price for your product or service, you should recognize that the relevant price is somewhere between the price floor that you established with your cost data and the price ceiling that is the maximum amount for which you could possibly sell your product or service.

THE IMPORTANCE OF THE PRICING DECISION

The decision as to what price to ask for your product or service exerts a major influence on several important areas. These include the following:

1. *Profit.* The price you select determines how much profit you will make.

2. *Recouping your investment.* The price at which you decide to sell your product or service will determine how quickly you will be able to recover the investment you made in developing and marketing your product or service.

3. *Resources available for promotion.* Your price will help determine the amount of financial resources you have at any given time to compete in the marketplace.

4. *Ability to penetrate a new market.* The price you select will determine whether or not you will be successful in getting into a new market.

5. *Image.* The price you select creates an image of the product and of your business. A high price may imply status and quality. A low price may imply economy.

THE EMPHASIS ON NONPRICE COMPETITION

With the considerable importance of pricing in determining the success of your business, you would think that every single business owner and manager devotes a great deal of thought to it. However, this is not true. One reason is that, even in today's economy, many consumers have much larger disposable incomes than in the past. Therefore, price may be of less importance, depending upon what you are selling. Also, with the many sophisticated marketing techniques available today, many marketers feel they don't need to use price as a means of attracting consumers. Some businesspeople are simply unaware of the sensitivity of demand in the marketplace to increases or decreases in price.

Perhaps those most aware are those dealing in direct response marketing, where testing of all types, including of different prices, is a must. For example, I once sold a four-volume set of booklets on how to become a published writer for $19.95. During testing I reduced the price to $14.95, wondering whether the increased number of sales would make up for the loss in contribution of each individual set sold. Note that I assumed that sales would go up as price was reduced. The results were quite surprising. Not only did I lose money because of the $5 differential in price for each unit sold, but the total number of sales actually went down. When I increased the price to $19.95, sales went up to their former level.

Some businessmen avoid serious pricing decisions because they feel there are fewer worries if they maintain a single stable price. They don't have to change the prices of the items in their literature or catalog, or reevaluate inventories for accounting, or renegotiate contracts. To them, price just isn't worth the worry. I hope to convince you in this chapter that this is not a good policy.

The fact that many business owners do not seriously price their products or services gives you an opportunity to win out over your competition and make a great deal of money by doing so.

WHEN SHOULD YOU CONSIDER PRICING OR REPRICING?

You should consider pricing or repricing what you are selling at any time, but especially in the following circumstances:

1. When you are introducing a new product or products
2. When there is an interrelated addition to your product line which may affect the pricing of older items already in the line
3. When you wish to penetrate a new market

4. When the competition has changed its price
5. During periods of inflation
6. During periods of depression
7. When you are about to change your strategy
8. When you are testing to find the "correct price"
9. When the product is in a different part of its life cycle

THE ECONOMIC THEORY OF PRICING

According to economic theory, price is determined according to the downward-sloping demand curve as shown in Figure 3.1. As prices increase, a smaller quantity of the product or service is demanded by your customer. The implication of the downward slope of the demand curve is that it takes a lower price to sell more. However, note that according to a new demand curve, D+1, which is higher than the other demand curve, D, in Figure 3.1, for the same price you can sell more products. The implication of this higher demand curve is that in order to shift the demand from D to D+1 you must take additional action, such as increased advertising or a sweepstakes or some other form of promotion. However, at the same price you may also sell fewer products if the demand curve shifts to D−1 as shown in Figure 3.1. This can happen as technology causes obsolescence of your product. When the slide rule was first replaced by the hand-held calculator, the demand curve shifted downward, and eventually the slide rule could no longer be sold. This shift could also be caused by a product failure, such as the crash of a certain model

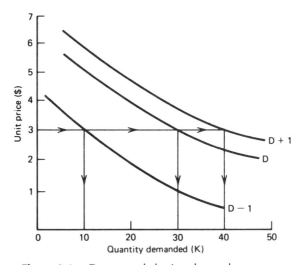

Figure 3.1. Downward-sloping demand curve.

of aircraft. Now, at the same price, a smaller number of that model of aircraft will be sold.

Now, even though this is true, a firm can sometimes charge more and sell more product; this is what happened with the mail order product I mentioned earlier. This is true because of selective demand for a specific product and the way the product is perceived. Some factors here are distinctive features, perceived value, and status.

HOW TO PRICE A NEW PRODUCT

Let's look first at perhaps one of the most difficult pricing tasks that any manager of a small business or even a giant business faces: the pricing of a new product not yet in the market. To price a new product, there are three steps you must take:

1. Determine your objective.
2. Find the demand versus the price.
3. Determine your basic pricing strategy.

Determining Your Objective

In any pricing decision that you make, you should think about what your overall objective is. Research in the United States showed that pricing decisions were made primarily for the following five business objectives:

1. To see a return on investment
2. To stabilize price and profit margin
3. To capture a target market share
4. To meet or prevent competition
5. To maximize profit

These pricing objectives show that your pricing decision should be based on a combination of goals that are internal to your company and the external market environment.

HOW TO ESTIMATE DEMAND VERSUS PRICE

Now that your basic objectives have been established, you must find some way to estimate the demand versus the price. The following methods have all been found effective in estimating this demand.

   1. *Ask customers.* From asking a sufficient number of customers about various potential prices, you will get some idea of how much of your product can be sold at each price. You may also learn the percentages of your potential customers that will buy at each price. For example, a survey may show that 80% of your customers would buy the product if the price were $5, 20% if $7, and 10% if $10. This information will also give you some indication of the profits that you might expect. The drawback here is that people will not always respond truthfully. (See Chapter 9, on marketing research, for more details.)

2. *Comparison with close substitutes or a replacement item.* We may compare the item we are going to introduce with similar items on the market today—what their prices are and how many are selling at those prices. If the product is totally new, then we may try to find a product it is replacing. For example, if we are introducing a new type of electronic watch, we may derive some initial price demand curves from the old design.

3. *Cost savings.* Sometimes, especially with industrial products, a price can be calculated based on the cost savings possible with the adoption of a new product. If you are going to price in this way, it will be important for you to promote the cost savings to your prospective customers.

4. *Test marketing.* Test marketing of the product is an outstanding way to derive demand versus product price. All that is necessary is that the product be offered at various prices to the same market. Because this type of testing requires the customer actually to put money on the barrel head for the product, it is much more accurate than simply asking the potential customer whether he or she would or would not purchase.

Once quantitative figures can be established for demand at various prices that we may set, we will consider the various pricing strategies that may be adopted.

Pricing Strategies for a New Product

For a new product, there are three basic pricing strategies. These are:

1. A high-price strategy known as skimming
2. A low-price strategy known as penetration
3. A meet-the-competition price strategy

Skimming. This strategy is used when the product is so new that basically there is no competition, or when you wish to give the product status through the price. You can skim the market using the high price, and later on, when competition enters the market, you can reduce the price to meet the competition. Such a strategy also enables you to have more resources available to meet the competition when that day comes.

Penetration. This strategy is used to get yourself into a new market by going in at a very low price. Some people will try your product simply because your price is significantly lower than the price the competition is charging. Naturally, you must be very careful when using this strategy because of the implications regarding quality and the possibility of getting stuck with a low-status image. Also, maintaining the low price with a lower contribution to profit margin means very high volume sales, which cannot always be achieved. Many companies using this strategy do so only to get the product tried by prospective customers, and once it has been adopted by a sufficient number the price is raised and the strategy changed to a meet-the-competition, or an even higher, price.

Meet-the-Competition.   According to this strategy, you are going to price your product or service at the same price as the competition's. If you are going to do this, you must have something else unique or people will not switch from the competition to your company unless they are thoroughly dissatisfied with the competition for some other reason. For example, perhaps you set the same price as your competition, but the quality of your product is much higher; or the reliability of your product is better; or your service is better and your employees more friendly. The point is that you must offer something different, something more than your competition, or people will have no reason to switch.

SECOND PHASE PRICING

After you have introduced a new product or service into the market, you may or may not wish to maintain the price. Perhaps you introduced a product that was totally new and for which you have no patent or other protection. After some time, the competition will enter the market with new products that are similar to yours. Perhaps they will be using a penetration price, or some price lower than the one you are offering. How do you react to this potential loss of your market? Perhaps your product has gone rapidly through the life cycle. Let us say you are selling an electronic calculator that technology has now rendered obsolete. In this case you may make the decision to do a remainder sale and sell everything out at a fraction of its initial high price, perhaps even at or below your cost. Whatever second phase strategy you work out, you must begin to think ahead even as you introduce a new product.

Here is an excellent example of a second phase strategy. The individual who used it actually increased his price when the competition entered with a penetration price. During one summer season, marketing genius Joe Cossman introduced the now common sprinkler hose with hundreds of tiny holes placed in a flexible tubing to allow water to sprinkle the grass or flowers in any desired pattern. This unique plastic hose was easily duplicated and no patent protection was possible. Therefore, Cossman expected and had many competitors during the second summer season. However, Cossman's method of distribution was not to sell direct but instead to sell through grocery stores to which he gave an approximate 50% discount from retail price. Instead of reducing his price when the competition came in, Joe actually increased his retail price. He passed the increased profit margin on to his distributors, the grocery stores. This increased their profits, and at the same time the image of the Cossman sprinkler was that it was of higher quality than the products of the competition. Cossman's innovative price strategy extended his control of the market, and he made more profit the second year with competition than he did the first year without.

Always think through your situation regarding distribution and other important factors in developing an innovative pricing decision.

WHAT TO DO IF NO ONE BUYS

If the market will not take your product or your service at the price you have established, to cover your costs and to allow you to make a desired profit, you have five alternatives:

1. *Lower the price.* This means you are accepting less profit in the hope that more of your profit or service will be purchased.

2. *Increase the price.* This means that you are repositioning your product as compared with that of the competition so your product will be perceived by your potential customers as being of higher quality or better in some other way.

3. *Reduce your costs.* In this way you can maintain the price and still be profitable with the amount you are selling.

4. *Drop the product completely.* This may sound drastic, but sometimes it is the wisest course

5. *Differentiate your product from that of your competition.* This is the same sort of thing you must do if you establish a meet-the-competition price for a new product. That is, you emphasize quality, service, product performance, delivery time, financing arrangements, discounting, or some other aspect that is important to your customer.

PRICING POLICIES

There are three basic pricing policy categories:

1. *Single price.* You have one price for all buyers regardless of timing, quantity purchase, and other factors.

2. *Variable price.* Price is always open to negotiation.

3. *Nonvariable price.* You offer the same price to all under similar conditions. Of course, under different conditions a different price is offered.

A single price has few advantages. The single price policy is used frequently in the consumer field or when selling to other small-purchase customers. The policy is, of course, easy to administer, and the emphasis is always on nonprice appeals, including all types of promotion such as face-to-face salesmen. Clearly, this policy will not be very attractive to individuals who buy in large quantities.

When selling to customers who make larger purchases, it is important to understand when it is best to have a nonvariable or a variable pricing policy.

As noted earlier, a variable price can be negotiated. This has the following advantages. First, you can make adjustments to your price instantly during the process of negotiation. Secondly, you can be flexible in your dealings. Whatever the competition does can be countered immediately, and you can easily respond to other changes in the marketplace during the negotiation process. Finally, you can vary your appeal to be based on price or nonprice promotionals according to the situation.

However, a variable pricing policy also has many disadvantages. Since the resulting price charged will be different from one customer to another, the potential exists for bad feelings on the part of those customers who pay more for the same product or service. Also, for very large contracts, it will take time to negotiate. It is often said that time is money, and when your own time or the time of valuable people resources in your firm is spent, costs will not be insignificant. Sometimes having a variable price means that you will not be able to negotiate yourself, in which cases you must delegate the pricing decision to someone working for you. This means loss of your control, to a certain degree, over the pricing in your firm. The potential also exists for abuse in this delegation since some of your people may resort to what amounts to price cutting instead of actually "selling." Finally, there are some legal complications which may result, growing out of a law known as the Robinson–Patman Act. We will discuss the implications of this act for a variable pricing policy shortly.

A *nonvariable price* has advantages as well. Clearly, it simplifies the selling process since no one except you has any authority to vary the prices. It is easy to administer such a policy, and clearly it is fair to all buyers. Naturally, you will avoid any legal complications of having a variable price, and you, of course, maintain control over the pricing decision.

DISCOUNT POLICIES

Discount policies can also affect sales very dramatically. One entrepreneur, the inventor of a unique item used by pilots, lost thousands of dollars in potential orders from the government simply because he had no discount policy. Discount policy may be classified in the following ways:

1. *A promotional discount.* This means special discounts to the consumer or perhaps within your distribution or organization to promote your product or your service.

2. *A trade discount.* This is a discount on the basis of the position in the distribution channel, such as a discount offered to a retailer or a wholesaler if you are a manufacturer, or anyone between you and the ultimate consumer of your product or service.

3. *A quantity discount to encourage large orders.* There are two types of quantity discounts. One is a noncumulative type, which is based purely on the quantity ordered at a specific period of time. Another is the cumulative discount, which is increased depending on quantities ordered by the same buyer over an indefinite period of time. Cumulative discounts tend to tie the buyer to the seller.

THE ROBINSON–PATMAN ACT OF 1936

The Robinson–Patman Act addresses price discrimination. Its intent is to regulate any tendency to injure competition. The Federal Trade Commission or a private complainant can initiate action against you for your pricing policies if you sell at different prices to two or more competing customers engaged in interstate commerce and your acts have a tendency to injure competition. There are certain defenses against these accusations. For example, it is not a violation of the act to sell at different prices because of cost differences, or to lower the price to one customer to meet the competition, or to lower the price because of changing market conditions. When in doubt, consult your attorney.

TWO CHECKLISTS FOR PRICING

The following checklists are provided to assist you in pricing. The first is a general pricing checklist for managers developed by Joseph D. O'Brien, associate professor of marketing at the College of Business Administration, Boston College, Boston, Massachusetts.[1] The second is a special pricing checklist for small retailers developed by Bruce J. Walker, associate professor of marketing at Arizona State University, Tempe, Arizona.[2]

Checklist One: Examining Costs, Sales Volume, and Profits

The questions following should be helpful when you look at prices from the viewpoint of costs, sales volume, and profits.

Costs and Prices

The small retailer who sets the price for an item by applying a standard markup may be overlooking certain cost factors connected with that item. The following questions are designed to help you gather information helpful for determining prices on specific types of items.

	Yes	No
1. Do you know which of your operating costs remain the same regardless of sales volume?	____	____

[1] Joseph D. O'Brien, *A Pricing Checklist for Managers*, Small Business Administration (1972).

[2] Bruce J. Walker, *A Pricing Checklist for Small Retailers*, Small Business Administration (1979).

	Yes	No

2. Do you know which of your operating costs decrease percentage-wise as your sales volume increases?

3. Have you ever figured out the break-even point for your items selling at varying price levels?

4. Do you look behind high gross margin percentages? (For example, a product with a high gross margin may also be a slow turnover item with high handling costs. Thus it may be less profitable than lower margin items that turn over quickly.)

5. When you select items for price reductions, do you project the effects on profits? (For example, if a food marketer considers whether to run canned ham or rump steak on sale, an important cost factor is labor. Practically none is involved in featuring canned ham; however, a rump steak sale requires the skill of a meat-cutter and this labor cost might mean little or no profits.)

Pricing and Sales Volume

An effective pricing program should also consider sales volume. For example, high prices might limit your sales volume while low prices might result in a large but unprofitable volume. The following questions should be helpful in determining what is right for your situation.

6. Have you considered setting a sales volume goal and then studying to see if your prices will help you reach it?

7. Have you set a target of a certain number of new customers for next year? (If so, how can pricing help you to attract them?)

8. Should you limit the quantities of low-margin items that a customer can buy when they are on sale? (If so, will you advertise this policy?)

9. What is your policy when a sale item is sold out before the end of the advertised period? Do you allow disappointed customers to buy the item later at the sale price?

Pricing and Profits

Prices should help bring in sales that are profitable over the long haul. The following questions are designed to help you think about pricing policies and their effect on your annual profits.

	Yes	No
10. Do you have all the facts on costs, sales, and competitive behavior?		
11. Do you set prices with the hope of accomplishing definite objectives, such as a 1 percent profit increase over last year?		
12. Have you set a given level of profits in dollars and in percent of sales?		
13. Do you keep records that will give you the needed facts on profits, losses, and prices?		
14. Do you review your pricing practices periodically to make sure they are helping to achieve your profit goals?		

Judging the Buyer, Timing, and Competitors

The questions in this part are designed to help you check your practices for judging the buyer (your customers), your timing, and your competitors.

The Buyer and Pricing Strategy

After you have your facts on costs, the next point of concern—whether you are changing a price, putting in a new item, or checking out your present price practices—must be the *customer*. Knowledge of your customers helps you to determine how to vary prices in order to get the average gross margin you need for making a profit. (For example, to get an average gross margin of 35 percent, some retailers put a low markup—10 percent, for instance—on items they promote as traffic builders and use high markup—sometimes as much as 60 percent—on slow-moving items.) The following questions should be helpful in checking your knowledge about your customers.

	Yes	No
15. Do you know whether your customers shop around and for what items?		
16. Do you know how your customers make their comparisons? By reading newspaper ads? Store shopping? Hearsay?		
17. Are you trying to appeal to customers who buy on price alone? To those who buy on quality alone? To those who combine the two?		
18. Do any of your customers tell you that your prices are in line with those of your competitors? Higher? Lower?		
19. Do you know which item (or types of items) your customers call for even though you raise the price?		
20. Do you know which items (or types of items) your customers leave on your shelves when you raise the price?		

	Yes	No
21. Do certain items seem to appeal to customers more than others when you run weekend, clearance, or special-day sales?	_____	_____
22. Have you used your individual sales records to classify your present customers according to the volume of their purchases?	_____	_____
23. Will your customers buy more if you use multiple pricing? (For example, three for 39 cents for products with rapid turnover.)	_____	_____
24. Do your customers respond to odd prices more readily than even prices, for example, 99 cents rather than $1?	_____	_____
25. Have you decided on a pricing strategy to create a favorable price image with your customers? (For example, a retailer with 8,000 different items might decide to make a full margin on all medium or slow movers while featuring— at low price levels—the remaining fast movers.)	_____	_____
26. If you are trying to build a quality price image, do your individual customer records, such as charge account statements, show that you are selling a larger number of higher priced items than you were 12 months ago?	_____	_____
27. Do your records of individual customer accounts and your observations of customer behavior in the store show price as the important factor in their buying? Service? Assortments? Some other consideration?	_____	_____

Pricing and Timing

Effective merchandising means that you have the right product, at the right place, at the right price, and at the *right time*. All are important, but timing is the critical element for the small retailer. The following questions should be helpful in determining the right time for adjusting prices.

	Yes	No
28. Are you a "leader" or a "follower" in announcing your price reductions? (The follower, even though he matches his competitors, creates a negative impression on his customers.)	_____	_____
29. Have you studied your competitors to see whether they follow any sort of pattern when making price changes? (For example, do some of them run clearance sales earlier than others?)	_____	_____
30. Is there a pattern to the kinds of items that competitors promote at lower prices at certain times of the month or year?	_____	_____

Yes   No

31. Have you decided whether it is better to take early mark-
    downs on seasonal or style goods or to run a clearance
    sale at the end of the season?   _____   _____
32. Have you made regular annual sales, such as anniversary
    sales, fall clearance, or holiday cleanup, so popular that
    many customers wait for them rather than buying in season? _____   _____
33. When you change a price, do you make sure that *all*
    customers know about it through price tags and so on?   _____   _____
34. Do you try to time price reductions so they can be promoted
    in your advertising?   _____   _____

Competition and Pricing

When you set prices, you have to consider how your competitors might react to
your prices. The starting place is learning as much as you can about their price
structures. The following questions are designed to help you check out this phase
of pricing.

35. Do you use all the available channels of information to
    keep you up-to-date on your competitors' price policies?
    (Some useful sources of information are: things your cus-
    tomers tell you; the competitor's price list and catalogs,
    if he uses them; his advertising; reports from your suppliers;
    trade paper studies; and shoppers employed by you.)   _____   _____
36. Should your policy be to try always to sell above or below
    competition? Only to meet it?   _____   _____
37. Is there a pattern to the way your competitors respond to
    your price cuts?   _____   _____
38. Is the leader pricing of your competitors affecting your
    sales volume to such an extent that you must alter your
    pricing policy on individual items (or types of items) of
    merchandise?   _____   _____
39. Do you realize that no two competitors have identical cost
    curves? (This difference in costs means that certain price
    levels may be profitable for you but unprofitable for your
    competitor or vice versa.)   _____   _____

Practices That Can Help Offset Price

Some small retailers take advantage of the fact that price is not always the determining
factor in making a sale. They supply customer services and offer other inducements
to offset the effect of competitors' lower prices, such as delivery service and comfortable

shoppers' meeting places. The following questions are designed to help you take a look at some of these practices.

		Yes	No
40.	Do the items or services you sell have advantages for which customers are willing to pay a little more?	_____	_____
41.	Based on personal observation of customer behavior in your store, can you tell about how much more customers will pay for such advantages?	_____	_____
42.	Should you change your services so as to create an advantage for which your customers will be willing to pay?	_____	_____
43.	Does your advertising emphasize customer benefits rather than price?	_____	_____
44.	Are you using the most common nonprice competitive tools? (For example, have you tried to alter your product or service to the existing market? Have you tried stamps, bonus purchase gifts, or other plans for building repeat business?)	_____	_____
45.	Should policies on returned goods be changed so as to impress your customers better?	_____	_____
46.	If you sell repair services, have you checked out your guarantee policy?	_____	_____
47.	Should you alter assortments of merchandise to increase sales?	_____	_____

Checklist Two: Pricing Checklist for Small Retailers

1. Is the relative price of this item very important to your target customers? The importance of price depends on the specific product and on the individual. Some shoppers are very price-conscious; others want convenience and knowledgeable sales personnel. Because of these variations, you need to learn about your customers' desires in relation to different products. Having sales personnel seek feedback from shoppers is a good starting point.   _____ _____

2. Are prices based on estimates of the number of units that consumers will demand at various price levels? Such demand-oriented pricing is superior to cost-oriented pricing. In the cost approach, a predetermined amount is added to the cost of the merchandise, whereas the demand approach considers what consumers are willing to pay.   _____ _____

3. Have you established a price range for the product? The cost of merchandise will be at one end of the price range

Yes   No

and the level above which consumers will *not* buy the
product at the other end.   _____   _____
4. Have you considered what price strategies would be compatible with your store's total retailing mix, which includes
   merchandise, location, promotion, and services?   _____   _____
5. Will trade-ins be accepted as part of the purchase price
   on items such as appliances and television sets?   _____   _____

Supplier and Competitor Considerations

This set of questions looks outside your firm to two factors
you cannot directly control—suppliers and competitors.
6. Do you have final pricing authority? With the repeal of
   fair trade laws, "yes" answers will be more common than
   in previous years. Still, a supplier can control retail prices
   by refusing to deal with nonconforming stores (a tactic
   that may be illegal) or by selling to you on consignment.   _____   _____
7. Do you know what direct competitors are doing price-
   wise?   _____   _____
8. Do you regularly review competitors' ads to obtain information on their prices?   _____   _____
9. Is your store large enough to employ either a full-time or
   part-time comparison shopper? These three questions emphasize the point that you must watch competitors' prices
   so that your prices will not be far out of line—too high
   or too low—without good reason. Of course, there may
   be a good reason for out-of-the-ordinary prices, such as
   seeking a special price image.   _____   _____

A Price Level Strategy

Selecting a general level of prices in relation to competition is a key strategic
decision, perhaps the most important.

10. Should your overall strategy be to sell at prevailing market
    price levels? The other alternatives are an above-the-market
    or a below-the-market strategy.   _____   _____
11. Should competitors' temporary price reductions ever be
    matched?   _____   _____
12. Could private-brand merchandise be obtained in order to
    avoid direct price competition?   _____   _____

Calculating Planned Initial Markup

In this section you will have to look *inside* your business, taking into account sales, expenses, and profits before setting prices. The point is that your initial markup must be large enough to cover anticipated expenses and reductions *and* still produce a satisfactory profit.

	Yes	No
13. Have you estimated sales, operating expenses, and reductions for the next selling season?	___	___
14. Have you established a profit objective for the next selling season?	___	___
15. Given estimated sales, expenses, and reductions, have you planned initial markup?	___	___

This figure is calculated with the following formula:

$$\text{Initial markup \%} = \frac{\text{Operating expenses} + \text{reductions} + \text{profit}}{\text{Net sales} + \text{reductions}}$$

Reductions consist of markdowns, stock shortages, and employee and customer discounts. The following example uses dollar amounts, but the estimates can also be percentages. If a retailer anticipates $94,000 in sales for a particular department, $34,000 in expenses, and $6,000 in reductions, and if the retailer desires a $4,000 profit, initial markup percentage can be calculated:

$$\text{Initial markup \%} = \frac{\$34,000 + \$6,000 + \$4,000}{\$94,000 + \$6,000} = 44\%$$

The resulting figure, 44 percent in this example, indicates what size initial markup is needed *on the average* in order to make the desired profits.

16. Would it be appropriate to have different initial markup figures for various lines of merchandise or services? You should seriously consider this if some lines have characteristics significantly different from others'. For instance, a clothing retailer might logically have different initial markup figures for suits, shirts and pants, and accessories. (Various merchandise characteristics are covered in an upcoming section.) You may want those items with the highest turnover rates to carry the lowest initial markup.   ___   ___

Store Policies

Having calculated an initial markup figure, you could proceed to set prices on your merchandise. But an important decision such as this should not be rushed. Instead, you should consider additional factors that suggest the best price.

	Yes	No
17. Is your tentative price compatible with established store policies? *Policies* are written guidelines indicating appropriate methods or actions in different situations. If established with care, they can save you time in decision making and provide for consistent treatment of shoppers.	_____	_____

Specific policy areas that you should consider are as follows:

18. Will a one-price system, under which the same price is charged every purchaser of a particular item, be used on all items?	_____	_____

The alternative is to negotiate price with consumers.

19. Will odd-ending prices, such as $1.98 and $44.95, be more appealing to your customers than even-ending prices?	_____	_____
20. Will consumers by more if multiple pricing, such as two for $8.50, is used?	_____	_____
21. Should any leader offerings (selected products with very low, less profitable prices) be used?	_____	_____
22. Have the characteristics of an effective leader offering been considered? Ordinarily, a leader offering must have the following characteristics to accomplish its purpose of generating shopper traffic: used by most people, bought frequently, very familiar regular price, and not a large expenditure for consumers.	_____	_____
23. Will price lining, the practice of setting up distinct price points (such as $5.00, $7.50, and $10.00) and then marking all related merchandise at these points, be used?	_____	_____
24. Would price lining by means of zones (such as $5.00–$7.50 and $12.50–$15.00) be more appropriate than price points?	_____	_____
25. Will cents-off coupons be used in newspaper ads or mailed to selected consumers on any occasion?	_____	_____

	Yes	No

26. Would periodic special sales, combining reduced prices and heavier advertising, be consistent with the store image you are seeking?

27. Do certain items have greater appeal than others when they are part of a special sale?

28. Has the impact of various sale items on profits been considered? Sale prices may mean little or no profit on these items. Still, the special sale may contribute to *total* profits by bringing in shoppers who may also buy some regular-price (and profitable) merchandise and by attracting new customers. Also, you should avoid featuring items that require a large amount of labor, which in turn would reduce or erase profits. For instance, shirts would be a better special sale item than men's suits, which often require free alterations.

29. Will "rain checks" be issued to consumers who come in for special-sale merchandise that is temporarily out of stock? You should give particular attention to this decision since rain checks are required in some situations. Your lawyer or the regional Federal Trade Commission office should be consulted for specific advice regarding the necessity of rain checks.

Nature of the Merchandise

This section will consider how selected characteristics of particular merchandise affect a planned initial markup.

30. Did you get a "good deal" on the wholesale price of this merchandise?

31. Is this item at the peak of its popularity?

32. Are handling and selling costs relatively great because the product is bulky, has a low turnover rate, and/or requires much personal selling, installation, or alterations?

33. Are relatively large levels of reductions expected as a result of markdowns, spoilage, breakage, or theft? "Yes" answers to the preceding four questions suggest the possibility of or need for larger-than-normal initial markups. For example, very fashionable clothing often will carry a higher markup than basic clothing such as underwear because the particular fashion may suddenly lose its appeal to consumers.

Yes   No

34. Will customer services such as delivery, alterations, gift
wrapping, and installation be free of charge to customers?
The alternative is to charge for some or all of these services.   _____   _____

Environmental Considerations

The questions in this section focus on three factors outside your business, namely
economic conditions, laws, and consumerism.

35. If your state has an unfair sales practices act that requires
minimum markups on certain merchandise, do your prices
comply with this statute?   _____   _____
36. Are economic conditions in your trading area abnormal?
Consumers tend to be more price-conscious when the
economy is depressed, suggesting that lower-than-normal
markups may be needed to be competitive. On the other
hand, shoppers are less price-conscious when the economy
is booming, which would permit larger markups *on a
selective basis.*   _____   _____
37. Are the ways in which prices are displayed and promoted
compatible with consumerism, one part of which has been
a call for more straightforward price information?   _____   _____
38. If yours is a grocery store, is it feasible to use unit pricing
in which the item's cost per some standard measure is
indicated?   _____   _____

Having asked (and hopefully answered) more than three dozen questions, you are
indeed ready to establish retail prices. When you have decided on an appropriate
percentage markup, for example, 35 percent on a garden hose, the next step is to
determine what percentage of the still unknown retail price is represented by the
cost figure. To do this, the basic markup formula is simply rearranged:

$$\text{Cost} = \text{Retail price} - \text{Markup}$$
$$\text{Cost} = 100\% - 35\% = 65\%$$

Then the dollar cost, say $3.25 for the garden hose, is plugged into the following
formula to arrive at the retail price:

$$\text{Retail price} = \frac{\text{Dollar cost}}{\text{Percentage cost}} = \frac{\$3.25}{65\% \text{ (or .65)}} = \$5.00$$

Yes   No

One other consideration is necessary:

39. Is the retail price consistent with your planned initial mark-ups? _____   _____

Adjustments

It would be ideal if all items sold at their original retail prices. Because we know that things are not always ideal, however, an examination of price adjustments is necessary.

40. Are additional markups called for because wholesale prices have increased or because an item's low price causes consumers to question its quality? _____   _____
41. Should employees be given purchase discounts? _____   _____
42. Should any groups of customers, such as students or senior citizens, be given purchase discounts? _____   _____
43. When markdowns appear necessary, have you first considered other alternatives, such as retaining price but changing another element of the retailing mix, or storing the merchandise until the next selling season? _____   _____
44. Has an attempt been made to identify avoidable buying, selling, and pricing errors that cause markdowns so that steps can be taken to minimize them? _____   _____
45. Has the relationship between timing and size of markdowns been taken into account? In general, markdown taken *early* in the selling season or shortly after sales slowdown can be smaller than *late* markdowns. Whether an early or late markdown would be more appropriate in a particular situation depends on several things: your assessment of how many consumers might still be interested in the product, the size of the initial markup, and the amount remaining in stock. _____   _____
46. Would a schedule of automatic markdowns after merchandise has been in stock for specified intervals be appropriate? _____   _____
47. Is the size of the markdown "just enough" to stimulate purchases? This question is difficult—perhaps impossible—to answer. You must carefully observe the effects of various markdowns for different kinds of merchandise to gauge which in fact are "just enough." _____   _____

                                                          Yes   No

48. Has a procedure been worked out for markdowns on price-
    lined merchandise?   _____   _____

49. Is the markdown price calculated from the off-retail per-
    centage? This question gets you into the arithmetic of
    markdowns. Usually, you first establish the tentative per-
    centage amount price must be marked down to excite con-
    sumers. For example, if you think a 25 percent markdown
    will be necessary to sell a lavender sofa, the dollar amount
    of the markdown is calculated as follows: _____   _____

    Dollar   Off-retail
    markdown = percentage × Previous retail price

    Dollar markdown = 25% (or .25) × $500. = $125.

    Then the markdown is obtained by subtracting the dollar
    markdown from the previous retail price. Hence, the sofa
    would be $375.00 after taking the markdown.

50. Has cost of the merchandise been considered before setting
    the markdown price? This is not to say that a markdown
    price should never be lower than cost; on the contrary, a
    price that low may be your only hope of generating some
    revenue from the item. But cost should be considered to
    make sure that below-cost markdown prices are the *exception*
    in your store rather than so common that your total profits
    are really hurt.   _____   _____

51. Have procedures for recording the dollar amounts, per-
    centages, and probable causes of markdowns been set up? _____   _____

Analysis of markdowns is very important because it can provide information that
will assist in calculating planned initial markup, in decreasing errors that cause
markdowns, and in evaluating suppliers.

    You may be weary from thinking your way through the preceding sections, but
don't overlook an important final question:

52. Have you marked the calendar for a periodic review of
    your pricing decisions?   _____   _____

This checklist should help you lay a solid foundation of effective prices as you try
to build retail profits.

SOURCES OF ADDITIONAL INFORMATION

Price and Price Policies, by Walton Hamilton, published by McGraw-Hill Book Co., 1221 Avenue of the Americas, New York, NY 10020.

Pricing Decisions in Small Business, by W. Warren Haynes, published by University of Kentucky Press, Lexington, KY 40506.

Pricing for Marketing Executives, by Alfred R. Oxenfeldt, published by Wadsworth Publishing Co., Inc., 10 Davis Drive, Belmont, CA 94002.

Pricing for Profit, by Curtis W. Symonds, published by AMACOM, a division of the American Management Association, 135 West 50th Street, New York, NY 10020.

Pricing for Profit and Growth, by Albert U. Bergfeld, James S. Earley, and William R. Knobloch, published by Prentice-Hall, Inc., Englewood Cliffs, NJ 07632.

Pricing Strategies, by Alfred R. Oxenfeldt, published by AMACOM, a division of the American Management Association, 135 West 50th Street, New York, NY 10020.

A Robinson-Patman Primer, by Earl W. Kintner, published by Macmillan Publishing Co., 866 Third Avenue, New York, NY 10022.

CHAPTER 4

ADVERTISING AND PUBLICITY

THE IMPORTANCE OF ADVERTISING

Millions of dollars are spent on advertising every year. In fact, from the time you were born until you reached the age of 21, you were exposed to about two million advertising messages. To prove the strength of these messages, see if you can answer these questions. What is a Bulova? What is a Bic? What is Bayer? What is Rinso? What is Ivory? What is a Mustang? What is Prell? What is Lowenbrau? Unless you neither read, nor watch television, nor listen to the radio, you probably answered most of these questions without difficulty. Now, let's try one a little more difficult. What do the letters "LSMFT" stand for? Research has shown that a significant number of people can answer this question, even among those who are now in their early twenties. "LSMFT" stands for "Lucky Strike Means Fine Tobacco." Yet the advertising message that included these letters hasn't been used since 1958!

Advertising is used for three basic purposes:

1. To promote awareness of a business and its product or service
2. To stimulate sales directly
3. To establish or modify a firm's image

YOU CAN COMPETE WITH THE BIG COMPANIES

Amazingly, even though some firms spend millions of dollars on their advertising every year, you can compete with them, and you can beat them if you get your money's worth for your advertising dollar. This is so because many firms, even large firms, advertise in an inefficient manner.

Let's look at some examples. For years, cigarette manufacturers fought to keep television advertising. When cigarettes were finally banned from advertising on television, tobacco companies predicted doom and stocks plunged. What happened to cigarette sales without television advertising? Sales went up! This showed that for more than 50 years the million dollars that had been spent had largely been wasted on ineffective television advertising.

Some years ago a major company, Lestoil, developed a new spray cleaner. This new cleaner, a disinfectant, cleaned so well that household germs were killed instantly. In order to convey this message, this new product was advertised under the name. "Clean and Kill." The result, however, was that the product was killed before the household germs. The advertising campaign was totally ineffective, possibly because housewives, the buying agent for this product, thought that the product was some type of poison.

Just as there have been major disasters in advertising, there have been tremendously successful campaigns. Can you imagine a company bragging about not being first? Well, that's what Avis Rent-A-Car did some years ago. Their message was "We're No. 2," and therefore, "We try harder." This made it very difficult for Hertz. How could Hertz retaliate without appearing to be the villain? The campaign was tremendously effective, and Hertz lost much of the power that should have come with being in first place.

Some years ago, Mercedes Benz produced its first diesel car of modern times. This was long before the time of the energy crunch. In fact, the diesel engine seemed to offer very few advantages since gasoline was relatively cheap. Even today, diesel fuel cannot be purchased everywhere; some 25 years ago diesel fuel was even more difficult to find. Also, diesel engines are very noisy compared with the standard gasoline engine. In despair, Mercedes Benz prepared to junk the production of the diesel engine car. But, as a last resort, they turned the project over to a direct marketing expert, Ed McLean. McLean wrote a direct sales letter targeted to individuals who had the money and might be persuaded to buy a Mercedes Benz. This sales letter turned the supposed disadvantages of the diesel engine around and made them advantages. The fact that diesel fuel couldn't be found everywhere meant that the automobile was exclusive. The noise of the engine was promoted as positive evidence that the engine was running. This letter was sent out to consumers on well-chosen mailing lists. The campaign was so successful that Mercedes Benz actually had to reopen the production line and manufacture more diesel engine automobiles! This advertising success won McLean the Golden Mailbox Award from the Direct Mail Marketing Association.

HOW TO DEVELOP AN ADVERTISING PROGRAM

Advertising, if you use it correctly, will work as well for a small firm as for a major multimillion-dollar corporation. To use advertising correctly, you must have an advertising program. To develop an advertising program, you must take the following steps:

1. Analyze the market.
2. Set concrete goals and objectives.
3. Set a budget.
4. Develop a creative strategy.
5. Choose your medium or media.
6. Evaluate the results.

Analyze the Market

To analyze the market, you've got to view your own product or service in terms of who can use it. That "who," whether it be male or female, child or senior citizen (or all of the above), is your target consumer (see Figure 4.1). Now, how are you going to reach that consumer?

CONSUMER PROFILE QUESTIONNAIRE

PERSONAL DEMOGRAPHIC INFORMATION

Mark the boxes that describe you.

1. Sex:
   ☐ Male
   ☐ Female

2. Age:
   ☐ Under 6
   ☐ 6 to 11
   ☐ 12 to 17
   ☐ 18 to 24
   ☐ 25 to 34
   ☐ 35 to 44
   ☐ 45 to 54
   ☐ 55 to 64
   ☐ 65 & over

3. Marital Status:
   ☐ Married
   ☐ Single (never married)
   ☐ Widowed
   ☐ Divorced or separated

4. Education:
   ☐ Grade school or less (grades 1–8)
   ☐ Some high school
   ☐ Graduated from high school (grades 9–12)
   ☐ Some college
   ☐ Graduated from college
   ☐ Some postgraduate college work

5. Principal Language Spoken at Home:
   ☐ English
   ☐ Spanish
   ☐ Other

6. Color:
   ☐ White
   ☐ Nonwhite

7. Employment:
   ☐ Not employed outside the home
   ☐ Employed outside the home
   ☐ Employed full time (30 hours per week or more)
   ☐ Employed part time (less than 30 hours per week)
   ☐ Not employed—looking for work

8. Occupation:
   ☐ Professional and technical
   ☐ Managers, officials, and proprietors, except farm
   ☐ Clerical
   ☐ Sales
   ☐ Craftsman
   ☐ Foreman
   ☐ Nonfarm laborers
   ☐ Service workers
   ☐ Private household workers
   ☐ Farm managers
   ☐ Farm laborers
   ☐ Farm foreman
   ☐ Armed services
   ☐ Retired
   ☐ Student
   ☐ Other

Figure 4.1. Consumer profile questionnaire. (From *Advertising Today* by J. Douglas Johnson. Copyright © 1978 J. Douglas Johnson. Reprinted by permission of the publisher, Science Research Associates, Inc.) (*Figure continues on p. 86.*)

9. Georgraphic Region:
   - [ ] Northeast
   - [ ] Metropolitan New York
   - [ ] Mid-Atlantic
   - [ ] East Central
   - [ ] Metropolitan Chicago
   - [ ] West Central
   - [ ] Southeast
   - [ ] Southwest
   - [ ] Metropolitan Los Angeles
   - [ ] Remaining Pacific

10. Geographic Area:
    - [ ] Central city
    - [ ] Urban fringe (suburbs)
    - [ ] Town
    - [ ] Rural

Population of city or town:
   - [ ] 4 million or over
   - [ ] Between 4 and 1 million
   - [ ] Between 1 million and 500 thousand
   - [ ] Between 500 thousand and 250 thousand
   - [ ] Between 250 thousand and 50 thousand
   - [ ] Between 50 thousand and 35 thousand
   - [ ] Under 35 thousand

11. County Size:
    - [ ] *A* county—one of the largest markets
    - [ ] *B* county—not included in *A* but area over 150,000 population
    - [ ] *C* county—not included in *A* or *B* but area over 35,000
    - [ ] *D* county—all remaining counties under 35,000

HOUSEHOLD DEMOGRAPHIC INFORMATION

Answer these statements about your family:

12. Household Sizes:
    - [ ] 1 or 2 members
    - [ ] 2 or 3 members
    - [ ] 3 or 4 members
    - [ ] 5 or more members

13. Number of Children:
    - [ ] None
    - [ ] Two
    - [ ] Three or more

14. Age of Youngest Child:
    - [ ] No child under 18
    - [ ] Youngest child 12 to 17
    - [ ] Youngest child 6 to 11
    - [ ] Youngest child 2 to 5
    - [ ] Youngest child under 2

15. Household income:
    - [ ] Under $5,000
    - [ ] $5,000 to $7,999
    - [ ] $8,000 to $9,999
    - [ ] $10,000 to $14,999
    - [ ] $15,000 to $24,999
    - [ ] $25,000 and over

16. Wage Earners in the Family:
    - [ ] Male head of household
    - [ ] Female head of household
    - [ ] Wife (nonhead of household)
    - [ ] One child
    - [ ] Two children
    - [ ] Over three children

17. Home Ownership:
    - [ ] Own home
    - [ ] Rent home

Five years prior to survey date:
    - [ ] Lived in same home
    - [ ] Lived in different house
    - [ ] in same county
    - [ ] in different county

18. Dwelling Characteristics:
    - [ ] House (unattached)
    - [ ] Attached home
    - [ ] Apartment
    - [ ] Mobile home or trailer
    - [ ] Single family dwelling unit
    - [ ] Multiple family dwelling unit

SOCIAL CLASS INFORMATION

Mark the group your family belongs to.

19. [ ] The local elite with inherited wealth and family tradition.
20. [ ] Top executive or professional manager or owner.
21. [ ] Business, industrial, or professional manager or owner.
22. [ ] White-collar worker in industry or government or small business owner.
23. [ ] Semi-skilled worker in construction or industry. Probably blue-collar union member.
24. [ ] Unskilled worker, perhaps unemployed.

PSYCHOGRAPHIC INFORMATION

Personality indicators

Mark the accurate statements about yourself.

It is my nature to:

25. [ ] Want to rival and surpass others.
26. [ ] Accept leadership and follow willingly.

Figure 4.1. (*Continued*)

27. ☐ Want things arranged, organized, secure, and predictable.
28. ☐ Want to be the center of attention.
29. ☐ Seek freedom, resist influence, and do things my own way.
30. ☐ Form friendships and participate in groups.
31. ☐ Want to understand others, examine their motives and my own.
32. ☐ Seek aid, help, and advice from others.
33. ☐ Want to control others and be the leader of groups.
34. ☐ Feel inferior, guilty, and accept blame easily.
35. ☐ Want to help others, be sympathetic and protective.
36. ☐ Look for new and different things to do.
37. ☐ Stick to a task and work hard to complete a job.
38. ☐ Am attracted by the opposite sex, go out and enjoy company.
39. ☐ Belittle, blame, attack, and want to punish people.
40. ☐ Have frequent daydreams and fantasies.
41. ☐ Experience times of tension, self-pity, and am restless or excitable.
42. ☐ Am self-confident in social, professional, and personal dealings.

LIFE-STYLE PREFERENCES AND ATTITUDES

Mark the answers that fit you best.

Leisure

43. ☐ Enjoy entertaining formally and going to movies, concerts, plays, dances, or dinner.
44. ☐ Habitually read newspapers, magazines, and books.
45. ☐ Spend a lot of time listening to music (not just as a background).
46. ☐ Think I have the right to do absolutely nothing some of the time.
47. ☐ Anxious to ι ; busy, go out and see people, participate in sports and other activities.
48. ☐ Would rather study or work than "waste time" playing.

Cooking

49. ☐ Want to prepare good, healthy meals and think I am good at it.
50. ☐ Like convenience foods that are frozen, in cans, or packaged as mixes.
51. ☐ Judge my achievement on the basis of compliments I receive for enjoyable meals.
52. ☐ Try to stay out of the kitchen as much as possible and hate the drudgery of cooking.
53. ☐ Enjoy preparing fancy, exotic, or unusual dishes "from scratch" and serving them in an unusual way.

Family

54. ☐ Think the man should be the boss and run the family.
55. ☐ Think the woman should be the boss and run the family.
56. ☐ Believe marriage should be a partnership with no bosses.
57. ☐ Think children should be considered in most family decisions.
58. ☐ Believe parents should make an effort to teach children and spend time with them.

Dress

59. ☐ Like to wear casual, comfortable clothes.
60. ☐ Want to look fashionable and stylish.

Physical Condition

61. ☐ Am in very good health.
62. ☐ Have an overweight problem.
63. ☐ Always on some kind of a diet.
64. ☐ Watch the scale, eat intelligently, and exercise.
65. ☐ Feel sickly much of the time.
66. ☐ Use over-the-counter drugs for minor ailments.
67. ☐ Seldom take anything for a headache or an upset stomach.

Finances

68. ☐ Have money in the bank and feel secure.
69. ☐ Just about break even every month.
70. ☐ Am in debt but believe the bills can be paid.
71. ☐ Am not optimistic about the financial future.

Risk

72. ☐ Am conservative and do not take chances.
73. ☐ Will take a calculated risk.
74. ☐ Take chances just to see what will happen.

Buying Style

75. ☐ Pick the same brand of products habitually.
76. ☐ Think about the products I buy and select them because they satisfy.
77. ☐ Look for bargains, deals, premiums, and usually compare prices.
78. ☐ Want quality in a product and will pay extra to get it.
79. ☐ Choose advertised brands and do not take chances on unknown products or manufacturers.
80. ☐ Keep trying new products to see what they are like.
81. ☐ Buy what I need when I need it and when a store is handy.
82. ☐ Plan shopping carefully with a list of needs and make an excursion out of the trip.

Figure 4.1. (Continued) (Figure continues on p. 88.)

83. ☐ Judge brands on the basis of ingredients, weight, and package size.
84. ☐ Never read the information on a package to find out what it contains.
85. ☐ Am attracted to a brand by its name, color of the package, and its design.
86. ☐ Usually buy what friends say is good.
87. ☐ Pay attention to advertisements and study them to make up my mind about what to buy.

88. ☐ Do not check into low-cost items much, but do shop intelligently and compare prices for high-priced products.
89. Respond to advertisements in:
   ☐ Newspaper
   ☐ Radio
   ☐ Magazine
   ☐ Television

MEDIA USE AND INTEREST

I use media at these times:

	Newspaper		Magazines		Radio		Television	
	Day	Wkend	Day	Wkend	Day	Wkend	Day	Wkend
90. 6 A.M. to 10:00 A.M.	☐	☐	☐	☐	☐	☐	☐	☐
91. 10:00 A.M. to 3:00 P.M.	☐	☐	☐	☐	☐	☐	☐	☐
92. 3:00 P.M. to 7:00 P.M.	☐	☐	☐	☐	☐	☐	☐	☐
93. 7:00 P.M. to midnight	☐	☐	☐	☐	☐	☐	☐	☐
94. Midnight to 6:00 A.M.	☐	☐	☐	☐	☐	☐	☐	☐

I pay attention to these types of stories or programs:

	Newspaper	Magazine	Radio	Television
95. Local news	☐	☐	☐	☐
96. National news	☐	☐	☐	☐
97. Weather	☐	☐	☐	☐
98. Sports	☐	☐	☐	☐
99. Business and finance	☐	☐	☐	☐
100. Editorials and interviews	☐	☐	☐	☐
101. Classified	☐	☐	☐	☐
102. Daytime serials	☐	☐	☐	☐
103. Comics or comedy shows	☐	☐	☐	☐
104. Crime news or programs	☐	☐	☐	☐
105. Adventure	☐	☐	☐	☐
106. Quizzes or game shows	☐	☐	☐	☐
107. Movies	☐	☐	☐	☐
108. Self-help stories	☐	☐	☐	☐
109. How-to-do-it	☐	☐	☐	☐
110. Theater, arts, and entertainment	☐	☐	☐	☐
111. Editorials	☐	☐	☐	☐
112. Interviews	☐	☐	☐	☐
113. Travel	☐	☐	☐	☐
114. Police shows	☐	☐	☐	☐
115. Romantic programs	☐	☐	☐	☐
116. Sexy stories and pictures	☐	☐	☐	☐
117. Cooking programs and stories	☐	☐	☐	☐

USE OF A PARTICULAR
PRODUCT OR SERVICE

(Statements must be adapted)

118. I am a
light _____
medium _____
heavy _____
or nonuser _____

119. I use your product/service
daily _____
once a week _____
once a month _____
once a year _____
120. I have used your product for a
short time _____
many years _____
121. I have tried similar products. The names are
_____

Figure 4.1. (*Continued*)

122. I use your product in combination with

_____

_____

123. I buy your product at a

supermarket _____

drugstore _____

department store _____

discount store _____

hardware store _____

or other store _____

124. The quantity I buy at one time is

a single package _____

several packages _____

many packages _____

TRADE WITH A PARTICULAR STORE

125. I shop in your store

more than once a week _____

at least once a week _____

every two weeks _____

once a month _____

once a year _____

126. The distance from my home to your store is

less than five blocks _____

one mile away _____

two or three miles _____

five miles _____

over ten miles _____

127. I usually buy these types of products at your store:

_____

_____

_____

_____

128. The part of my shopping I do at your store is:

All _____

Most _____

129. My favorite stores that are similar to yours (and including it) are:

First choice _____

Second choice _____

Third choice _____

130. Each year I spend this amount in your store

$ _____

Figure 4.1. (*Continued*)

Along these lines, marketing and advertising experts have developed a very useful concept called *market segmentation*. If you use the market segmentation concept, instead of trying to sell to the entire market, you zero in on a specific segment of the population that is most interested and can best be served by buying your product or service. The segmentation concept makes sense. You cannot satisfy the entire market with one specific item, and further, you will always have limited resources with which to advertise and promote your products or services.

Advertisers employ segmentation through their application of strategies: positioning, media, and creative. *Positioning strategy* refers to how your product is positioned in comparison to the competition. For example, Colonel Sanders' Kentucky Fried Chicken was successful when aimed at buyers who are mainly housewives with a contemporary state of mind—busy, active, finding it hard to prepare meals for their family on a daily basis. Yet at first Kentucky Fried Chicken was a failure when positioned mainly as a countrified, folksy product.

Use of *media strategy* by advertising means selecting the appropriate medium or media to reach the segment that is most interested or would be most interested in buying your product. For example, why are beer, razors, and similar male-oriented products advertised on television during sporting events? Clearly because this is when and where the main user of these products is available as an audience for the advertising.

Creative strategy concerns the copy (writing) in the advertisement, the graphics, pictures, or photographs, and the ideas that combine these into an effective ad. For example, Mark O. Haroldsen wrote a book called *How to Wake Up the Financial Genius Within You*. His message for the opportunity-seeker's market in magazines such as *Salesman Opportunity, Spare Time Opportunities*, and the like, used the title of the book as the headline. Yet in advertising placed in the *Wall Street Journal*, Haroldsen used an entirely different advertisement: the headline read, "How to Avoid Paying Taxes Legally." Why did he use this different creative strategy for the *Wall Street Journal*? In the first case he was appealing to individuals who wanted to grasp an opportunity to make money. In the *Wall Street Journal* he was appealing to professional managers and entrepreneurs who were already making money and were interested in reducing their considerable taxes.

Nowadays, advertisers segment the market in many ways. Here are just a few categories that you might consider for your product or service.

Age. Advertisers tend to spend the most money trying to gain the attention of individuals in the age group 18 to 34 because, statistically, this group spends the most money on consumer products. However, this is certainly not true for all types of products or services. For example, record manufacturers go primarily to the age group 12 to 19, and those who sell luxury items appeal to the age group 34 to 49.

Sex. Here again you can see a segmentation. Mennen Speed Stick underarm deodorant is sold to men. Women will buy a different brand even though the chemical composition may be almost identical to that of Mennen Speed Stick. Or, more obviously, men buy *Playboy*; women buy *Playgirl*.

Income, Education, and Occupation. Income, education, and occupation are frequently considered together because they are related. For instance, a medical doctor generally has a high income and a considerable education. However, this is not always true. Many blue-collar workers earn as much as or more than their white-collar counterparts. In fact, one of the problems that Robert Oppenheimer had when he headed the Manhattan Project, which developed the atom bomb, was that his electricians made as much as his scientists and engineers; when his professionals discovered this they complained bitterly about "inequity." Many tradesmen such as plumbers and certain mechanics, make high salaries. And, of course, if you are self-employed you have the potential for making much more money than salaried professionals.

Geographic Location. Winter weather implies certain types of products just as sunny Miami or California implies other types. If you are selling beach clothes, your product would direct you to the location of your potential sales.

Marital Status and Family Size. Certain types of products and services will segment according to these factors. Video dating services, travel and tour services, singles bars, and nightclubs, for example, will all segment the market in advertising depending on marital status. Certain types of products are segmented by family size when a giant economy size is offered.

Ethnic Group.   Segmentation by ethnic group occurs because some groups prefer certain types of products over others. Soybean products, for example, such as tofu or soybean milk, are sold mainly to Asian communities. Certain types of delicatessen products are sold mainly to Jewish, Italian, or German communities. Other types of foods, cosmetic products, or luxury items must also be segmented by ethnic group.

Subculture.   Subcultures such as "yuppies" or "over 65" can also be effectively segmented from the mass market and therefore advertised to. For example, for the over-65 group, market research has shown a greater tendency to do comparison shopping, to buy mainly nationally known name brands, and to shy away from shops that are believed to cater exclusively to older customers. In fact, some years ago a nationally known baby food company lost millions of dollars in sales because it introduced a special line of senior foods, which was ignored by its intended market.

Social Class.   Different social classes tend to prefer and read different types of publications. For example, *Reader's Digest* and *Ladies' Home Journal* are in one class; *Time* and *Sports Illustrated* in another; the *New Yorker* and *Vogue* magazine in yet another.

Of the categories previously discussed, age, sex, marital status, family size, income, education, and occupation, and geographical location are all known as *demographic* factors. Subculture, ethnic group, and social class are known as *social culture* factors. Segmentation in advertising is increasing for psychographics and life style categories. These include activities, interests, and opinions, product usage, new product adoption behavior, and family decision making. To accomplish segmentation by psychographics or life style factors, special research is conducted to measure aspects of human behavior including what products or services are consumed, the activities, interests, and opinions of respondents, special value systems, personality traits and conception of self, and attitudes toward various product classes.

Recently, additional special groups have been identified as being especially good targets for segmentation. Some of these new groups are as follows.

College Students.   Individuals selling to the market of more than 11 million college students have made millions of dollars. Computer dating was originated in 1966 by a college student who became a millionaire prior to graduation through market segmentation.

The Hispanic Market.   This viable market, which includes more than 15 million people, has become so strong that special courses in marketing to this segment have been offered at some of the nation's largest universities.

Divorces. While divorce may not be desirable in any society, it is a significant factor in ours. The average marriage today lasts only six years. As a result, divorcees today are one-half of the single population.

Individuals Living Together. Today, the two million individuals who are living together constitute a segment in themselves.

The Working Woman. Today, two-thirds of women are working, and more than 50% of mothers are working; this is a truly gigantic segment.

Health. There's a tremendous interest in health in the United States. Vitamin sales have doubled in 10 years. The readership of magazines pertaining to health, such as *Prevention*, is steadily growing, with new magazines and newsletters appearing every day. There are 60 million individuals in the United States who are overweight, and two-thirds of these individuals are women. As a result, diet books and other products and services are of continual interest to this segment. There is almost always at least one diet book on the *New York Times* Best Seller List.

Children with Money. Today, children ages 6 through 11 receive allowances the average of which approaches more than $100 a year. The result is 2.5 billion dollars in spendable income, making this segment a tremendous buying force.

Sports Enthusiasts. Jogging, tennis, bicycling, swimming, and even the martial arts are nosing out more traditional sports such as football and basketball in popularity. There is a tremendous interest in all sports and a tremendous market segment to be served.

Spiritual and Mind Power. Recent popular interest in such subjects as yoga, mysticism, New Age, Scientology, and Silva Mind Control has grown among an increasingly large segment of the population. This group constitutes a segment completely separate from religion in the traditional sense.

To learn how best to reach your customer, some sort of market research will be necessary. One way of doing this is with your own survey of your customers or potential customers. A form for you to use is shown in Figure 4.1, a consumer profile questionnaire.

A useful book is *Do It Yourself Marketing Research*, by George Edward Breen, published by McGraw-Hill Book Co., 1221 Avenue of the Americas, New York, NY 10020.

Set Concrete Goals and Objectives

Once your analysis is completed, your job is to establish the goals and objectives of your advertising program. What do you want to happen? You should answer the question in precise, concrete terms so that you can measure your results at a later time. And by when do you want it to happen? Establish a specific time frame. For example, a suitable advertising objective might be to increase by 20% over the next three months the number of males ages 15 to 25 who walk into your retail establishment and make a purchase. That says precisely who, what, and when.

The Advertising Budget

Once goals and objectives have been established, you must look to your advertising budget. In some cases your budget will be established before goals and objectives because of your limited resources. It will be a given, and you may have to modify your goals and objectives. If money is available, you can work the other way around and see how much money it will take to reach the goals and objectives you have established.

The professionals use several methods to establish an advertising budget:

Percentage of anticipated or past year's sales
Arbitrary approach
Quantitative models
Objective and task approach
Affordable approach
Competitive approach

Of these methods, a recent survey shows that the most popular method used today is that of *percentage of anticipated sales*. This means that you must forecast your sales for the future period and then allocate a fixed percentage. This fixed percentage is usually found by comparing the advertising in your industry by other firms that are of your size and who offer a similar product. Obviously, this method has an advantage over taking a fixed percentage of a past year's sales since you are looking to the future. On the other hand, it says little about the advertising program and has nothing to do with the objectives and goals that you have established.

The *arbitrary approach* means simply that you pull a figure out of the air and decide that this is how much money will be devoted to advertising. This method has little to recommend it.

Quantitative models can be extremely sophisticated. However, because of their complexity and the many factors that must be considered, such models are little used and probably not desirable or even workable for a small firm. In fact, even by major firms the quantitative model method is little used.

With the *objective* and *task approach*, you relate your budget to the goals and objectives you have established. While the percentage of sales or profits or percentage of any approach first determines how much you'll spend without much consideration of what you want to accomplish, this method establishes what you must do in order to meet your objectives—only then do you calculate its cost. For a small firm, it must frequently be used with the affordable approach since in some cases, and as mentioned previously, you may set objectives that can only be reached at a much higher budget than you can afford. In this case, you must scale down your objectives.

In order to use the objective and task method, you break down the cost of your budget by calendar periods, by media, and perhaps by sales areas. Breakdown by calendar periods means that you divide the advertising plan on a monthly or weekly basis. Media breakdown denotes how much money you will place in each advertising medium, such as television, radio, newspaper, direct mail, and so forth. Sales areas are the areas in which you will spend your advertising budget. That is, if you are going after different market segments simultaneously under one advertising program, you must decide how much money each market segment will get. Use the form in Figure 4.2 to assist you in preparing your advertising budget.

With the *affordable approach*, you don't go for the optimum, but only what your firm can afford.

Finally, with the *competitive approach*, you analyze how much the competitor is spending and spend more, the same, or less depending upon your objectives.

Cahners Publishing Company publishes a *Work Book for Estimating Your Advertising Budget*. The guidelines in the work book are based on 10 decision rules, which

Account	Month		Year to Date	
	Budget	Actual	Budget	Actual
Media 　Newspapers 　Radio 　TV 　Literature 　Direct Mail 　Other Promotions 　Exhibits 　Displays 　Contests 　Sweepstakes Advertising Expense 　Salaries 　Supplies 　Stationery 　Travel 　Postage 　Subscriptions 　Entertainment 　Dues				
Totals				

Figure 4.2. Advertising budget. (Adapted from *Advertising Guidelines for Small Retail Firms*, by Ovid Riso, SMA 160, Small Business Administration [1980]).

define conditions requiring higher advertising expenditures. The research that resulted in these decision rules was conducted for Cahners by the Strategic Planning Institute of Cambridge, Massachusetts. Here are the 10 decision rules as to when higher expenditure is required:

1. When you seek to maintain or increase market share
2. When you seek higher new product activity
3. When you seek faster growing markets
4. When you seek lower plant capacity
5. When you seek lower unit price
6. For products that do not represent a major purchase for your customers in terms of total dollars
7. If your products are either high (or premium) priced or low (or discount) priced
8. If your products are of higher quality
9. If you have broad product lines
10. If your products are standard as opposed to made-to-order

You can get a free copy of this workbook from Cahners Publishing, 221 Columbus Avenue, Boston, MA 02116.

Creative Strategy

Creative strategy involves planning what you will say in your advertising message, how you will say it, and any artwork to be included. Unless you are a professional in this area, or your ad is very simple, it is better to get expert, professional help in preparing creative work. You can find these professionals fairly easily in your phone book. For artwork, look under Artists—Commercial or Advertising Artists. Do the same for photography and for copywriters.

If you intend to write your own copy, I would recommend the book *How to Write a Good Advertisement*, by Victor O. Schwab, published by the Wilshire Book Co., 12015 Sherman Rd., North Hollywood, CA 91605.

If you are going to write your own copy, observe the following guidelines.

First, make the headline appeal to self-interest, offer exciting news, or rouse interest in your consumer. The headline should be positive, not negative. The headline should suggest that the reader can obtain something easily and quickly. Make the headline stress the most important benefit of your product or service, and write it so that it grabs the reader's attention and causes him or her to read further. Also, be sure that the headline is believable and, of course, make sure that it ties in with what you write later in the body.

In the copy content itself, you should try to gain interest immediately. If you have enough room in your copy, use a story or a startling or unusual statement or quote; use news if you don't have enough room. Show the benefits and advantages so as to appeal to emotional needs; make what you offer irresistible through what you say. If you can, add credibility to your copy through the use of testimonials. These are statements made by other people who have used your product or service and are happy with it.

Always remember when you are writing copy that you are writing to communicate; write in a conversational tone that flows quickly. Use short words, short sentences, and short paragraphs, and lots of subheadings throughout. If you want your copy to be read, it must be interesting and easy to read. I have found Rudolf Flesch's book, *The Art of Readable Writing*, published by Harper and Row Publishers, Inc., to be of considerable help here.

These principles in copywriting should apply whether your advertisement is to appear in print or on radio or television. Only minor modifications should be necessary depending on limitations of these different media.

Medium and Vehicle Selection

Each of the advertising media categories (print, television, radio, etc.) has several vehicles: magazine or newspaper, and the type thereof; radio or television show, and the type thereof, and so on. There are four major considerations when you make you selection of medium (assuming you're using just one) and vehicle. These are as follows:

1. *Budget match.* The medium and vehicle you use must be consistent with the money available in your budget.

2. *Medium and vehicle and target consumer match.* The medium and vehicle that you select must be seen, heard, or read by your target consumer market.

3. *Medium and vehicle market mix relationship.* The medium and vehicle you select also must be reflected in the emphasis you place on the marketing mix. The marketing mix is made up of various inputs of product, price, the distribution method that you use, and promotional factors. What is the relationship between medium and vehicle and market mix? Let's take a new product. With a new product you may choose to use TV as your medium because with TV you can reach the most people in the shortest amount of time. Also, the product must fit the medium or vehicle. Some years ago, entrepreneur Joe Cossman sold over one million plastic shrunken heads. Obviously *Vogue* magazine was never considered as a vehicle for this particular product. High price denotes a certain medium and vehicle, as does low price. Matching must also be followed with distribution and promotional factors.

4. *Creative medium and vehicle marriage.* Certain appeals are best for certain media and vehicles, as shown earlier in the example of Mark O. Haroldsen's book, *How to Wake Up the Financial Genius Within You*. To reach those interested in getting rick quick, the vehicle selected was *Specialty Salesmen* and similar magazines. To reach those interested in tax shelters, the vehicle selected was the *Wall Street Journal*.

The Categories of Media.   All the categories of media should be considered as you plan for your advertising campaign. These include:

1. Print (newspapers, magazines)
2. Broadcasts (radio, TV)
3. Direct mail (letters addressed directly to lists of potential buyers in your target consumer market group)
4. Specialty items (pens, pencils, or other gadgets with the name of your firm embossed on them)
5. Directories (Yellow Pages advertisements, advertisements in association membership directories, and so forth)
6. Outdoor (billboards, transit posters)
7. Movie theater advertisement
8. Others, such as matchbook covers

Audience. One publication that will greatly assist you in planning your campaign is the *Standard Rate and Data Service* or SRDS. The SRDS publishes a set of periodically updated volumes including:

1. Consumer magazines
2. Farm publications
3. Business publications
4. Newspapers
5. Weekly newspapers
6. Network radio and TV
7. Spot radio and TV
8. Transit
9. Mailing lists

While major advertisers and advertising agencies are the usual subscribers to SRDS, many libraries carry these volumes. You will find them extremely useful in matching your target audience and selecting the media and vehicles that you can use.

Making Intermediate Comparisons. Each medium has its advantages and its disadvantages for your particular situation. For example, television, which has a broad reach and offers opportunities for a dynamic demonstration, is expensive and does not allow for demographic selectivity to any great extent. Newspapers may be relatively cheap; however, they offer little secondary readership, limited color facilities, and little demographic selectivity possibilities. To assist you in making intermedia comparisons, consider Figure 4.3, the advertising media comparison chart developed by the Bank of America.

Advertising Planning Concepts. Some of the concepts that you should consider in your planning in addition to cost are reach versus frequency; continuity; target market, marketing and advertising objectives; the marketing mix of product, price,

ADVERTISING MEDIA

Medium	Market Coverage	Type of Audience	Sample Time/Space Costs
Daily Newspaper	Single community or entire metro area; zoned editions sometimes available.	General: tends more toward men, older age group, slightly higher income and education.	Per agate line, weekday; open rate: Circ: 8,700: $ .20 19,600: $ .35 46,200: $ .60 203,800: $ 1.60
Weekly Newspaper	Single community usually; sometimes a metro area.	General; usually residents of a smaller community.	Per agate line; open rate: Circ: 3,000: $ .35 8,900: $ .50 17,100: $ .75
Shopper	Most households in a single community; chain shoppers can cover a metro area.	Consumer households.	Per agate line; open rate: Circ: 10,000: $ .20 147,000: $ 2.00 300,000: $ 3.20
Telephone Directories	Geographic area or occupational field served by the directory.	Active shoppers for goods or services.	Yellow Pages, per half column; per month: Pop: 14-18,000: $ 15.00 110-135,000: $ 35.00 700-950,000: $ 100.00
Direct Mail	Controlled by the advertiser.	Controlled by the advertiser through use of demographic lists.	Production and mailing cost of an 8½" × 11" 2-color brochure; 4-page, 2-color letter; order card and reply envelope; label addressed; third class mail; $.33 each in quantities of 50,000.
Radio	Definable market area surrounding the station's location.	Selected audiences provided by stations with distinct programming formats.	Per 60-second morning drive-time spot; one time: Pop: 400,000: $ 35.00 1,100,000: $ 90.00 3,500,000: $ 150.00 13,000,000: $ 300.00
Television	Definable market area surrounding the station's location.	Varies with the time of day; tends toward younger age group, less print-oriented.	Per 30-second daytime spot; one time; nonpreemptible status: Pop: 400,000: $100.00 1,100,000: $300.00 3,500,000: $500.00 13,000,000: $600.00
Transit	Urban or metro community served by transit system; may be limited to a few transit routes.	Transit riders, especially wage earners and shoppers; pedestrians.	Inside 11" × 28" cards; per month: 50 buses: $ 125.00 400 buses: $1,000.00 Outside 21" × 88" posters; per month: 25 buses: $1,850.00 100 buses: $7,400.00
Outdoor	Entire metro area or single neighborhood.	General; especially auto drivers.	Per 12' × 25' poster; 100 GRP* per month: Pop: 21,800: $ 125.00 386,000: $ 135.00 628,900: $ 150.00
Local Magazine	Entire metro area or region; zoned editions sometimes available.	General; tends toward better educated, more affluent.	Per one-sixth page, black and white; open rate: Circ: 25,000: $ 310.00 80,000: $ 520.00

*Several boards must be purchased for these GRPs.

Figure 4.3. Advertising media comparison chart. (Reprinted with permission from Bank of America, NT & SA, "Advertising Small Business," *Small Business Reporter*, Vol. 15, No. 2, Copyright © 1976, 1978, 1981.)

COMPARISON CHART

Particular Suitability	Major Advantage	Major Disadvantage
All general retailers.	Wide circulation.	Nonselective audience.
Retailers who service a strictly local market.	Local identification.	Limited readership.
Neighborhood retailers and service businesses.	Consumer orientation.	A giveaway and not always read.
Services, retailers of brand-name items, highly specialized retailers.	Users are in the market for goods or services.	Limited to active shoppers.
New and expanding businesses; those using coupon returns or catalogs.	Personalized approach to an audience of good prospects.	High CPM.
Businesses catering to identifiable groups: teens, commuters, housewives.	Market selectivity, wide market coverage.	Must be bought consistently to be of value.
Sellers of products or services with wide appeal.	Dramatic impact, wide market coverage.	High cost of time and production.
Businesses along transit routes, especially those appealing to wage earners.	Repetition and length of exposure.	Limited audience.
Amusements, tourist businesses, brand-name retailers.	Dominant size, frequency of exposure.	Clutter of many signs reduces effectiveness of each one.
Restaurants, entertainments, specialty shops, mail-order businesses.	Delivery of a loyal, special-interest audience.	Limited audience.

Figure 4.3. (Continued)

promotion and distribution, and promotional variables; competitive advertising activity; the size of your budget; and your creative strategy.

All of these have been discussed previously except for reach versus frequency and continuity.

Reach versus Frequency. Reach is the total number of households that will be exposed to an advertising message in a particular vehicle or medium over a certain period of time. It is expressed as a percentage of the total universe of households. Frequency is the number of exposures to the same message each household receives. Therefore, average frequency would equal the total exposures for all households sampled, divided by the reach. Even at tremendous expense, you cannot reach 100% of your target market. Therefore, the key is trying to estimate the point at which additional dollars should go into frequency after the optimal reach has been achieved. Some pointers that will assist you in making this decision are as follows:

Go for greater reach

1. . . . when you are introducing a new product to a mass market and want as many people as possible to know about it.
2. . . . when your advertising message is so compelling that most people will react to the initial exposure.
3. . . . when your product or service message is in itself newsworthy and will itself demand attention.

Go for higher frequency

1. . . . when your competitor is going for high frequency against the same segment as you.
2. . . . when you are seeking direct response; that is, when you want individuals to order the product or respond to the service directly from the ad.
3. . . . when you want your target consumer to act within a certain limited time period.
4. . . . when there isn't too much to differentiate what you are offering from what your competition is selling.

Continuity. Continuity has to do with the length of time that your medium schedule should run. Obviously, you can run a medium schedule continuously or periodically; once a day, once a week, or even more infrequently. Here again, you should consider the various factors that may influence success as a tradeoff against cost and limited resources. For funding optimal frequency, experts have developed something called the "three-hit theory." The basis of the theory is that there is an optimal range after which you are wasting money. This range, according to the theory, is three receipts of your message or "hits." Three hits will insure that the customer learns of your product or service through your advertising message. To get the three hits, you need 11 to 12 potential advertising exposures. Therefore, the average potential frequency should be 11 to 12 times.

Once you have decided upon the medium (or media), you must then decide upon the vehicle(s). To do this, you use demographics, that is, the demographic research that you have done against that supplied by the vehicle in question. In this regard, you should know that every magazine or television or radio show can offer a current demographic profile of its readership or listenership. It is therefore a question of matching up their information with your research of your target customer.

Negotiating and Special Discounts.   Many small business advertisers don't realize that they could advertise for much less than they are doing now if they knew about the special negotiating possibilities and discounts that are offered. These include the following:

1. Mail order discounts
2. PI (per inquiry) deals
3. Frequency discounts
4. Stand-by rates
5. Help if necessary
6. Remnants and regional editions
7. Barter
8. Bulk buyers
9. Seasonal discounts
10. Spread discounts
11. An in-house agency
12. Cash discounts

If you are a mail order advertiser, many magazines realize that you must make money directly from your ad or you cannot stay in business and will not advertise again. In addition, with this type of advertising it is easy to know immediately whether you are doing well and whether it made money for you. Accordingly, many magazines will give special *mail order discounts*, sometimes up to 40%, to mail order advertisers. Therefore, if the advertisement normally costs you $200, you need only pay $120. This is a big discount and certainly nothing to pass by. Even for many national mail order advertisers, it may spell the difference between a profitable ad and failure.

A *PI deal* is one in which you agree to pay the publication only for those inquiries or sales that the ad itself brings in. This may be on radio, television, or in a magazine. As a result, in return for this agreement, the magazine will run your advertisement with no money from you up front. Certainly this is a major advantage for a small businessperson. Usually the mail is sent to the vehicle, which will sort it and keep the records for you. At other times the ad is keyed and the mail sent directly to you. You must turn a percentage of each order over to the vehicle at fixed periods that you agree upon. If the orders go to the vehicle, they will send you the names of those who order so that you can respond and send the product to the customer. They will also send that amount owed you for each product. A typical PI deal will usually cost something like 50% of the selling price to the publication vehicle.

Frequently it is difficult to locate PI deals, and you need to talk to the salesperson representing the vehicle. Few magazines, radio stations, or television stations like their regular advertisers to know that they accept PI deals, so don't expect them to be advertised as such. They are not easy to find, but they are worth the trouble of looking for them.

Most media will offer *frequency discounts*. Therefore, if you advertise more than once or more than what is standard, you can expect a lower cost than what you might otherwise achieve. Be careful, however, in committing yourself to long-range advertising programs until you know whether or not the campaign is going to work.

Most vehicles are committed to publication or broadcast on a regular basis. At certain times, not all advertising may be sold outright up to the last minute. The vehicle therefore has a choice: it can either sell this advertising at a greatly reduced amount—*stand-by rate*—or put in some sort of editorial content that does not generate additional profits. To get the stand-by rate, you must first let the different vehicles know that you are interested in this type of deal, and they must be able to get hold of you quickly by telephone. Sometimes a stand-by rate is available only after you advertise with this publication or station for some time. Then, the people know you and trust you. This is important since the deal is closed verbally—no money from you in advance. The advantage of the stand-by rate is well worth it. Again, you may pay as little as 40 to 50% of the normal cost of advertising.

Help if necessary is applicable usually to mail order advertisers and, again, is in recognition of the fact that the mail order advertiser must make money from the ad in order to stay in business. What it means is that if the ad is not profitable, the publication may agree to run the ad and repeat it if necessary until you at least break even. Help may not assist you in making additional money, but it sure can prevent you from losing a lot of money. Therefore, you should always check into the possibility of help-if-necessary deals if you are a mail order advertiser.

Many national magazines today will allow advertisers to buy space only in certain regional editions rather than in every edition appearing nationally. This situation works to your advantage in reduced advertising costs; sometimes the regional editions will not be sold out in advertising and space may go begging. You can get *remnants in regional editions* at a discount of as much as 50%. To locate remnant advertising possibilities, talk to salespeople representing the advertising vehicle.

Sometimes a publication or station may be willing to *barter*, that is, to take products or services in exchange for advertising. This occurs where the vehicle has an interest other than publishing or broadcasting. Barter is a great way to go since it allows you to increase sales without using up capital resources.

Bulk buyers are purchasers of huge amounts of advertising from advertising media. Because of the quantity in which it is bought, they pay much less. The bulk buyer then resells the advertising space. The price you pay to a bulk buyer will vary greatly and it will be negotiable. Toward the end of the advertising period, if this space isn't sold, you may be able to get discounts as large as 50% of what you would normally pay.

Certain media do not do well during certain seasons of the year. As a result, during these periods they offer substantial *seasonal discounts* over their normal rate. If your product or service sells well during that season, you should seriously consider seasonal discounts in your advertising. On the same principle, your product may cost a great deal to sell during prime time on television or radio. However, there may be no need to sell during prime time. In fact, your product may sell better in other than prime time. Therefore, you should consider nonprime-time discounts much in the line of seasonal discounts.

If you are a big advertiser and advertise on two or three pages or more of a particular issue of a magazine, you may be able to get a special *spread discount*. This may or may not be on the vehicle's rate card, which describes its advertising costs, so you must ask about it. Again, discounts can run as high as 50% of the normal cost.

Advertising agencies get an automatic 15% discount from any vehicle in which they place your ad. This is one way they have of making money. As a result, many small businesspeople form their own *in-house agency* to take advantage of the 15% discount for themselves. Most vehicles say they will not deal with in-house agencies and will not accept advertising from them at the 15% discount. However, what they are really saying is that they will deal with you as long as you're not obvious about being an in-house agency. Merely indicate that you're placing the ad for the company indicated and give other instructions in accordance with the rate card or the *Standard Rate and Data Service* publication. Therefore, for the cost of registration of a name other than that of your regular company, and stationery specially printed with this name, you can get a 15% discount every time you advertise.

Many advertisers overlook the fact that most vehicles will give a *2% cash discount* for payment of cash within the first ten days. However, if you do not take this discount, very few vehicles will automatically return your money. So, look for this information on the rate card you request from the vehicle. If you can get a 2% discount, you can save a lot of money. Even small firms are saving as much as $50,000 a year this way, once they become large advertisers.

Evaluation of Results

Unless you know how well your advertising is doing, much or all of your money could be wasted. Therefore, it is important to establish some measurements of the effectiveness of your advertising. There are several methods of doing this:

1. Direct response
2. Involuntary methods
3. Recognition and awareness tests
4. Recall tests
5. Focus group tests

Direct Response. This is probably the best means of measuring the effectiveness of your advertising, because you measure actual responses to your ad. In order to do this, simply code the advertisement so that you'll know which response is from which advertisement. A typical code uses "Suite," "Room," "Drawer," or sometimes even different initials before the name of the company, or different initials after the box number. For example, a letter can stand for the vehicle in which the advertisement appears, and a digit following the letter can denote the month. Let us say that you advertised in *Outdoor Life* magazine in January. "A" could stand for *Outdoor Life*, and the digit "1" could stand for advertisement in January. The simple addition to your address of "Suite A-1" or "Room A-1" would tell you immediately the vehicle and the exact advertisement.

Involuntary Methods. These methods of measuring advertisement effectiveness are usually pretesting methods. They record involuntary responses over which neither the subject nor the researcher has control. They are objective, but they are also expensive. They are also done in an unnatural setting. One device, called a pupilometer, measures the dilation of the pupil while the individual is observing advertising. The device is unwieldy and uncomfortable, and it certainly isn't the way that the reader usually sees advertising. One very simple involuntary method is called the "down the chute" test. It consists of having someone read advertising copy while you watch his eyes. If there are no problems with comprehension or readability, it is presumed that the individual's eyes will keep moving from left to right, left to right, as he goes line by line down the page. But if the pupils stop moving, there could be a problem, and at this point you should ask the reader what he is reading. You note the problem and then continue the procedure.

Recognition and Awareness Tests. In recognition and awareness tests, consumers who have read or seen an advertisement are asked whether they remember the ad. One limitation is the possibility of confusion of your ad with similar ads, and the sample size used is usually small compared to the total number of readers.

The oldest type of recognition test is a readership test called the "Starch." In the Starch system, the interviewer shows the magazine to the subject, and if the subject says he or she has read it, the interviewer goes through the magazine ad by ad with the subject indicating whether he or she has "noted the ad," which means has seen it; "associated it," which means he or she remembers the brand name; or "read most," which means that he or she has read at least half of the copy. The Starch system reports the percentage of ads "noted," "associated," and "read most" for each subject.

Awareness tests measure the cumulative effect of advertising. Test subjects are consumers in the target consumer group for the ad. First, demographic information is gathered to determine if they are likely customers. Then, they are asked the question "Have you seen the ads lately for (name of product)?" The problem with this type of test is that there are too many variables that can affect the response.

Recall Tests.   In a typical recall test, the prospects are first screened and asked questions about their attitude. They are then asked to watch a program, while those in a control group are asked similar questions but do not watch. The effectiveness of recall is determined later when brand awareness is measured in both groups and the results are compared.

Focus Group Tests.   The focus group has grown as a method of pretesting in recent years. It is relatively low budget in that 8 to 10 representative consumers are invited in. It is therefore not a quantitative but rather a qualitative measure of reactions to help you decide whether to run one ad or another.

The small businessperson can adopt many of these methods to help in determining the effectiveness of advertising. The key is to keep your methods simple, hold down costs, and be careful about drawing inferences if you use a very small sample size.

SHOULD YOU EMPLOY AN ADVERTISING AGENCY?

Whether or not to employ an advertising agency depends a great deal on how large a company you have and what an advertising agency can do for you. Many of the things that an advertising agency can do, such as media selection, copywriting, supplying artwork, and so forth, you may do for yourself, in which case it may be better to establish your own in-house agency as described earlier and save 15%. On the other hand, all these activities take up your resources, and an agency can tie everything together and probably do a more professional job for you. The problem here is that many of the best agencies will only work for your firm when you become a major advertiser. If you are big enough, the services provided by an agency may cost you nothing since the agency receives 15% commission from the medium or media used. If you are not a major advertiser, the agency will bill you for services rendered on an hourly, daily, or project basis.

If you do decide to employ an advertising firm, do not engage the first one that you contact. First, talk to the principals of the agency and get some definite information about them. This should include: the size of the agency, that is, last year's billing, how long the principals have been with the agency; their general philosophy of positioning; whether they deal mainly with industrial accounts or with consumer accounts; and what some of their accounts are. You should also query them to find out in which areas of your business they would like to become involved. Some agencies will handle everything for you. Others will develop and place your ads, and that's it. Ask who at the agency would be working directly on your account and his or her title, and who would be responsible for supervision on a day-to-day basis. You should also ask for representative accounts—accounts similar to yours—with which the advertising agency has experience so that you may contact those firms. Naturally, you should ask about compensation arrangements. If you are going to be doing a considerable amount of advertising, it is perfectly legitimate to ask for a speculative presentation by the agency. In fact, you should ask for a proposal from several different agencies. During these speculative presentations, you can get a feel for what the agency can do and whether you like or dislike the people and services you will be paying for. There are, however, certain disadvantages to asking several agencies for proposals. They will have competitive information on your firm, and some agencies will see this as exploitive inasmuch as they obviously must pay for this proposal whether or not they get your business. In general, it is better not to ask for a speculative proposal unless the agency is a serious candidate.

Consider the following factors in making your decision to "hire" an agency:

1. Is the agency size consistent with your needs and growth plans?
2. Is the agency's philosophy of positioning compatible with your own?
3. Is the agency's management strength compatible with your firm?
4. Is the agency well equipped to offer overall marketing counsel?
5. Is there a similarity among the agency's other accounts and your firm?
6. Do you have a good opinion of the account team assigned by the agency to be responsible for working with you and doing your advertising?
7. Does the agency have a good research capability?
8. Does the agency have a good creative capability?
9. Does the agency have a good media planning capability?
10. Is the agency in good financial shape?
11. How did the references check out?

Of course, as mentioned earlier, one of the problems that you will have as a small firm is interesting an agency in working with you. One way to do this is to stress your tremendous growth potential. If you don't have much cash, try barter. That is, trade your product or services for their services. Finally, you could offer stock in your company in exchange for their services.

HOW TO GET FREE ADVERTISING THROUGH A PUBLICITY RELEASE

Every magazine is constantly looking for new ideas, new news, and new information to tell its readers. So, whenever you have a new product or service or something

Mr. A. B. Jones
Editor
World Military Gazette
101 New State Drive
New York, NY 10065

Dear Mr. Jones:

I am writing to you because my company, Global Associates, has just developed a new product that will have a tremendous effect on casualty reduction in military operations. This new product is a personal protective body armor that is half the weight of current models but gives slightly more than double the level of protection.

This amazing armor is called "KPC composite." It is soft and flexible although it has five times the tensile strength of steel. A special patented carrier has been developed for the KPC Composite material. The whole unit is called "The Commando MK III Armor Jacket."

I know that your readers will be interested in learning not only of the existence of this life-saving garment, but also that individual soldiers can order their own Commando MK III Armor Jackets directly from Global Associates at $300 per unit, insurance and postage costs included. I have enclosed a publicity release along with a photograph for your use if desired.

Sincerely,

President
GLOBAL ASSOCIATES

Figure 4.4.   Letter to the editor for a publicity release.

different happens with regard to your current product or service that might be of interest to a magazine's readers, many magazines will be happy to publicize it for you and will charge you nothing. This has an additional advantage. Editorial coverage of your product or service is usually more effective than your own advertising. You should understand that magazines will not run every idea or product publicity release you submit. In order to reach those that will, you must run a direct mail campaign. Your campaign package should consist of three basic elements:

1. A sales letter to the editor
2. Suggested editorial material about your new product or service (called the "release")

3. Either the product itself or a 4-by-5 inch glossy photograph of the product (generally a photograph is just as good, unless your product is a book or a booklet)

Figure 4.4 is a letter to the editor for free advertising for a body armor product I sold several years ago. Follow this general format when asking for free advertising in a letter. Do not mention that you may become a paid advertiser later. If you are sending money to the magazine for a paid advertisement, do not send it with a letter to the editor requesting free editorial mention. Do not mention whether you're currently an advertiser in the magazine.

Figure 4.5 shows a typical publicity release that might accompany a letter such as the one shown in Figure 4.4. Note that the publicity release is typed and need not be printed. Figure 4.6 shows a photograph of the product. Photographs can be reproduced in quantity rather cheaply, although usually not by a standard commercial photographer. For example, a 4-by-5-inch glossy in quantities of 100 can be obtained for as little as 30¢ a copy by a duplicate photograph service, which you can find in your Yellow Pages. One that I have used and recommend is Duplicate Photo Laboratories, Inc., P.O. Box 2670, 1522 North Highland Ave., Hollywood, CA 90028.

FOR IMMEDIATE RELEASE

New Body Armor Announced

Global Associates, a body armor company, announced the development of a new personal protective body armor today. The new armor, known as KPC Composite, is half the weight of current body armor, but offers twice the level of protection. The armor also has the unusual properties of being soft and flexible although it displays five times the tensile strength of steel. The armor has defeated projectiles travelling as fast as 2000 feet per second. It has also been tested against and has stopped various small-arm ammunition, including .38 caliber, .45 caliber, .22 magnum, 9mm, .41 magnum, and .44 magnum. A special patented carrier has been designed for the armor and designated the Commando MK III Armor Jacket. This garment itself has many unusual features. It is worn like a jacket, with a closure in the front. This permits increased ventilation during use and allows the armor to be donned or doffed without removing the helmet or other headgear. In addition, a special lockstrap suspension system has been developed. Although the straps cannot be pulled apart, under emergency conditions the armor can be completely jettisoned in less than three seconds. For normal armor closure, a protected slide fastener is provided. The entire ensemble comes in three sizes—small, medium, and large. It weighs just 4½ pounds. Interested buyers can purchase the Commando MK III Armor Jacket by sending $300 to Global Associates, 56 N. Sierra St., Pasadena, California 91109

Figure 4.5. Publicity release.

Figure 4.6. The Body Armor Product

HOW TO GET NEWSPAPERS ALL OVER THE COUNTRY
TO GIVE YOU FREE PUBLICITY

Another type of promotion you can do is one that I did for my book *Building a Mail Order Business* (John Wiley & Sons, 1982, 1985, 1991). I wrote to editors of the family or general interest sections of newspapers all over the country. I offered each exclusive use in their geographic area of a short article I had written called "Can Anyone Make a Million Dollars in Mail Order?" Naturally I mentioned my book. You can see my letter in Figure 4.7 and a sample of the results in Figure 4.8. Note that the editor changed the title in this instance. This got me countrywide newspaper coverage and eventually led to numerous appearances on radio and TV. The result was that we sold thousands of books that we would not otherwise have . sold.

WILEY SERIES ON BUSINESS STRATEGY
JOHN WILEY & SONS, INC., 605 THIRD AVENUE,
NEW YORK, N.Y. 10158
Series Editor:
DR. WILLIAM A. COHEN

Recent research that I completed has uncovered a business that can be run out of the home on a part-time basis, yet which can and has produced a number of millionaires. In fact, its current sales volume exceeds $100 billion every year, and it is so lucrative that more than half of the "Fortune 500" companies are engaged in it.

The business that I am referring to is the mail order business . . . and readership demand for information about the subject is so great that many major book publishers, include McGraw-Hill, Prentice-Hall, and Harper and Row have published a book on the subject. Several of these publishers have more than one book on mail order in print. Interestingly, almost all stay in print over the years and continue to sell. For example, one of Prentice-Hall's books on mail order is in its 24th printing. John Wiley has just published my book entitled BUILDING A MAIL ORDER BUSINESS: A COMPLETE MANUAL FOR SUCCESS.

The reason that I am writing to you is that I have just completed a short article that explores the question, "Can Anyone Make a Million Dollars in the Mail Order Business?" I know that the answer, which is based on the research that I did for my book, will surprise you. It certainly surprised me . . . and I know that it will surprise and interest your readers as well.

I am enclosing this article for your review. I can offer it on an exclusive basis to your newspaper in your city. However, as with many hot items that may be due in part to present economic conditions, the demand for this information is time sensitive. Therefore, I can only reserve my offer to you for 30 days. Please let me hear from you as soon as possible.

Sincerely,

William A. Cohen, Ph.D.
Professor of Marketing

Figure 4.7.   Letter to newspaper editors.

Imagination is the key to making a million

By DR. WILLIAM A. COHEN

More than eighty years ago. Richard Sears and Julius Rosenwald got together to build Sears. Roebuck & Co. into what would eventually become a $10 billion corporation. In the process, these two entrepreneurs built themselves into the world's first mail order millionaires.

Since the time of Sears' beginning, countless part time and full time entrepreneurs have been attracted by the apparent ease with which inexperienced business people could enter this profession of selling products through the mail and emerge with a fortune. What is surprising is not that many have failed. Many have. But the unexpected fact is that in both good times and bad, many have succeeded.

Just before the depression of 1929, a young man by the name of Robert Collier wrote a book on "The Secret of the Ages." In the first six months after writing the book. Collier made more than a million dollars selling the book solely through the mail. He went right on selling the book through the 1929 depression. In fact, although the book has never appeared on any best seller list, it wouldn't surprise me if "The Secret of the Ages." was one of the biggest sellers of all time since it has never been withdrawn and is still being sold through the mail today.

Now it could be that Collier's achievement was a fluke ... if so many others hadn't done the same thing with similar products.

Brainerd Mellinger, famous for his self-published course on import-export. built a huge multi-million dollar business around his product. Joe Karbo wrote his book. "The Lazy Man's Way to Riches" in 1973. Before he died in 1980. he sold more than a million copies and that dollars each. His family continues to sell the book today.

Melvin Powers, a famous mail order publisher in North Hollywood. started with a single small book on hypnotism. Today he has more than 400 books in print and has sold millions of books in the interim.

Of course, there are a great many products besides books which are sold through the mail. In a recent year, more than $2.7 billion in general merchandise including home furnishings, housewares and gifts were sold as well as another billion dollars each in ready to wear clothing and collectibles. This is the stamping ground of mail order wizards like Joe Sugarman in Chicago who built a $50 million a year business selling electronic products in only seven years right out of his garage.

Sixty-nine year old A. J. Masuen of LeMars. Iowa, went from door-to-door salesman to more than $1 million a year selling first aid kits and supplies through a mail order catalog. Two high school boys. Len and Rick Hornick started their multi-million dollar mail order business selling hand-carved wooden ducks to hunters and collectors. Today they employ more than 100 expert craftsmen to make their ducks, and they mail out a 32-page catalog to almost a million customers four times a year.

What qualities does the would-be mail order entrepreneur need? Three qualities are ab-

solutely essential: imagination. persistence. and a high degree of honesty. Imagination is needed in order to be able to visualize the special appeal which will compel a potential customer to buy your product. If you have imagination. you can sell almost anything by mail.

Mail order pro Ed McLean proved this by selling thousands of an unpopular model of a Mercedes-Benz automobile which conventional automobile dealers hadn't been able to sell. Mail order experts Hank Burnett. Christopher Stagg. and Dick Benson proved it by selling sixty airplane tickets at $10.000 each for an around-the-world flight. But perhaps the king is Joe Cossman. With no more business experience than being an ex-serviceman. Cossman sold 2.118.000 ant farms. 1.583.000 potato spud guns. 1.600.000 imitation shrunken heads. and 1.508.000 home garden sprinklers and many other products ... all by mail.

Persistence is required because success is rarely instantaneous and there are always obstacles and set-backs. Cossman spent over a year working on his kitchen table encountering false leads. problems. and failures at the same time holding down a full time job during normal working hours before he finally hit his first success. And even that first successful project required hard work and numerous obstacles that had to be overcome. Less persistent entrepreneurs would have quit long before.

Absolute honesty is required because a successful mail order business is built on trust. repeat sales. and satisfied customers.

After all. you are asking your customers to send money. sometimes a great deal of money. to someone he does not know and cannot see. Cheat your customer even a little. and you've lost that customer forever. Without that repeat customers. you might just as well invest your time and energy in a dried up oil well. The potential for a successful enterprise might have existed once, but now its gone for good.

The basic principles which you must understand to be successful in mail order have to do with product selection. structuring your offer. testing. where and when to advertise. and what to put into your advertisements. It takes a book to do justice to all of these subjects in detail. so we'll look only at the rudiments.

While it is true that a mail order expert can sell just about anything through the mail. some products just naturally make better mail order products than others. To increase your chances of picking a winner. look for a product that is light weight. nearly unbreakable. has a broad appeal to a large segment of the population. and has a large margin for profit. This last requirement means you have to be able to buy low. and sell high. Believe me. you are going to need this high profit margin in order to pay for your advertising costs. and at first to pay for your mistakes during the learning process.

You should try to get a product which allows you to sell it at three or four times the cost of the product to you. Now clearly you can't do this with a high priced product. But for most

products under $25 this should be your goal.

This brings us to the important subject of testing. Successful mail order dealers test almost everything. They test which offer is best. They test different types of appeals. They test different prices. And they test different media in which to advertise. Testing is mail order's secret weapon. It is also the secret which allows a mail order operator to fail with four products out of five and still walk away with a million dollars or more.

How is it done? You spend a little money for a test. A complete failure tells you to drop the whole project. A marginal failure or a marginal success says to experiment and rework some aspect of the project. A major success gives you the green light for a larger investment. In this way you can afford to lose a little money on several dismal failures. But when your testing indicates a clear success. you can move immediately to capitalize on what you know to be a winner. The idea is not to risk a lot of money until you are certain of success.

While there are no guarantees. the potential does exist for just about anyone to make a million dollars or more in this business if they have imagination. persistence. and honesty and if they follow the basic principles that have proven to be successful.

[Dr. Cohen is professor of marketing at California State University, Los Angeles. He has just published a book entitled. "Building A Mail Order Business: A Complete Manual For Success." which is in its second printing.]

Figure 4.8. Resulting newspaper notice.

SOURCES OF ADDITIONAL INFORMATION

How to Advertise—A Handbook for Small Business, by Sandra Linville Dean, published by Enterprise Publishing, Inc., 725 Market Street, Wilmington, DE 19801.

How to Advertise and Promote Your Business, by Connie McClung Siegel, published by John Wiley & Sons, Inc., 605 Third Avenue, New York, NY 10158.

How to Be Your Own Advertising Agency, by Herbert J. Holtje, published by AMACOM, a division of the American Management Association, 135 West 50th Street, New York, NY 10020.

How to Get Big Results from a Small Advertising Budget, by Cynthia S. Smith, published by Hawthorne Books, Inc., 260 Madison Avenue, New York, NY 10016.

How to Write a Good Advertisement, by Victor O. Schwab, published by Wilshire Book Co., 12015 Sherman Road, North Hollywood, CA 91605.

Risk Free Advertising, by Victor Wademan, published by John Wiley & Sons, Inc., 605 Third Avenue, New York, NY 10158.

Tested Advertising Methods, by John Caples, published by Reward Books, Englewood Cliffs, NJ 07632.

The Successful Promoter, by Ted Schwarz, published by Contemporary Books, Inc., 180 North Michigan, Chicago, IL 60601.

CHAPTER 5

PERSONAL SELLING

THE IMPORTANCE OF PERSONAL SELLING

As a method of promotion, personal selling of your product should be given major consideration. Unlike other methods of promotion, including advertising, publicity releases, contests, and sweepstakes, personal selling involves face-to-face communication and feedback. That gives it a tremendous edge.

THE ADVANTAGES OF PERSONAL SELLING

Personal selling has six advantages over other promotional methods:

1. *Flexibility.* Your salespeople can vary and tailor the sales presentations they make depending upon the customers' needs, behavior, motives, and special situations.

2. *Immediate feedback.* Salespeople can vary their presentation and approach depending upon the reaction as they proceed.

3. *Market pinpointing.* Much advertising is wasted because you pay for sending your message to individuals who may be readers or viewers of a vehicle but are not real prospects for your goods or service. With face-to-face, personal selling, greater pinpointing of the target consumer is possible than with any other means of promotion.

4. *On-the-spot sales.* Personal selling is the only method of promotion by which you can sell the product and receive money immediately.

5. *Not just sales.* Your salespeople can perform other necessary services while making sales calls. For instance, they can do customer research, relay customer complaints, develop credit information, and verify the reality of customer prospects.

6. *No time limit.* An advertisement gets read. It either does its work or is disregarded. But until they get thrown out, your salespeople can keep trying to make the sale.

THE BIG DISADVANTAGE OF PERSONAL SELLING

Face-to-face selling has one single disadvantage, and it is a big one: its high cost. The cost of recruiting, motivating, training, and operating a sales force is not to be underestimated. Finding the caliber of people necessary to do the job may be extremely expensive. As energy costs have skyrocketed, so has the cost of each individual sales call. In many parts of the country today, a single sales call costs $150 or even more.

Because of this major limitation, sales forces and face-to-face selling must be used wisely and efficiently. This chapter will show you how to accomplish this.

WHAT DIFFERENT SALES JOBS DO SALESPEOPLE DO?

Salespeople do a variety of sales jobs. Some sales jobs simply require order taking rather than actually persuading an individual to buy something. Others require the sale of complicated, sophisticated, and expensive machinery. The different sales jobs are sometimes placed into seven groups.

Group 1: Product delivery persons. With this type of sales position, selling is actually secondary to delivering the product, be it milk, fuel oil, soft drinks, or whatever. This type of salespeople rarely originates sales. Therefore, a persuasive personality is not required, although an individual who performs good service and is reasonably pleasant may ultimately increase sales over a period of time.

Group 2: Inside order-takers. Inside order-takers are salespeople who generally work inside, behind retail counters. In this case, and in the majority of situations, the customer has already entered the store in order to buy. These salespeople primarily service the customer. Sales can be increased by the order-taker's helpful attitude, but usually not significantly so.

Group 3: Outside order-takers. Outside order-takers are salespeople who work in the field outside of the store. Their job generally involves calling on retail food establishments. They do little or no selling, but, like the salespeople in the first group, are primarily delivery people.

Group 4: Missionary salespeople. The primary job of missionary salespeople is to build good will while performing promotional activities or providing other services to a customer. Examples of this type of salespeople are those detail men and women who service physicians and the pharmaceutical industry. They may or may not be expected or even permitted to solicit orders.

Group 5: Technical salespeople. Technical salespeople such as sales engineers don't need persuasive powers as much as they need technical, in-depth knowledge of the product or service they can display when dealing with the customer. No matter how persuasive, a technical salesperson cannot be successful without this technical background.

Group 6: Creative sellers of tangibles. These are salespeople who must sell tangible products through creative selling. That is, they must actually persuade people to purchase. Now, we are getting into a more difficult sales job since the customer may not be aware of a need for the product or how the product can satisfy his or her needs better than other products or services he or she is currently using. The creative seller may sell a product that is also technical; however, in this case persuasiveness and other sales traits are as important as or more important than the technical knowledge. Sellers of tangible products sell everything from encyclopedias to airplanes.

Group 7: Creative sellers of intangibles. This is probably the most difficult of sales positions. Not only must the salesperson be persuasive and able to sell, but he or she must sell a product that is not easily demonstrated and cannot be shown to or touched by the customer. Products that fall into the intangibles category include such items as insurance, consulting services, and advertising.

Knowing what kind of salesperson you want is very important. If you get the wrong type for your sales job, you might fail to get sales or waste money on qualifications you do not need.

THREE KEYS TO IMPROVING SALES BY DEVELOPING A SUPERIOR SALES FORCE

Your sales force can do a poor, mediocre, or terrific job in selling for you. It all depends on you and your ability to develop your sales force. Here are three keys to success:

1. *Selection.* You've got to find the best salespeople. It is a challenging problem, but if you succeed, it will make a major contribution to the overall sales ability of your organization.

2. *Training.* Once you have superior people, they must be given the correct training to enable them to maximize their sales ability.

3. *Compensation.* Compensation plans depend on many factors. They are critical in sales because compensation is what motivates your salespeople and makes them perform. Performance cannot be measured simply in terms of sales volume. While the importance of sales volume cannot be overemphasized, other factors—including service, providing information to customers, and creating good will—may be very important to your organization.

Selecting Salespeople

To begin the selection process, you must identify what type of salesperson you need. Next, you must establish a job description and specification. Armed with these, you can search for sources of available salespeople and finally implement your selection system.

Sources of Salespeople. While you can use sources described earlier in your recruiting and selection of a sales force, salespeople fall into a special category. For example, a research study in the insurance industry revealed that there were four primary sources for prospective insurance salespeople:

1. Salespeople personally known by the hiring sales manager
2. Individuals with influence
3. Individuals selected from the present sales force and given new geographical territories or sent to new locations
4. Salespeople recruited through direct mail advertising

Which of these groups do you think did best? Those recruited from the present sales force did five times as much business the first month as those recruited cold through direct mail advertising. Also of interest is the fact that it took six times as long to complete negotiations and start the new sales recruits doing business from groups 3 and 4 as it did to start those from groups 1 and 2.

Other sources of salespeople which you should consider in your sales force recruiting are as follows:

1. *Those working for you who are not currently in sales.* Be alert for the bright, persuasive individual with a "sales-type personality" who is interested in selling. Such an individual may be moved from another position in your company to become very effective for you in a sales position.

2. *Word of mouth from present customers.* Your current customers may assist you by recommending effective salespeople.

3. *Local schools and universities.* New graduates are always looking for opportunities, and sales is a great way to start. Schools and colleges will assist you in finding candidates from among their students.

4. *Recommendations from your present sales force.* Your present sales force frequently comes in contact with other salespeople from other companies and in other industries. They may have some excellent recommendations for new recruits.

The Six Elements of a Sales Force Selection System. The six elements of your selection system are as follows:

1. Application forms
2. References
3. Interview
4. Intelligence and aptitude tests
5. Physical examination
6. Field observations of candidates

While application forms, references, and interviewing have all been discussed in an earlier chapter, it is important to realize that here the most important qualities in a candidate are his or her readiness and ability to sell. Therefore, you should not hesitate to emphasize this aspect, especially in checking on references and in the personal, face-to-face interview.

In fact, in order to make the personal interview more objective, some interviewers of potential salespeople use a form having a semantic differential intensity scale to note differences. In this manner, various attributes can be more or less objectively rated immediately through judgment. A typical judgment chart is shown in Figure 5.1.

As recommended in an earlier chapter, the prospective candidate should be interviewed by more than one individual in your firm so that opinions can be compared. This is especially true when seeking salespeople who must have considerable persuasive abilities—who must actually inform and persuade people regarding their needs and wants and the ability of the product or the service to fulfill them. First, you want some objective opinion about this ability. But second, if the candidate has it, you don't want to miss some key point because of his or her ability to persuade you.

Tests, physical examinations, and field observations have not been discussed previously for other types of jobs. They are particularly important, however, for sales positions. Because the sales job itself may require considerable field work, good health and personal appearance may have a direct bearing on success or failure. Therefore, if the job is at all demanding physically, a physical examination should be required prior to hiring. Some types of intelligence and aptitude tests for selling

1. General appearance	5. Imagination
poor 1 2 3 4 5 6 7 8 9 excellent	poor 1 2 3 4 5 6 7 8 9 excellent
2. Dress	7. Attitude toward work
poor 1 2 3 4 5 6 7 8 9 excellent	poor 1 2 3 4 5 6 7 8 9 excellent
3. Verbal communication	8. Intelligence
poor 1 2 3 4 5 6 7 8 9 excellent	poor 1 2 3 4 5 6 7 8 9 excellent
4. Manners	9. Ability to sell himself or herself
poor 1 2 3 4 5 6 7 8 9 excellent	poor 1 2 3 4 5 6 7 8 9 excellent
5. Persuasiveness	10. Overall handling of interview
poor 1 2 3 4 5 6 7 8 9 excellent	poor 1 2 3 4 5 6 7 8 9 excellent

Figure 5.1. A differential intensity scale for use in interviewing potential sales personnel.

were extremely popular in the late 1950s and early 1960s. They are currently controversial because they are far from perfect and many eliminate a few excellent candidates while allowing some poor candidates to get through. However, psychological testing will eliminate candidates who are totally unsuited for selling. Administering these tests has one additional advantage. It will impress the potential employee of the importance that you place on the sales position. This can have a motivational effect on the candidates you hire.

Remember, be very careful with psychological testing. Have a professional evaluate the results. You can find such psychological testers listed in the Yellow Pages under Aptitude and Employment Testing. Do not attempt to purchase the test and evaluate the results on your own. One firm that did this eventually discovered that candidates it hired who got top scores on a test were much poorer performers than those who scored less well.

For some very important positions, on-the-job observation may be necessary to determine whether the salesperson is suitable or not. This can be done through a conditional hire, which makes permanent hire contingent on acceptable performance under personal observation.

Do's and Don't's of Salespeople Selection

Kenneth Grubb, president of Kenneth Grubb Associates of Princeton, New Jersey, developed the following list of do's and don't's for selection of salespeople.[1]

In thinking about tips on selecting salesmen, look first at the "Do's."

Do—Write a Job Description. The starting point in selecting salespeople is a job description. You should, if you haven't already done so, spell out the duties and responsibilities required for your selling job.

This description should define the type of selling that the job requires. Do you sell a product, a service, or a combination of the two? Selling a service, or a product and its related service, often requires your salesman to have a technical background or an aptitude for absorbing technical information.

As a counterpart to the job description, main specifications should also be prepared. Spell out in as much detail as you can the abilities and qualities an applicant needs to be successful in selling your product or service. There is no substitute for knowing what you are looking for.

Do—Select for Initiative and Perseverance. Salespeople have to be self-starters because they are among the least supervisable of employees whether "on the road" or on the sales floor. They either make themselves work, or they don't. At best, evaluation and incentive plans are a poor substitute for spontaneous self-drive, and

---

[1] Kenneth Grubb, *Tips on Selecting Salesman MA No. 196*, Small Business Administration (1976).

self-policing. You or your sales manager, if you have one, cannot generate initiative in a dead battery.

How much of a self-starter you need depends on the job to be done. If your salespeople check into the office each morning, for example, they can be reminded, if necessary, to call on particular accounts. But if they are on the road all week, they must remind themselves.

Do—Look for Reliability.   An applicant salesman must be reliable because you will have to trust him to do his job. He also will have to gain the confidence of customers; the test of his reliability is their reactions to him. It boils down to his being a "straight shooter."

Straight shooting starts at home. In encouraging salesmen to do the right thing, three rules of thumb apply. First, the owner-manager should not fool himself about what his policies are. For example, if he has to withhold certain information for competitive reasons from his salesmen, he should not kid himself or them by pretending that they have all the information.

Second, the owner-manager should keep in mind that any failures in ethics that a salesman possesses will usually be turned first against his employer. If a company condones shady practices when they benefit the company, the salesman is likely to use this attitude as license to put his own interests above those of the company.

Third, to many customers and to the public, almost the only "picture" they get of a company is the salesman whom they see. Moreover, they often see through a salesman more quickly than either the salesman or his company may believe. If he is not reliable, customers may realize it before the owner-manager does.

Do—Seek Mental Ability.   The amount of brainpower a salesman needs depends on the selling job. Some jobs require only enough to memorize sales talks and put one foot in the door. Other jobs require a high degree of imagination, intelligence, and sometimes technical education.

In many small companies, the difference between a large and a small sales volume lies in the salesman's ability to understand quickly the key points in a customer's problem and to come up with an imaginative solution. Other small companies build a big sales volume on the salesman's ability to see new ways to redesign particular products. Such ingenuity enables the owner-manager to get a jump on his competitors. In selecting a salesman, make sure his mental ability matches the requirements of selling your product.

Do—Look for Willingness to Travel.   If extensive travel is part of your selling job, make sure that the applicant is willing to travel. If he doesn't know it already, make him aware that the comforts and pleasures of normal home and social life are often impossible in a traveling job.

Your objective is to forestall trouble. If the wife wants her husband at home, or he wants to be with his family, all sorts of problems ensue.

On the other hand, some men like travel. They don't like the routine of calling on the same customers over short periods. They like to be away because it's so nice to come back. They like the attention they get from their families when they return from their trips.

When this is the case, you're lucky. This type of "travel-happy" salesman doesn't need the "diversions of the road," which can tarnish a company's reputation.

Do—Look for Willingness to Take Punishment.   Many salesmen are paid to take punishment from which other employees would shrink. They receive rough and even rude treatment from the hard-to-see prospect, not to mention his secretary and other office help with instructions to keep salesmen away from his door.

Sometimes a sales manager hands out, in a different way, as much punishment as the salesman receives from customers. At best, the push for large quotas turns into a battle of wits between the salesman and his boss.

In some companies, the punishment includes the risk of alcoholism. The owner-manager feels—not always correctly—that his salesmen must drink freely with all customers. When, and if, this is part of the selling job, applicants should be told.

Do—Select Emotionally Balanced People.   Selling is often a sort of schizophrenic job. The demands and pressures split some men in two.

Most salesmen have to appear cheerful and unworried during frequent discouragements. For example, they have to be polite to a rude prospect when they would prefer to respond in kind.

Even with the most pleasant customers, the salesman often has to repress his desires out of deference. He may have to bend over backwards to satisfy some customers. Often he has to listen when he would prefer to talk. A liking for people helps to cushion the pressures. When a salesman likes people, it is easier for him to put his preferences in the background when he needs to.

The pressures on salesmen are bad enough when times are good. They can become terrific when there is a temporary drought in sales. The boss may blame him and push for sales—sometimes where none are to be had. To add insult to injury, sometimes the factory may let him down on delivery dates he has promised customers. In addition, some customers—often big volume accounts—may jump on the bandwagon. They seem to sense that the salesman is "down" and try to browbeat him.

Under such topsy-turvy pressures, only an emotionally balanced person can survive. If a salesman is inclined to upset easily, he may start acting less than rationally. Or he may quit his job, and you lose your investment in him.

Whether the pressures are heavy or light, the effective salesman has to surmount them. Preoccupation with his own problems make him insensitive to the unspoken shifts in attitudes and interests of his customers. Also, he needs to be emotionally mature to handle success—to resist the temptation to coast during good times.

In selecting salesmen, the "don't's" are as important as the "do's." A few of the negative aspects follow. They may remind you of others that are particular to your situation.

Don't—Pick Only for Selling Skills.   Contrary to folklore, skills and experience in selling may be the last thing to look for in selecting a salesman. If you already have a successful sales organization, your best bet is probably to select people who can be trained in your methods. When the candidate's other qualifications (for example, he knows your industry and the needs of customers) are sound, he can usually be taught the necessary selling techniques fairly quickly.

On the other hand, when you hire an "experienced" salesman, you may be buying trouble. He may have to unlearn old ways before learning new ones. "Experience" includes bad practices, tricks, habits, and abuses, which may handicap him in learning your ways of selling. For example, he may be in the habit of overstocking customers.

In a fairly new company, the owner-manager may have to hire experienced salesmen because no one in his company really knows how to sell. If such is your case, make sure that you select salesmen whose skills and experience are sound for your type of selling job.

Don't—Pick for Control of Accounts.   Some owner-managers are tempted to hire men from competitors on the theory that such salesmen bring business with them. If you are thinking in that direction, keep in mind that there is a strong tendency to exaggerate the extent to which salesmen can "take customers with them" and hold such business.

Don't—Pick for Trade Secrets.   Some companies hire a competitor's salesman for the information they hope to gain rather than for the selling the man can do.

The owner-manager who hires with the expectation of gaining trade secrets or accounts should keep one fact in mind: Benedict Arnolds are always available to the highest bidder. Money draws them from one company to another.

Don't—Pick Only for Wide Acquaintance.   The owner-manager who hires a salesman because he is widely known among potential customers may be kidding himself. He may be the kind of salesman from whom customers run if they see him coming. His faults may outweigh the advantages of knowing the prospects you are trying to reach. Worthwhile prospects are ready to listen to salesmen who show promise of helping them to have fewer headaches and make more money.

Don't—Expect the Impossible.   Some owner-managers expect their salesmen to do the impossible. They do little planning and preparation and expect the salesman to steamroll his way to a large sales volume. Even the best salesman is handicapped when the home office makes faulty marketing plans, such as insufficient advertising or a tight billing policy.

Often, when an owner-manager expects to get by with little or no planning, he picks men who have strong compulsions to get ahead fast. "We pay a high commission," he says, "and expect top results." The salesman drives himself, often sacrificing his personal life, to make such big money. Some individuals crack under such pressure. Others, addicted to big money, change jobs for greener pastures.

In this same vein, an owner-manager should not expect his salesmen to do what he wouldn't do himself. For example, he would not himself be a doormat for customers to wipe their feet on. Nor would he deliberately lie to customers.

It is important also to caution your men about leading customers to expect the impossible. For example, a salesman should not sell more than you can ship. Nor should he "oversell" a customer on the benefits of your products.

Finally, if you hire a relative as a salesman, do it with your eyes open. It is one thing if he has proved his ability by selling for another company. It is another thing if his most prominent quality is kinship with you.

Use Your Own Judgement

These do's and don't's are suggestive. You may think of others that are pertinent to your situation.

Keep in mind the importance of doing your own thinking about the kind of salesmen you need. They develop procedures that will help in selecting individuals who meet the requirements of your situation.

In selecting salesmen, there is always the question: How do you tell whether the candidate is qualified? How does the owner-manager determine whether the candidate has initiative, reliability, mental ability, and other requirements for the job?

You have to make a judgment based on what you can learn about the candidate. His application form gives you some information. Yet get additional facts and impressions about his past performance by talking at length with him. Sometimes you may test him by asking critical questions about your industry and its customers. Or you might use tests prepared by firms that specialize in their preparation.

Above all, it is important to check his references before making a decision. Use the telephone or a face-to-face contact because a former employer may be too busy, or reluctant, to express himself freely in writing.

Training Salespeople

There are four main areas in which training will contribute to success of your sales force regardless of the type of selling in which it is engaged:

1. Knowledge
2. Work habits
3. Selling skills
4. Attitude

Knowledge.   A salesperson must have knowledge of the product, of the company, of the sales environment, and of the entire environmental situation in which he or she is operating. Only with knowledge can the sales individual best explain the product or the service to the customer.

Work Habits.   The salesperson's work habits are responsible for great success stories as well as great failures. An individual's work habits can also spell the difference between sales success and failure in your company. With sales calls as expensive as they are, a salesperson who makes few calls a day can ruin you in short order. Making calls is a matter of mental attitude and selling work habits.

Selling Skills.   There are so-called "natural salespeople." But while some individuals may be naturally better suited for selling than others, sales skills can be learned and mastered by many people. These skills include establishing rapport and empathy, making effective presentations, handling objections, and closing.

Attitude.   A critical factor in performance in selling is attitude. In fact, it is so important that many books by successful salespersons emphasize this one factor. Elmer G. Leterman, who sold over $300 million worth of life insurance policies more than 30 years ago, said in his book, *The New Art of Selling*,[2] that the first law of creative success is to quit looking outside ourselves for solutions to our problems. In other words, it is the salesperson's attitude that spells success or failure.

Methods of Training Salespeople

There are several methods you can use to train your salespeople to become sales "superstars."

   1. *Indoctrination training.* With indoctrination training, you give your salespeople basic orientation as to the sales job and how it is done. In many cases, your sales manager will accompany the new salesperson to help him learn the job by observation. As the salesperson gets more and more experience, he or she takes over more and more of the job, and finally the manager backs off entirely and the salesperson is on his or her own.

   2. *Job rotation training.* Job rotation training is generally for larger companies. A salesperson spends a certain amount of time in a variety of jobs, which may include positions

---

[2] Elmer G. Leterman, *The New Art of Selling*, Harper and Brothers, New York (1957).

in the factory, in production, in research and development, in the office, and in a sales branch. This way he or she gets a better idea of how the salesperson's job fits into other company operations.

3. *In-class training.* When field experience cannot be easily given, or sometimes even if it is, classes can be conducted to train salespeople how to do their job. This training is particularly effective for providing new information on products, the company, the market, and so forth. The classroom can also be used for motivation. Also, selling skills can be taught and assimilated through various types of role-playing. However, in-class training is time consuming. In a very small company, extensive classroom training may take too many of your resources. Even so, one multimillion-dollar executive recruiting operation started with a solid week of training for everyone hired and maintains this policy to this day.

4. *Sales meetings.* Sales meetings act as a training ground for new employees who are salespeople as well as older ones. In sales meetings, they can trade experiences and build friendly competition. You can also give additional or new training to help salespeople increase their job effectiveness.

5. *Seminars.* Many training companies around the country have training programs especially designed to train new salespeople. There are many training organizations, both national and local, that can provide training needs for your salespeople. These companies can be located in the Yellow Pages under Training—Sales or Sales Training headings. An investment of this type can pay off tremendously in the effectiveness of your new sales employees.

Compensating the Salesperson

The compensation plan for salespeople is particularly important, and it has definite aims. These aims include encouraging the highest volume of sales for your most profitable items while at the same time providing motivation and incentive for your salespeople to work harder. Specifically, your compensation plan must have objectives both for your company and for your salespeople.

Objectives for your salespeople:

1. To receive compensation in direct proportion to sales accomplishments
2. To be compensated for time spent with the customer that does not directly result in sales, such as "missionary" work and service to the customer
3. To have provisions for security, retirement, and possible seasonal or other slumps in selling
4. To receive compensation on a par with what could be earned selling for other companies or for other lines of products or services
5. To have a sense of *esprit de corps*, not only in the sales force but with other employees

Objectives for your company:

1. To motivate and inspire your salespeople to increase sales
2. To encourage your salespeople to sell high-profit items

3. To enable your firm to maintain the maximum of profit consistent with other factors, including compensation for your salespeople who meet all criteria listed as objectives
4. To maintain the maximum control possible over your sales force and your salespeople's activities
5. To encourage cooperation among your salespeople and with other functional areas and people in your company
6. To encourage company *esprit de corps*

The Three Basic Means of Compensating a Sales Force.   There are three basic means of compensating a sales force. These are: (1) salary, (2) commission, and (3) combination plans. Each has its advantages and its disadvantages.

With a *salary* plan, you have an arrangement whereby you pay a defined amount of money, weekly, monthly, or annually, in return for whatever work is required by the sales force. It has the following advantages:

1. It is easy for the company to budget and administer.
2. Since the compensation is guaranteed so long as the salesperson works for you, it allows for the greatest amount of control over your sales force.
3. It is generally easier to recruit salespeople for this type of compensation plan.
4. Since compensation is guaranteed, extravagant promises or overselling by your salespeople will be discouraged.
5. It is easier to arrange for your salespeople to accomplish nonselling activities since their "time is not money."
6. The system encourages the maximum cooperation among salespeople and other members of your company.
7. It is easier to transfer salespeople to other territories using this plan.

However, this compensation plan also has disadvantages:

1. There is a lack of incentive for high sales.
2. Salary is a fixed cost unrelated to sales revenue.
3. So-called "super" salespeople are rarely attracted by a straight salary since they can make much more money on a commission system.
4. If business activity is declining, it is very difficult to adjust salaries. You will be forced to discharge some of your salespeople. This means morale problems and additional costs for training and hiring when business conditions improve.
5. Salaries must be paid whether or not there are sales.

Straight salary plans are usually most useful under any of four conditions:

1. For compensating new salespeople who are not yet ready to assume their full responsibilities
2. For compensating missionary salespeople whose duties are not to make an immediate sale, but whose work eventually leads to sales over a period of months or even years

3. For opening new territories in which you have not formerly been selling
4. For sales of sophisticated or technical products requiring lengthy negotiations

A compensation plan using sales *commissions* is simply an agreement on your part to pay the salesperson a percentage of each dollar of a product or service sold. In such a plan, the salesperson is usually entirely on his or her own. A successful salesperson can make a lot of money. An unsuccessful salesperson makes nothing. In some states the straight commission plan has been modified since minimum wages must be paid. However, the basic principle is the same. The amount earned is directly related to sales made.

Advantages of the commission plan are as follows:

1. A company with limited capital can fully staff its sales force without high overhead commitments.
2. This method provides direct incentive for high sales.
3. A commission plan attracts more aggressive and persuasive salespeople since these are the only ones who can make it work successfully.
4. The costs of sales are automatically reduced if and when sales decline.

Naturally, the commission plan has its disadvantages, although at first it may appear that the system is absolutely ideal for any company. The disadvantages of the commission system of compensation are as follows:

1. There is a great deal of difficulty getting salespeople to devote time to sales tasks which may be important to your company but for which no commission is paid.
2. There is great danger in overselling the customer and possibly incurring customer ill will.
3. There is a great deal of bookkeeping involved.
4. There is potentially greater difficulty in recruiting.
5. There is less cooperation within the company among salespeople and among other functional areas.

Because of the potential difficulties with straight commission plans, modifications have been made. Here are the primary changes that have been introduced.

With the *commission against draw* modification of the straight commission, a salesperson is allowed to draw a certain amount of money ahead of his or her sales against commissions that will be earned later. This sales advance or draw allows the salesperson to have living expenses even during a slump. As soon as the first commissions are earned, they are used to pay the draw that the salesperson has already been advanced.

With the *modified commission scale*, a commission rate is established by a series of steps. It is frequently used with the draw in order to help the salesperson pay off the money advanced as rapidly as possible. In order to do this, a higher commission may be paid on the first sales until the money advanced is covered; then the commission rate may drop to lower levels or steps depending upon the scale that is constructed. Of course, this is also advantageous to the company if sales are greater than anticipated since the commission will be less on the higher amount of sales. The approach, however, does have a disadvantage; some companies take the opposite tactic and increase commission percentage for higher amounts of sales. In some cases this increase is effected through a bonus plan, a bonus being paid for effort resulting in increased sales or sales above a certain set goal or quota. Let us say that you are paying 10% commission and have established the quota for salespeople of $20,000 in sales per month. The bonus would come into play if this $20,000 per month were exceeded. Perhaps you would offer an additional 5% bonus for sales exceeding the quota. Thus, if a salesperson only met this quota, he or she would receive $20,000 times 10%, or $2,000 commission. But for sales of $30,000 a month, your salesperson would receive $30,000 times 10% or $3,000, plus an additional 5% of the $10,000 difference between $20,000 and $30,000, or an additional $500. Therefore, the total amount of compensation would be $3,000 plus $500, or $3,500.

Commission plans work well under the following circumstances:

1. Where considerable incentive and motivation are needed to get high sales
2. Where very little missionary work or other sales assistance that does not have to do with closing out a sale is required
3. Where the company is not so strong financially that it can afford large amounts of overhead to compensate salespeople whether or not sales are made
4. Where salespeople can operate independently

Combination plans offer a fixed compensation element plus a variable element made up of a commission on sales or a bonus based on volume. In combination plans, the fixed portion is a salary. The variable portion is used to motivate sales and to achieve many of the benefits of the commission type of compensation plan. The variable element of the combination plan may include payments on sales volume, payments on a performance evaluation, a combination of volume and a performance evaluation, or some type of bonus.

The advantages of combination plans are:

1. Flexibility in dealing with the overall job of selling the company's product or service
2. Flexibility in making changes in territory assignment or assignment of customers
3. Choice among the various factors that will motivate the salespeople to work independently to achieve high sales
4. Ability to group salespeople for team selling situations of major products while applying direct incentive as well as salary compensation to motivate this performance

The disadvantages of combination plans are:

1. Complexity in construction of the plan
2. Amount of time required for administration and bookkeeping
3. Difficulty of explaining the plan to salespeople
4. The need for constant review to be sure that the factors being used as part of the overall compensation are doing what they are supposed to

The combination plan can work well for many companies, but in order to use it you must balance the best features of the salary plan and the commission plan while at the same time trying to eliminate their disadvantages. This isn't always easy and requires considerable thinking and planning ahead of time. It should be used when (1) a complex selling task is to be rewarded, and (2) factors other than volume are considered important and yet an incentive element is definitely required.

HOW TO MEASURE THE PERFORMANCE OF YOUR SALES PERSONNEL

Until you know how your sales force is performing, you have no way of making meaningful changes to improve performance. Therefore, it is necessary to develop a means of evaluation. In general, evaluation is based on two sets of factors: quantitative and qualitative. Quantitative factors generally are easier since they are specific and objective. Sales volume either goes up or it does not. You see the results in black and white. Qualitative factors must rely on subjective judgment. However, in many types of sales operations, qualitative factors must be considered because of the extent of their influence on company objectives.

Quantitative Factors

The following are factors in sales that are useful in comparing quantitative performance:

1. Sales volume segmented as to areas, products, customer groups, and so forth
2. Sales volume as a percentage of a predetermined quota or calculated territorial potential
3. Gross profit
4. Sales that may be segmented by number of orders, average size, or similar factors
5. Closing ratio (a ratio of the number of sales closes divided by the number of calls made)
6. Percentage of new accounts sold
7. Number of new accounts sold
8. Number of new accounts sold divided by number of new accounts called on

Qualitative Factors

The following are factors that should be considered in evaluating your sales force on a qualitative basis:

1. Analytical ability
2. Company knowledge
3. Competition knowledge
4. Customer relations
5. Decision-making ability
6. General attitude
7. General knowledge of sales environment, the customer, legal aspects, and the product
8. Health
9. Organization and management of time
10. Personal appearance
11. Personality
12. Preparation for presentations and sales calls
13. Product knowledge

HOW TO IMPROVE YOUR SALESPERSON'S PERFORMANCE

Raymond O. Loen of R. O. Loen Company, Management Consultants of Lake Oswego, Oregon, developed the following guide to bringing about improvements in sales performance in three steps[3]: planning, measuring, and correcting.

Planning

Get the sales representative's agreement about goals to meet or exceed in the next year:

1. Total profit contribution in dollars
2. Profit contribution in dollars for:
   Each major profit line
   Each major market (by industry or geographical area)
   Each of 10–20 target accounts (for significant new and additional business)

Get the sales representative's agreement about expenses to stay within for the next year:

1. Total sales expense budget in dollars
2. Budget in dollars for: travel, customer entertainment, telephone, and other expenses

Measuring

Review at least monthly the sales representative's record for:

---

[3] Raymond O. Loen, *Measuring Sales Performance MA 190*, Small Business Administration (1978).

1. Year-to-date progress toward 12-month profit contribution goals
2. Year-to-date budget compliance

Correcting

Meet with sales representatives if his or her record is 10 percent or more off target. Review the number of calls made on each significant account plus what he or she feels are his or her problems and accomplishments. In addition, you may need to do some of the following to help improve performance:

—Give more day-to-day help and direction
—Accompany on calls to provide coaching
—Conduct regular meetings on subjects representatives want covered
—Increase sales promotion activities
—Transfer accounts to other sales representatives if there is insufficient effort or progress
—Establish tighter control over price variances allowed
—Increase or reduce selling prices
—Add new products or services
—Increase financial incentives
—Transfer, replace, or discharge

WHETHER TO USE SALES TERRITORIES

A sales territory is a geographical area in which a salesperson does his or her business. His or her activities may or may not be limited in certain areas. Further, he or she may or may not have an exclusive over a certain area. Establishing sales territories has the following advantages:

1. It fixes precise performance responsibilities.
2. It helps a salesperson to organize his time.
3. It helps maximize customer service.
4. It cuts down on overlapping of sales efforts.
5. It fosters competition and comparison among salespeople in different territories.
6. It helps equalize opportunities in various territories among different salespeople.
7. It makes for adaptation of certain background personality factors and desires of salespeople to their customers.
8. It helps control the overall sales operation.
9. It ensures that all of your salespeople have ample opportunities to sell.
10. It helps maintain total and efficient coverage of your entire market.

However, in certain circumstances, it is better not to limit your salespeople to distinct territories. This may be true if you don't have sufficient salespeople to cover all the territories that might be available; or if certain of your salespeople seem to operate better when they are freewheeling; or if you feel you can get best results out of all of them if you do not establish territorial rights. Sometimes you will not be able to establish territory divisions fairly. In this case it is better not to establish them at all. And in some industries, such as executive recruiting, for example, it may make sense not to establish territories in a geographical sense but rather to group your salespeople depending upon the functions of the various individuals whom they are trying to recruit. Finally, if you are introducing a new product and you want to saturate the market as quickly as possible, the restrictions of sales territories may slow down some of your people.

HOW TO ESTABLISH SALES TERRITORIES

1. If you're going to establish sales territories, it is important first to establish them fairly. There must be some basis of comparison. Usually, a market index or indices relating to the product or the service that you are selling are selected. These indices are usually based on one or more demographic factors, such as income, which would represent buying power or segments of the population that would be interested in the product or the service. For example, if you were selling a high-priced automobile, how many families in the area or the potential area that would constitute a geographical territory could afford such a car? Or, if you had a product that went in the home, how many homes that use such a product are in the territory? Sometimes a combination of different factors is used with a weighting system applied depending upon the relative importance of the factor. In this fashion, territories are divided with indices resulting in approximately the same sales potential.

2. The next problem is to determine how wide an area a salesperson can handle. Factors such as distance, call frequency, as well as numbers that a salesperson can process must all be considered. This will impact on the size of the different territories that are divided, and will also let you know how many salespeople you will need to cover a particular area.

3. At this point you may begin allotting the various territories based on market potential to salesmen. Various adjustments may be necessary depending on local conditions, demand, competition, transportation factors, the product, and other of the strategic and environmental variables that we will discuss in Chapter 7. For example, if a newer product is being sold, the territory may be expanded to give the salesperson having to sell this new product greater opportunity to sell a profitable volume. Each factor for adjustment should be considered on an individual basis so that the net result is territories with essentially identical market potential and number of accounts that can be serviced by the salesperson. Territory allotment should be done so that the servicing of the territories will be profitable to you and profitable to the individual doing the selling.

WHETHER TO USE A SALES REPRESENTATIVE

A sales representative is a special type of sales agent who is independent and sells for a number of different companies for the commission that he or she is paid. Selling using a sales representative has some particular advantages for a small firm with a limited product line. First, you don't have to pay money up front to hire salespeople to sell your product. You pay only the commission after the product is sold. Second, you do not have to recruit except to locate the sales representative. And third, with a limited product line and your own salespeople, you must amortize the cost of selling over a limited line of products. Each call is therefore that much more costly and less profitable. There are other advantages to using a sales representative. These include:

1. Immediate entry into a specific territory or a more general market
2. Regular calls on your customers and prospects
3. Quality salesmanship with no need for you to train
4. Cost as a predetermined selling expense—a percentage of sales as commissions

However, there are also disadvantages you must consider if you are going to use a sales representative:

1. You have limited control over a sales agent as opposed to a salesperson, who is your own employee, who reports to you, whom you train, and who is directly dependent on you for compensation.
2. On very large volumes of sales, the selling expense will be much larger than with your own employees.
3. An independent agent's allegiance to your products and your company is not total since he or she also serves other clients who are selling similar (but noncompeting) products or services. Therefore, such individuals must have special incentives to push your products over others.
4. If and when you terminate a contract with a sales representative, the sales representative may take your customer with him or her to a new client who is a competitor.

HOW TO SELECT A SALES REPRESENTATIVE

If you do decide that it is worthwhile for your business to employ a sales representative, you must get someone who is right for you and your company, and who will build profits. Therefore, selecting a sales representative should not be done hastily. Edwin

E. Bobrow, of Bobrow-Lewell Associates, Inc. of New York, recommends that you ask yourself the following questions in matching an agent to your company's character and image.[4]

What sort of selling skills are necessary for selling my products? Does the agent need technical knowledge and experience in addition to personal selling ability?

What marketing functions, if any, do I need in addition to selling?

Must the agent service my product as well as sell it?

Do I need a one-man or one-woman agency or an organization? If the latter, how large an organization?

What is the agent's record of success in products and territories similar to mine?

How long has the agent been in business? What is the agent's reputation? How well can I trade on it?

Are the other lines carried by the agent compatible with mine? Will the agent's contract for his or her existing lines help gain entry for my line?

Is the trade the agent specializes in the one I want to reach?

Does the agent cover the geographic area I need covered and in what depth?

Do the character, personality, values, and integrity of our two organizations correspond?

Can the "reps" who are the employees of the sales agent sales manage their own territories or will they need management and guidance from the agent? Or from me?

Is the agent the type who merely follows instructions or does the agent have a reputation for offering constructive suggestions? Which type do I need?

Is the chemistry right? Will we enjoy working together?

In my own businesses I have used a special form that all potential manufacturers' representatives or sales representatives are required to complete. This is shown in Figure 5.2. You may incorporate it or design a similar one for your own firm.

SOURCES FOR FINDING SALES REPRESENTATIVES

The following are sources of sales representatives for your company:

1. The Manufacturers and Agents National Association (P.O. Box 16878, Irvine, CA 92713) publishes a directory, *The Manufacturers and Agents National Association Directory of Members*, that may be available in your public library.
2. *The Directory of Manufacturers Agents* is published by McGraw-Hill Book Co., 1221 Avenue of the Americas, New York, NY 10020.
3. Recommendations from customers, sales managers of noncompeting companies, as well as editors, salesmen, and trade magazines can all be useful.

---

[4] Edwin E. Bobrow, *Is the Independent Sales Agent for You? MA 200*, Small Business Administration (1978).

GLOBAL ASSOCIATES
Protective Armor Systems
56 N. SIERRA ST.
PASADENA, CALIFORNIA 91109
U. S. A.

Representative's Application Form

This application is for sales representatives of Global Associates' armor product lines on a commission basis for the territory indicated.

Name of firm _____

Address _____

_____

_____

Year established _____ Number of salespeople _____ Annual sales _____

Managers' or partners' names _____

_____

Territory covered _____

Territory desired _____

References _____

_____

Firms now represented/products

_____

_____

_____

Figure 5.2.   Form for evaluating potential sales representative.

4. If you are exporting, contact the Department of Commerce. They may be able to find a manufacturers' representative for you abroad through their computerized system.
5. You can place classified ads in trade magazines whose readership includes the type of manufacturers' representatives you are seeking.

IMPORTANT ADVICE ABOUT WORKING WITH A SALES REPRESENTATIVE

It is better to have a written contract with an agent so that both sides know exactly what they are going to do. Typically, this contract should spell out that either side may terminate the relationship with the other given 30 days' notice.

When dealing with a new sales representative, you should also be very choosy about granting wide territories. Unfortunately, a few sales representatives will take many more territories than they actually can service well, and some that they do not work in at all. But remember that under the terms of the contract, any sales made in any of those territories, whether directly or indirectly by the sales representative, will ensure him or her of a commission. Therefore, until you understand the situation fully, it is better to limit sales to those territories in which the sales representative has accomplished sales in the past, so that you can be reasonably sure he or she will be able to do so for you in the future.

Even after you have begun a relationship with a sales representative, look for ways to maximize the relationship. Seek ways that you can promote your products or your service with the agent. Remember that you are dealing with a human being; it is not simply a matter of dropping the whole thing in the agent's lap and letting him or her run. You must give encouragement and reason to excel. You must motivate this individual who is selling for you. Never forget that his or her prime incentive is to build his or her own company. Your sales representative cannot afford to push your products or your services if they are unprofitable. Therefore, you must do what you can to insure that these products or services are profitable. Get feedback regarding customer relations and what features are liked and what features are not, and how your products and services can be improved.

Always involve the sales representative in all phases of your marketing. Invite him or her back for meetings either annually or semiannually at your company. Take his or her suggestions regarding packaging, promotion, and marketing. Make your manufacturer's representative or sales agent a part of your team.

However, do not burden your sales agent with confusing details. He or she must go out and make the sale. So, make your instructions clear-cut in order to make it easier for your representative to achieve this goal.

SOURCES OF ADDITIONAL INFORMATION

How I Raised Myself from Failure to Success in Selling, by Frank Bettger, published by Prentice-Hall, Englewood Cliffs, NJ 07632.

How to Develop Successful Salesmen, by Kenneth B. Haas, published by McGraw-Hill Book Co., 1221 Avenue of the Americas, New York, NY 10020.

How to Sell Well, by James F. Bender, published by McGraw-Hill Book Co., 1221 Avenue of the Americas, New York, NY 10020.

The Lacy Techniques of Salesmanship, by Paul J. Micali, published by Hawthorne Books, Inc., 260 Madison Avenue, New York, NY 10016.

Management of the Sales Force, by William J. Stanton and Richard H. Buskirk, published by Richard D. Irwin, Inc., 1818 Ridge Road, Homewood, IL 60430.

The New Art of Selling, by Elmer G. Leterman, published by Bantam Books, Inc., 666 Fifth Avenue, New York, NY 10019.

The Sales Managers Handbook, 13th edition, edited by John C. Aspley, published by The Dartnell Corp., 4660 Ravenswood Avenue, Chicago, IL 60640.

Sales Planning and Control, by Richard D. Crisp, published by McGraw-Hill Book Co., 1221 Avenue of the Americas, New York, NY 10020.

CHAPTER 6

HOW TO MAKE MONEY WITH TRADE SHOWS

WHAT IS A TRADE SHOW?

Trade shows have been held since medieval times, providing sellers with an opportunity to get together to display their products. It has been estimated that there are over 35,000 trade events in the United States alone every year, and more than 7,800 trade shows. Taking proper advantage of the unique potential offered by a trade show can make a great deal of extra money for you by boosting your sales. On the other hand, incorrect use of this promotional opportunity will waste your money, time, and resources.

ADVANTAGES OF TRADE SHOWS

Trade shows offer unique advantages over other means of promotion. Here are several:

1. You can meet with many of your customers and potential customers at one time. You can demonstrate your products and give your customers an opportunity to see and handle them.
2. You can meet with your sales representatives and bring them up to date on your latest products, techniques, and plans, and you can also locate new sales representatives.
3. You can promote your company image in a certain business or industry.
4. Because the trade show itself will be promoted to interest a certain target group of potential customers, you will be furnished with a pre-selected audience having interests matched with your products or services.

137

5. You can rapidly test new products to see whether there is interest from customers and sales representatives.

6. You can distribute additional information regarding your products or services to qualified buyers, potential buyers, sales representatives, and other interested people.

7. You will be able to reach some people who ordinarily are not accessible.

8. Other companies in your industry, both competitors and suppliers, will often be demonstrating their products at the same trade show. This gives you a look at your competition as well as the opportunity to talk to the top people in firms important to your business.

9. You will be able to develop inquiries and leads for expanding your mailing list into new markets you haven't yet entered.

10. You will be able to make large numbers of potential contacts in a relatively short interval of time.

11. You will complement your other promotional activities through your trade show participation.

SETTING OBJECTIVES

In order to maximize the benefits that you will receive, it is necessary that you set definite objectives prior to your participation. That is, you should sit down and work out exactly what you wish to accomplish by your participation in the trade show. Study the list below and consider which objectives are applicable in your case.

1. To test market a new product
2. To recruit new sales personnel or new sales representatives or dealers
3. To develop new sales territories or new distribution channels
4. To encourage your customers to bring their technical problems to you for solutions
5. To introduce new products or new services or policies
6. To make sales
7. To demonstrate equipment that could not otherwise be shown easily to a customer
8. To bring together your representatives, internal sales and marketing people, and other key executives for conferences during the trade show
9. To expand your list of potential customers
10. To check on your competition and what they are offering
11. To increase the morale of your sales personnel and representatives and encourage them to work together
12. To build your company's image in the industry
13. To demonstrate your interest in and support of the sponsoring association

Please note that this list of objectives is not all-inclusive. There may be other goals or objectives unique to your situation that you should identify prior to trade show participation.

HOW TO DECIDE WHICH TRADE SHOWS TO ATTEND

With the large number of trade shows being held worldwide every year, it is clear that you cannot attend them all. It is therefore extremely important that those that you do attend are the most beneficial in boosting your sales and accomplishing the objectives that you establish. In order to make your plans, you must first know what shows are going to be held. The following are sources of information:

1. *Successful Meetings Magazine*, 1422 Chestnut St., Philadelphia, PA 19102, publishes an annual exhibit schedule.
2. *World Meetings, United States and Canada*, and *World Meetings Outside the United States and Canada* are directories available from the Macmillan Publishing Co., 866 Third Ave., New York, NY 10022.
3. *Exhibits Schedule* is published by Bill Communications, Inc., 633 Third Ave., New York, NY 10017.
4. Check your trade or industry magazine. Frequently a calendar of upcoming trade shows and conventions is furnished.

From any of these sources, make a list of shows that interest you and seem to be right for your business. Then, write the management of each show and ask for the literature that it has prepared. Specifically, you are interested in obtaining answers to the following questions:

1. Who has attended in the past and who are the people that these shows attract
2. How many attend
3. The geographical areas from which the attendees come
4. The industries and markets the attendees represent
5. The job titles and responsibilities held by the attendees
6. The topics of seminars, workshops, and events that may be offered at the show
7. The physical location of various exhibit booths available and the location relative to other events going on, entrances, exits, and so forth
8. Other services provided by the show sponsors

You should keep in mind that the information provided to you is a sales document and will therefore present everything in the best possible light. Therefore, one additional source of information obtained from this document that you can and must put to use is the list of prior exhibitors. If you contact these individuals, you can ask directly whether they were able to reach their objectives and whether they think your needs will be met by the trade show in question. Ask a lot of questions. The more you can learn about the show, the more information you have to make your decision.

Harvard professor Thomas V. Bonoma recommends making trade show spending decisions according to a nine-cell matrix as shown in Figure 6.1. Note that the idea

Firm's Marketing Communication Strengths

	Getting Customers	Keeping Customers	Other Objectives
Getting Customers	Low Investment	High Investment	Maintenance Investment
Keeping Customers	High Investment	Low Investment	Maintenance Investment
Other Objectives	Low or Maintenance Investment	Maintenance Investment	Maintenance Investment

Trade Show Strengths

Figure 6.1. Making Trade Show Spending Decisions. Source: Adapted from Thomas V. Bonoma, "Get More Out of Your Trade Shows," *Harvard Business Review*, Vol. 61 (January–February, 1983), p. 82, Exhibit II.

is to look at your communication strength versus the strengths of the trade show in three areas: getting customers, keeping customers, and other objectives. This tells you whether you should make a high, low, or maintenance investment in the show.

HOW TO CALCULATE THE SPACE YOU WILL NEED FOR YOUR EXHIBIT

In order to calculate how much space you will need, you must consider your objectives and what will go into your exhibit. Every display, exhibit, or piece of furniture will require a certain amount of square footage. In addition, you will probably have salespeople on duty in the booth, and they too will require space. Therefore, you must decide how many salespeople you should have and how much footage you should allow for this.

Robert B. Konikow, public relations counsel for the Trade Show Bureau in New York City, recommends finding out first how many of the people visiting the trade show are likely prospects. You do this using the prospects that you received in the mail from the trade show. Try to ascertain the number of visitors with meaningful titles or groups that you would be interested in talking with. Clearly, you won't be able to get all of these people to your booth, but you should be able to fit at least half of them. Take the total number of prospects of the type you are seeking and divide by two. Divide this number by the total number of hours the show will be open. From this calculation you can obtain the average number of visitors per hour.

A salesperson can typically handle approximately 15 prospects per hour. This is a good figure to use for your next calculation unless your own experience has shown that your salespeople handle more or less. Take the hourly visitor rate you have calculated previously and divide it by 15. From this you will get the average number of salespeople you should have on duty in your booth to handle the number of visitors you expect.

For each sales representative you have on duty, you must allow approximately 50 square feet of space. With less than 50 feet of space, the visitor will have a feeling of being crowded. But with more space, the visitor gets a feeling of loneliness and is unwilling to intrude on your salespeople! So, multiply the number of salespeople that you have calculated by 50 and you will get the amount of clear space you will need. Add this to the space that you've calculated previously for your demonstration equipment and furniture and you will come up with how large a booth you are likely to need in square feet.

Let's look at an example. Assume that your furniture and equipment to be displayed occupy 5 square feet of space. Let us say that you have decided from the prospectus that 1,200 prospects are likely to attend the show. Dividing this figure by 2 gives you 600, the number likely to visit your booth. Further, the show will be open a total of 20 hours. Dividing 600 by 20 gives you 30 visitors per hour. Dividing the 30 visitors per hour by the 15 prospects that a salesperson can see per hour on the average gives us 2 salespeople who should be on duty. Multiply 50 by 2 to get 100 square feet of space necessary for your salespeople. Add 100 to 5 for the furniture and equipment you're going to display for a total of 105 square feet necessary. Now, as it happens, most standard booths are 10 by 10, or 100 square feet. The extra 5 square feet can be easily absorbed and a standard booth will fill your bill. On the other hand, if the amount of space you need is much larger than the standard size, perhaps you should consider either two standard booths or an irregularly sized booth, if available.

HOW TO DESIGN YOUR DISPLAY

You must design your display to meet your own requirements as well as to conform to those of the trade show. You should also consider the following factors:

1. You cannot show more than your budget will allow.
2. You want to attract only good prospects who will meet the objectives you have established.
3. You want to demonstrate the uniqueness of whatever it is that you are selling.

You must consider your booth just as you would an advertisement. That is, it must first attract attention, then gain interest, then create a desire to step in, and finally encourage action by your prospect whether he or she is a potential customer, potential sales representative, or whatever.

Remember that just as the headline in a good display or space advertisement attracts a reader to a specific ad, your trade show booth should, through its appearance, attract the people you want to see to your booth. It is best to use live demonstrations and other displays that are different from those of your competition and demonstrate benefits to your customers or to the prospects you are trying to attract. Participation demonstrations will spur interest and are much better than static exhibits or presentations that prospects merely watch.

Demonstrations can be very simple and yet still carry the message across to the audience you wish to reach. A manufacturer of a new safety lens that is much more protective than the ordinary safety lens developed a simple but highly effective demonstration. He arranged a table like a small shooting gallery, with a pellet gun mounted in a transparent, protective case. The handle and trigger of the gun were exposed so that it could be fired. A regular safety lens and this manufacturer's lens could be shot by interested prospects. The regular safety lens shattered easily. This manufacturer's new safety lens did not. This was the hit of this particular trade show and resulted in numerous sales. Go to other trade shows in your area even if you are not exhibiting and check out the exhibits that are attracting large numbers of prospects. This will give you many good ideas when you design your own exhibit.

THINGS TO DO BEFORE THE SHOW

After you have selected your trade show or (shows), designed your exhibit, and made other arrangements, you can greatly increase your ability to capitalize on a trade show's advantages if you venture into some of the following preshow activities:

1. Feature a unique item. Focus the activities around this unique item brought in especially for the show. Naturally, the unique item should support the objectives that you have established previously.

2. Contact local media for publicity. Write letters to newspapers, radio and television stations, and other media in the city where the trade event will be held. With the letter, send a publicity release as described in Chapter 4. Feature the unique item you have developed for the show and ask to have your publicity release printed. Make yourself available for personal interviews.

3. Publicize to your industry. Send the publicity release that you have developed on your unique item for the show to all trade magazines in your field. Again, promote this unique product or service to the maximum extent possible and ask to have your publicity release printed.

4. Mail special letters with the publicity release to your customers, sales representatives, and others who may be interested. Give them a special invitation to see you at your booth and see your new item or the item you are promoting. Be sure that you indicate the exact location of your booth.

5. Send letters with the publicity release and with your invitation to other interested parties who might not normally attend a trade show for your particular industry or association. For example, if you were a small book publisher exhibiting a special health food diet cookbook, you might also do a mailing to all the health food stores in the city in which the show is being held. These individuals might not normally attend a book or publisher's trade show, but a special invitation promoting an item they are interested in might get them there and to your booth.

6. Obtain and prepare additional promotional material, such as posters in your show windows or stickers to affix to your normal correspondence, which announce the fact that you will be in a trade show. This will have the additional advantage of promoting your image to your customers and suppliers even if they do not go to the show.

7. Prepare brochures or other information about your products or services to distribute to prospects at the show. Make sure this information is to the point, directly relates to what you are selling, and, of course, is interesting. However, unless your product is highly technical and is an expensively priced item, do not go overboard on this. Remember that there are many show attendees who do nothing more than collect brochures and throw them away later.

You should also be concerned with the following tasks, many of the details of which were probably covered in the prospectus sent to you by the trade organization. They are important, so don't neglect them.

1. Be sure that you have insurance covering your trade show activities.

2. Prepare and prefabricate as much of your booth as possible prior to shipping. Labor costs for doing this at shows are high.

3. Be sure you've timed your packing and shipping so everything arrives well ahead of time.

4. Select your booth location. The better locations sometimes cost more money. However, many experts say that the location of the booth is a major factor in trade show success.

5. Be sure that you have your hotel reservations and also a rental car reserved if you will need it.

6. Have an emergency plan concocted in case your booth is lost or delayed in shipment. You might be able to fall back on displays put up through your local representatives or other equipment that you might carry with you. Always expect the best but be prepared for the worst.

7. Have certain items duplicated and carry them with you in case they are lost or damaged in shipment, and have a tool kit for emergency repairs.

THINGS TO DO DURING THE SHOW

In order to maximize the benefits of a trade show, you should not simply go and have a good time. You should make a list of specific things you intend to do and then do them. Your list may including the following:

1. Contact the local media if they haven't already contacted you after a mailing. Try to get additional exposure through interviews, appearing on television and radio talk shows, and so forth.

2. Contact local customers, suppliers, and other interested prospects. If you cannot do this face to face, use your telephone. Personal contact while you are in town will be of considerable assistance to your business.

3. Meet and talk with other exhibitors. Sell to them, if possible. Think creatively about ways in which other exhibitors may help you in your business. One exhibitor made thousands of dollars in sales simply by noting that his product fit naturally as a lead-in item to a higher-priced item sold by another exhibitor. His proposal was to give this other exhibitor exclusive sales rights in his industry, which was totally different from the industry for which the product was usually sold. Be alert to opportunities at exhibits.

4. Use your local sales representatives to the fullest extent possible. They will be able to profit heavily from the fact that you are exhibiting in their city. They can help you prepare your booth and be your local contact point.

During the exhibit, you will meet many people and will obtain sales cards from many. It is a sad fact that when you talk to many people, one after the other, you will not remember later what these business cards are for. One way of dealing with this problem is to write what the individual wants on the back of the business card as soon as you receive it. An even better way is to use a pocket tape recorder and record this information.

The Trade Show Bureau publishes a number of reports on trade shows that you can obtain by writing to 1660 Lincoln St., Suite 2080, Denver, CO 80264, or by calling (303) 860-7626. A list of reports follows; contact the Bureau for current prices.

Marketing/Communications

Ten Years of Trade Show Bureau Reports in Ten Minutes—10 × 10 (MC #12). This unique Bureau report distills research findings into an attractive, easy to read, multicolor booklet. It defines the dynamic advantages of the trade show and exposition as a cost-effective and productive selling medium.

Exhibiting By Objectives (MC #11). This booklet by Fred Kitzing is designed to show exhibitors how to improve productivity by setting objectives prior to show participation, thereby realizing the greatest return on their marketing investment.

Trade Shows—This Marketing Medium Means Business (MC #10). This article, written by W. Mee, past president of the Bureau, is a reprint from Association Management Magazine and combines a variety of Bureau statistics and data on industry trends.

Coping with Trade Show Overload: Strategies for Participants, by Audrey J. Mahler and Ann Duke *(MC #9).* Trade shows invite participants to investigate current industry trends, products, and projections. This article presents a model for setting goals, planning a strategy, implementing the plan and measuring the results. Follow Mahler & Duke's model and you will win the jackpot at the next trade show you attend.

Trade Show Selection Criteria (MC/RR #23). An analysis of the most important factors in exhibitors' selection of which trade shows they select for participation.

The Role of the Advertising Agency Involvement in Trade Show Participation (MC/RR #25). An analysis of how advertising agencies perceive trade shows, how they are, or plan to be, involved with this marketing medium.

Spotlight Your New Product Via Trade Shows (MC #8). An article by Robert B. Konikow, reprinted from *Marketing Times*, outlines the special requirements of new product introduction at a trade show.

Trade Show Marketing & Sales 1—A System for Selling in Trade Shows; Trade Show Marketing & Sales 2—A Guide to the Many Uses of Trade Shows in Business Marketing (MC #7). These two booklets, prepared by Fred Kitzing, maximize performance at expositions. They provide an understanding of the opportunities offered, along with the basic guidelines to capitalize on the opportunity. Sold as a set.

Expositions Work—A Management Guide for Exhibitors, by Edward A Chapman, Jr., CME *(MC #6).* The success or failure in participating in major marketing/

selling events is contingent on an understanding of and an adherence to basic marketing fundamentals. This 30-page booklet details the elements essential for success, and how those elements must be applied. It is an essential marketing guide for novices as well as seasoned practitioners.

The Effect of Booth Size and Booth Traffic (MC/RR #5020). The relationship between the size of an exhibit booth and the traffic generated has not previously been reported. This analysis by exhibit surveys of 77 exhibits at the 1987 IFT Food Expo provides a "first-time look" at the effect of booth size on achieving higher traffic density.

Expositions—They Mean Business (MC #5). This report, a succinct summary of Bureau research, defines the importance of expositions in the marketing mix. It clearly demonstrates the cost effective and productive ways in which this marketing/ selling medium can improve the productivity of the marketing plan.

Pre-Show Promotion: Its Role in New Product Introduction (MC #4). Pre-show promotion is an essential ingredient in introducing new products. Mark Noble, in a case history, explains how, through effective brand marketing, product positioning, and a dynamic pre-show promotion campaign, a company can introduce a new product line in a very mature and competitive market. He chronicles his company's success in bringing 94 out of 100 key prospects to its trade show booth.

The NCC, A Grand Daddy Trade Show: AT&T—A Case Study (CS #18). This case study examines show managers and exhibitors working more closely together to produce the results they want, where exhibitors create their own marketing communications events tied in with the shows. AT&T and its approach to a single show.

The Effect of Advertising on Booth Traffic at the 1987 Institute of Food Technologists Food Expo (MC/RR #5030). This study is an extension of the Trade Show Bureau Report #27 (October 1985), which established a direct correlation between the frequency of advertising and booth traffic, specifically for advertisers in *Food Technology*. This survey of the 1987 IFT Food Expo is an expansion of the previous research.

The Effect of Advertising on Booth Traffic (MC/RR #27). An analysis of the relationship between advertising consistency and booth traffic: a study of exhibitors at the Food Exposition of the Institute of Food Technologists—comparing booth traffic with exhibitors' advertisers in the Institute's journal *Food Technology*, and those exhibitors who did not advertise.

Success in Trade Show Exhibiting—It's Dependent On an Application of Marketing Skills—Skillfully Applied, by Gerald Sanderson *(MC #3).* Successful participation in a major trade exposition requires the dedicated application of a variety of marketing skills. Failure to do the "necessary homework" can result in frustration and failure—evidenced by some exhibitors in the high technology field. Gerald Sanderson provides an insight into the elements that do guarantee success and provides the reasons why these elements must be addressed.

On Being an Exhibitionist! (MC #2). This reprint from *Medical Conference Planner*, by Jan M. Spieczny, claims that a blend of showmanship, sellmanship, and salesmanship is essential to get the most out of your exhibit dollar.

What Makes Visitors Remember Your Trade Show Exhibit (MC/RR #11). This study looks at the effect of a number of characteristics on the proportion of visitors who remember a booth, including booth personnel, company awareness, industry leadership, and exhibit approach.

The Exhibit Management Function—Perceptions of Exhibit Management and Marketing Executives (MC/RR #2040). An authoritative report by the Center for Marketing Management Studies, Southern Methodist University, on the exhibit management function focusing on the ways exhibit management perceives the function and comparing it with the perceptions of their marketing management.

Exhibit Management Practices—Setting Objectives and the Evaluation of Results (MC/RR #2010). An extensive analysis by the Department of Marketing, University of Massachusetts at Boston, of exhibit management practices, with particular emphasis on the setting of objectives and the evaluation of show results.

A Formula for Determining Exhibit Staff and Space Needs, by Jenny Tesar *(MC #1).* In an article for *Successful Meetings*, Jenny Tesar reviews the tested formula developed by Exhibit Surveys, Inc., of Middletown, New Jersey, to determine trade show staffing and space requirements.

Exposition Attendance Promotion—Effective Communication Practices (MC/RR #5010). An overview of how trade shows are promoted, the magnitude of the funds expended in the process, and the various media utilized in show promotion is provided in this report. It is based on a sample of 538 managers of expositions greater than 10,000 sq. ft., and in addition to reporting on the most effective advertising and promotional techniques, the analysis provides data by show type, including attendance promotion expenditure per registrant.

Sales/Measuring Return

Five Tips for Measuring Exhibit Impact. by E. Jane Lorimer *(SM #16).* This article gives five practical tips for measuring your exhibit impact for shows where sales are not a primary objective. This system measures performance in terms of exposure.

Secrets of the Aisle by Dr. Allen Konopacki *(SM #15)*. Dr. Konopacki defines eight factors that will insure the maximum return on show attendance, and double your productivity.

How Trade Shows Continue to Influence Sales (SM/RR #28). U.S. trade shows are moving closer to their European counterparts as important sales vehicles. This conversion study of the 1984 National Computer Conference compares the dynamic sales results of the 1984 show with that held in 1978–79.

How Trade Shows Influence Sales (SM/RR #1110). This report gives an analysis of on-site registrants at the 1986 PC Expo in New York and provides a breakout of the purchases made by "resellers" and corporate volume buyers within a nine-month period following the show. It also analyzes the degree of influence the show had on purchase decisions planned for the next 12 months or within 21 months following the show.

Why Some Exhibits Pay Off, by Arthur L. Fiedman *(SM #14)*. Success through trade show participation is no accident. This report adapted from a presentation at "Meeting World," utilizes a series of case histories to help exhibitors maximize their return on show investment.

How to Improve Your Trade Show Performance Measurably, by Richard Swandby *(SM #13)*. Measuring the effectiveness of participation in trade shows. The report provides trend data on audience quality indicators.

20 Ways to Turn a So-So Show Into a Bonanza (SM #12). Robert Letwin, in this reprint from *Successful Meetings*, lists 20 essential steps you should take to get a good return on your investment in a trade show exhibit.

Measuring Trade Show Results (SM #11). A member of one of the nation's foremost exhibit research firms, Jonathan M. Cox, in this reprint from *Successful Meetings*, focuses on the most important element in any marketing activity—evaluation results.

What a Lead Conversion Program Should Do for You (SM #10). In this penetrating analysis from *The Exhibitor*, Charyn Ofstie details how knowledgeable exhibitors can cover the costs of a lead-tracking program with the conversion of one qualified lead.

Trade Show Lead Systems—A Faster Track to Sales, by Charyn Ofstie *(SM #9)*. Lead generation is one of the most important trade show benefits. Following through on those leads is particularly critical—and often overlooked. This report provides a precise and defined method to insure the full return on the show investment.

Do You Know How Much You Can Accomplish by Attending a Trade Show (SM #8). A concise guide to assist show visitors in getting the maximum return from show attendance.

Number of Calls to Close a Trade Show Lead (SM/RR #18). The report provides, for the first time, data on the number of follow-up calls required on average to close a trade show lead.

You Make the Difference—A Guide to Getting Sales Results Through Trade Shows (SM #7). The second edition of this popular publication. Tips on how to maximize sales at trade shows. In booklet format.

How Much Must You Spend to Reach a Prospect? (SM #6). A graphic comparison of the cost of an industrial sales call with the cost of a qualified exposition lead to reach a prospect.

Does Your Staff Practice "Boothpersonship" (SM #5). Reprint from *Business Marketing* of an article by Bob Dallmeyer on the importance of understanding the uniqueness of trade show selling.

The Trade Show Audience: The Source for Unknown Prospects (SM/RR #22). A study of visitors to 13 regional and 15 national shows indicates that the vast majority of them were not called on by salespeople from companies whose exhibits they had visited. The study also compares traffic density and the performance of booth personnel at regional and national trade shows.

Trade Shows Continue to Reach Prospects Less Expensively than Personal Sales Calls (SM/RR #2070). The Trade Show Bureau's annual cost analysis, comparing "Cost of an Industrial Sales Call" with "The Average Exhibit Cost Per Visitor Reached."

How Is the Exhibit Dollar Spent (SM/RR #2060). This cost analysis defines the ways in which exhibitors allocate their expenditures for the various elements making up the exhibition budget. In addition, it provides the cost information on the various types of exhibits utilized.

Exhibitors—Their Trade Show Practices (SM/RR #2050). The rapid expansion of the trade show industry in the past 10-year period is a reflection in part of exhibitors' changed perception of the productivity and cost effectiveness of expositions. The advantages of trade show participation have been widely publicized, resulting in an influx of new exhibitors, currently exceeding 7% annually.

How to Boost Your Exhibit's Prospect Appeal (SM/RR #13). A study by Robert T. Wheeler, Jr., examines what exhibitors can do before and during a show to get more qualified visitors to their space.

The Effect of Booth Location on Exhibition Performance and Impact (SM/RR #20). According to this study, the location of the exhibition within the hall is neither a positive nor negative factor.

The following are brief comparison summaries of data extracted from publications RR #18 and RR #2060.

How Much Will It Cost to Book an Order? (SM #4). A brief evaluation of McGraw-Hill's number of sales calls to book an order with the cost to close a trade show lead.

How Many Calls Must You Make to Book an Order? (SM #3). A summary of the number of calls needed to close an order compared to the number of sales calls needed to close a qualified trade show lead.

How Much Should You Spend to Reach a Prospect? (SM #2). A summary comparing cost to reach a prospect in the field versus contacting a qualified prospect in a trade show booth.

What Is the Cost to Book an Order from a New Customer? (SM #1). A summary comparison of the cost of closing an order from a new customer versus the cost of closing an order from a trade show lead.

Attendee/Exhibitor Characteristics

Reaching the Unknown Prospect—Trade Show Visitors Not Reached by Regular Sales Calls (AC/RR #1120). This report, the 1990 version of the Bureau's first audience analysis, verifies the dynamic ability of expositions to reach an exclusive and highly qualified audience of buying influences not reached by the typical sales call. It is this unusual ability of expositions that has been one of the driving forces behind the growth of this industry.

Analysis of Trade Show and Conference Attendees Regarding Their Opinions of Why (or Why Not) They Attend Trade Shows and Conferences (AC/RR #1100). This report details the thought processes of quality decision makers as to why they do or do not attend trade shows. In addition, it provides information on the data visitors need in order to commit to attending these marketing events.

Attendee Purchase Behavior at a Consumer Show (AC/RR #1090). This analysis of the Atlanta Home Show provides a penetrating insight into attendee demographics, buying plans, shopping patterns, and plans for future purchases. This meaningful data can help exhibitors improve their show productivity and assist show organizers to better target their attendance promotion efforts. Full study available.

Attitudes and Opinions of Computer Executives Regarding Attendance Information Technology Events (AC/RR #1080). This B. R. Blackmarr & Association study details the important role played by exhibitors in attendance promotion, providing information on how expositions can be planned more effectively to boost attendance.

Attendee Purchase Behavior at an Industrial Trade Show (AC/RR #1070). This study analyzes a typical large industrial trade show. It covers the important factors that influence attendees' purchase behavior.

Trade Show Visitor Floor Traffic Analysis (AC/RR #1060). This report provides data on how attendees plan their show visit and how they cover the floor once on-site. Understanding attendees' show visit behavior is helpful in achieving successful exhibition performance.

The Effect of Economic Recessions on Trade Shows (AC/RR #1050). This study was undertaken to determine what effects business recessions have on the quality and quantity of attendees at trade shows. The report provides an insight into the changes that have taken place in the industry, using 1968 as the base year.

Trade Shows—An Optimum Selling Environment/Audience Survey and Sales Conversion Study: The World of Concrete 1986 Show (AC/RR #1040). A before-and-after analysis of one of the nation's major industrial expositions—evaluating attendees' plans to purchase versus actual purchases.

Corporate Executives' Perceptions of Trade Expositions—Factors Which Influence Attendance Decisions (AC/RR #1030). An analysis by B. R. Blackmarr & Associates sought out the attitudes of and comments from decision makers who do not regularly attend trade shows. These studies identify decision makers' rationales for nonattendance and contain significant information for show management and exhibitors—all of whom are seeking to attract corporate management executives believed to control key purchase decisions.

Attendee Purchase Behavior at a Retail Trade Show—Who Are the Buyers (AC/RR #1020). This study, undertaken for the Bureau by Georgia State University, looks at the attendees at a major retail buying show. It provides an audience overview of who attends, what they purchase, how they arrive at their buying decisions, and how much they spend.

An Audience Survey of the 1985 National Plastics Exposition (AC/RR #1010). A dramatic analysis of the Society of the Plastics Industry's Chicago exposition providing data on buying plans by product category, and projecting total sales generated by this major industry event.

Characteristics at Regional and National Trade Shows (AC/RR #21). Questionnaires returned by 18,341 visitors at 30 regional and 31 national trade shows are studied to determine audience quality, job function, distance traveled to reach show, other shows attended, time spent in exhibits, and other related data.

Reaching the Unknown Prospect (AC/RR #2). An analysis of the trade show audiences' buying influence level—identifying the percentage of buyers not normally reached by the sales personnel. Limited quantities (updated by AC/RR #1120).

The Trade Show Audience (AC/RR #3). What is the make-up of the people who attend trade shows? An analysis of visitors from 22 shows.

Each of the following studies examines the audience at a single show, looking at its buying influences, show experience, time spent on floor, and other related data.

Radiological Society of North America (AC/RR #16).

New York Gift Show (AC/RR #15).

Office Automation Conference (AC/RR #10).

New York National Boat Show (AC/RR #9).

AWS Welding Show (AC/RR #8).

National Computer Conference (AC/RR #6).

1986 Radiological Society of North America—Exhibit Personnel Behavioral Study and Traffic Floor Analysis (AC/RR #4000). Attendee's evaluation of booth personnel performance at the world's largest health care conference.

The Exhibitor/Their Trade Show Practices (AC/RR #19). A study of the organizations and practices of companies that participate in trade shows, with 1982 compared to 1978.

International

Participation in International Trade Fairs—A New Direction (IN #4). The changes in the Commerce Department's "Overseas Trade Fair Certification Program," a joint private sector/government initiative, are designed to further encourage show management organizations to more actively pursue the international expansion of their show sponsorship. The timing of this policy change coincides with the governments' establishment of the privatization panel, and the pressing need to address aggressively the balance of payments deficit.

Dispelling the Myths of Foreign Trade Shows (IN #3). A concise booklet listing the seven myths that tend to restrain exhibitors from taking advantage of the selling opportunities in overseas trade fairs.

You've Got an Uncle in the Overseas Trade Show Business (IN #2). Traditionally wary of government programs, U.S. companies, especially small to medium-sized firms, often overlook the assistance available to make their presence in an overseas trade show a success. Government services can make the experience a productive one.

Trade Fair Certification (IN #1). This article reprinted from *Business America* defines how the Commerce Department and the private sector work together to encourage U.S. exhibitor participation in international trade fairs.

A Case Study—Forum Communications (CS #15). Steve Sanbeck, President of Forum Communications, Inc., an advertising and public relations firm specializing in international trade, provides an insight into a unique aspect of trade show marketing. Forum is involved in marketing Hanover Fairs, the West German trade show organization, to the U.S. marketplace, as well as using their American expertise to help other European clients become successful in the United States.

A Case Study—Anderson & Lembke (CS #11). Hans Ullmark, Executive Vice President of Anderson & Lembke, an international network of business-to-business agencies, describes how Anderson & Lembke took an unconventional route to introduce a new product for a client into a closed market. Through an aggressive pre-show promotion program, they achieved 100% turnout of their prospects at a key trade show.

Trade Shows: Opportunities to Sell—A Case Study of Hanover Fairs CeBIT September 1988 (CS #1). Nowhere is the value of expositions as a marketing/selling medium better appreciated and more effectively executed than in Europe. This report defines how 2,730 exhibitors from 35 nations make Hanover Fairs CeBIT a leading showcase for office, information, and telecommunications technology. It also shows how U.S. technology can secure the fastest entry into world markets at the lowest possible cost.

Industry Trends

Convention Center Industry Growth 1980–1987; Projected Growth 1988–1995, by Robert Black, founding publisher, *Tradeshow Week (IT #5)*. This study meets two objectives: to determine growth rates in the U.S. Convention Center Industry 1980–1987, in terms of number of facilities offering 25,000 square feet or more of exhibit space, total exhibit space inventory; and distribution of facilities geographically and by size of exhibit space. In addition, it forecasts the probable percentages of growth in the U.S. Convention Center Industry 1988–1995, in terms of number of facilities and total exhibit space inventory.

Trade Show Space Usage—Convention Center Space Capacity, by Robert Black, founding publisher, *Tradeshow Week (IT #4)*. What are the facts on trade show growth? And can these growth trends be relied on to project convention center requirements for the future? This report answers these questions.

Convention Center Planning, by Robert A. Sowder, vice president and director of the Convention Center Facilities Group, Danial, Mann, Johnson & Mandenhall *(IT #3)*. Too often, market studies fail to address the critical issues involved in the planning of a complete convention/exhibition facility. This thoughtful analysis addresses design criteria from the three user-requirement points of view—the visitors/attendees, event managers and exhibitors, and facility management.

The Trade Show Marketplace—New Growth, New Dimensions, by Robert Black, founding publisher, *Tradeshow Week (IT #2)*. In a presentation developed for the Exposition Services Contractors Association, one of the industry's foremost authorities and statesmen provides an incisive overview of the trade show industry.

Trade Show Industry Growth 1972–1981; Projected Growth 1981–1991 (IT/RR #17). An examination of 10 years' activity, and a projection, based on responses from show managers, on what lies ahead.

The Trade Show Industry—Management and Marketing Career Opportunities, by Robert Black, founding publisher, *Tradeshow Week (IT #1)*. A reprint of a lecture presented at Cornell University under the auspices of the Cornell University Department of Communications. This presentation reports on the growth and dynamism of the trade show industry and the career opportunities it provides.

Industry Resources

Source Directory (IR #5). A booklet containing lists of associations, books, periodicals, and audio-visuals concerned with trade show, marketing, booth design and other related subjects.

Speakers Directory (IR #4). A source of men and women who can speak with authority on various aspects of the industry. This directory is divided by industry and by geographic location.

Exhibitor Handbook—A Guide for Successful Exhibiting (IR #3). This manual for exhibitors, edited and published by the National Association of Exposition Managers, provides answers to the many logistical questions faced by the new exhibitor, and serves as a refresher for the experienced practitioner. A 26-page report.

Can Your Property Attract Trade Shows? (IR #2). A reprint of an August 1986 article from *Hotel and Resort Industry* that lists the ways experienced hotel operators capture this meaningful business.

Convention Center—1990 Annual Report—Laventhol & Horwath (IR #1). A detailed analysis of operating performance of all convention facilities with over 100,000 square feet of exhibit space.

Audio-Visual Presentations

Ten Years of Trade Show Bureau Reports in Ten Minutes—10 × 10 (AV #2 A/B). This unique Bureau report distills its research findings into an easy-to-follow presentation. It defines the dynamic advantage of the trade show and exposition as a cost-effective and productive selling medium. #2A—35 mm slides. #2B—8½" × 11" overhead transparencies.

The Bottom Line (AV #1). A 12-minute film presentation demonstrates why the trade show properly positioned in the exhibitor's marketing plan provides a cost effective means of securing sales objectives. ½" VHS.

Case Studies

The NCC, A Grand Daddy Trade Show: AT&T—A Case Study (CS #18). This case study examines show managers and exhibitors working more closely together to produce the results they want, where exhibitors create their own marketing communications events tied in with the shows. AT&T and its approach to a single show.

Advertising Agency Case Study Series

How Advertising Agencies Participate in Trade Shows (CS #17). As trade exhibitions have matured into major marketing events, exhibitors have increasingly turned to their advertising agencies for those professional communications skills essential to secure the maximum return on the show investment. This executive summary provides a brief description of the ten case studies of advertising agencies who are actively involved in their clients' trade show programs.

A Case Study—Fleishman & O'Conner Marketing, Inc. (CS #16). An increasing number of agencies are getting involved in their clients' trade show programs. In addition to working with clients who are exhibiting at trade shows, this agency acts as marketing and public relations advisor to show management for shows it produces.

A Case Study—Forum Communications (CS #15). Steve Sanbeck, president of Forum Communications, Inc., an advertising and public relations firm specializing in international trade, provides an insight into a unique aspect of trade show marketing. Forum is involved in marketing Hanover Fairs, the West German trade show organization, to the U.S. marketplace, as well as using their American expertise to help other European clients successfully in the United States.

A Case Study—O'Neal & Prelle (CS #14). William O'Neal, president of O'Neal & Prelle, an advertising agency based in Hartford, Connecticut, describes his company's involvement in trade show programs—making the trade show part of the firm's overall marketing and communications program. He demonstrates that trade show programs deserve the creative input that an advertising agency can provide.

A Case Study—Shapiro & Conner (CS #13). In this case study, Jenny Tesar interviews Alan Shapiro, president of Shapiro & Conner, an advertising agency in Norristown, Pennsylvania. Shapiro describes his firm's involvement in its clients' trade show programs and how trade shows can play a central role in launching and selling products and services.

A Case Study—Simms & McIvor (CS #12). Simms & McIvor, an advertising agency in Bound Brook, New Jersey, is closely involved in its clients' trade show programs. With many of its clients in the pharmaceutical and health care field, McIvor reveals some valuable insights about pre-show and show promotion for health care shows. He shows how an advertising agency can make the trade show program a dynamic and vital part of its clients' entire marketing plan.

A Case Study—Anderson & Lembke (CS #11). Hans Ullmark, executive vice president of Anderson & Lembke, an international network of business-to-business agencies, describes how Anderson & Lembke took an unconventional route to introduce a new product for a client into a closed market. Through an aggressive pre-show promotion program, they achieved 100% turnout of their prospects at a key trade show.

A Case Study—Cummings Advertising Inc. (CS #10). Cummings is a medium-sized industrial agency deeply involved in the trade show activity of most of its clients. While its clients are in many industrial fields, the greatest concentration is in food processing.

A Case Study—Barbeau–Hutchings (CS #9). Barbeau–Hutchings has solid technical experience in its clients' industry—analytical instrumentation and semiconductor markets. They develop creative themes for pre-show promotion and play a vital role in clients' trade show participation.

A Case Study—The Barth Group (CS #8). As an advertising and public relations firm that is actively involved in its clients' trade shows, the Barth Group creates marketing strategies and special events for the nation's major trade show producers.

A Case Study—Andrews/Mautner Inc. (CS #7). This agency is concerned with the coordination of trade show participation with the other elements of its clients' marketing programs and the supporting activity that is essential to achieve the maximum effectiveness of the trade show budget.

Trade Shows: Opportunities to Sell Series

Trade Shows: Opportunities to Sell—A Case Study of the Hotel Purchases Exchange (CS #6). This case study describes how both hoteliers and companies selling to the hospitality industry maximized selling opportunities at the first Hotel Purchasing Exchange.

Trade Shows: Opportunities to Sell—A Case Study of the Supermarket Industry Convention (CS #5). This case history presents a detailed view of the world's largest food marketing exposition and technical conference. FMI has become a truly international marketing event (3,721 registrants from 48 foreign countries), and a showcase of the latest products and merchandising trends representing the state of the art in exposition management.

Trade Shows: Opportunities to Sell—A Case Study of the National Sporting Goods Association's World Sports Expo (CS #4). Few industry groups utilize the exposition medium more productively and innovatively than do the manufacturers of sporting goods. The World Sports Expo dramatically combines the excitement and the selling dynamics of the market NSGA makes for this important industry. It is a major industry marketing event, and its essence is captured in this report.

Trade Shows: Opportunities to Sell—A Case Study of the 1988 Winter Consumer Electronics Show (CS #3). More than 15,000 exhibitors filled 749,909 square feet of exhibit space in three convention areas in Las Vegas. Exhibits ranged in size from 10′ × 10′ booths to 4,000 square feet. This report uses specific examples to relate how show management and exhibitors work together to create a dynamic selling environment.

Trade Shows: Opportunities to Sell—A Case Study of the Sporting Equipment Super Show (CS #2). The emphasis at trade expositions is on sales results, and nowhere is this more evident than in modern major retail shows. Here cost effectiveness is the focus for attendees and exhibitors alike: an opportunity to capitalize on the efficiencies offered at a dominant industry gathering.

Trade Shows: Opportunities to Sell—A Case Study of Hanover Fairs CeBIT September 1988 (CS #1). Nowhere is the value of expositions as a marketing/selling medium better appreciated and more effectively executed than in Europe. This report defines how 2,730 exhibitors from 35 nations make Hanover Fairs CeBIT a leading showcase for office, information, and telecommunications technology. It also shows how U.S. technology can secure the fastest entry into world markets at the lowest possible cost.

THINGS TO DO AFTER THE SHOW

The trade show itself will generate many potential sources of business for you. But you must follow up immediately so that all this potential business does not grow cold. Consider the following suggestions:

1. Write up another publicity release and mail it to all prospects that you met during the show. If the show provides a registration list of the names of companies and other persons attending the show, use this and add it to your mailing list.
2. Mail a publicity release to all your sales representatives throughout the country and promote your participation at the show to them. If you got good results during the trade show, let your sales representatives know about it. It will stimulate them to do more and better work for you.
3. Go over the business cards that you obtained and make certain that each one is individually handled and that what the prospect wanted is furnished.
4. Go over the objectives you established for the trade show and ask yourself whether these objectives were met. This will provide you with important information as to whether the trade show was worthwhile and whether you should attend next year. If you decide that this trade show was worthwhile, start planning immediately. Make reservations right away.

SOURCES OF ADDITIONAL INFORMATION

Creative Selling Through Trade Shows, by Al Hanlon, published by Hawthorne Books, Inc., 260 Madison Avenue, New York, NY 10016.

The Exhibit Medium, by David Maxwell, published by *Successful Meetings Magazine*, 1422 Chestnut Street, Philadelphia, PA 19102.

How to Get Big Results from a Small Advertising Budget, by Cynthia S. Smith, published by Hawthorne Books, Inc., 260 Madison Avenue, New York, NY 10016.

How to Participate Profitably in Trade Shows, by Robert B. Konikow, published by Dartnell Corp., 4660 Ravenswood Avenue, Chicago, IL 60640.

Trade Show Exhibit Planning Guide, published by Guideline Publishing Co., 5 Holmes Road, Lexington, MA 02173.

CHAPTER 7

HOW TO DEVELOP A MARKETING OR BUSINESS PLAN

A MARKETING PLAN CAN MAKE YOU RICH

For a small business, the marketing plan and the business plan are identical. Both must have hard financial information. This plan is essential for efficient and effective marketing of any product or service, and every entrepreneur or small business marketer should be able to develop a marketing plan that will ultimately lead to success. Seeking a project success without a marketing plan is like trying to navigate a ship through perilous waters with neither charts nor a clear idea of your destination. Therefore, the time it takes to develop a marketing plan is well worthwhile and will allow you to visualize clearly both where you want your business to go and what you want it to accomplish. At the same time, a marketing plan maps out the important steps necessary to get from where you are now to where you want to be at the conclusion of the planning period. Further, you will have thought through how long it will take to get where you want to go and what resources in money and personnel will be needed and must be allocated from within your company. In fact, to obtain this allocation of resources, a competent and thoroughly thought-out plan is essential. Without a marketing plan, you will not even know whether you have reached your objectives or not.

WHAT A MARKETING PLAN WILL DO FOR YOU

A marketing plan accomplishes the following:

1. Acts as a road map
2. Assists you with management control

160

3. Helps you in briefing new employees and other personnel recently assigned to the project
4. Helps you in your briefings to higher management and in obtaining allocations of resources
5. Enables you to see problems and opportunities that may lie along the pathway to project success

A Marketing Plan as a Road Map

If you were traveling from point A to point B and you had never been to point B before, you would almost certainly consult a road map if you had any distance at all to travel. If you didn't use a map, you could drive around in circles for hours trying to locate point B, and if you couldn't ask anyone for directions, you probably would not get there. Unfortunately, some marketers attempt to do the same thing in the marketplace. The usual result is failure. However, with a marketing plan used as a road map, everything is made much simpler. You can follow a precise route from where you are presently to where you want to go. Of course, sometimes something occurs during travel which cannot be foreseen on the map—perhaps the road is closed or blocked, requiring the driver to take a detour. Even when this happens, the map assists the driver by helping him or her choose the best alternative route to the destination. The marketing plan, or the marketing road map, works in the same way. A marketing plan, which documents and shows exactly how to reach carefully defined business goals, serves the same function as a road map for the driver of a car and will enable you to reach corporate goals much more quickly and with much less effort and more efficient utilization of resources than would otherwise be possible.

Management Control

As you enter the process of starting up and implementing a project, you will encounter various problems that cannot be foreseen. In fact, it is almost certain that nothing will go exactly as planned. However, in thinking through your project and laying out a full and complete plan, you will be able to spot many potential problems ahead of time. Furthermore, with the help of a documented plan leading directly to the goals you have established, you will be able to see clearly the difference between implementation and intention. This gives you control of the situation and lets you see more clearly the corrective action necessary to keep your project on the proper course to achieve the goals you have set.

A good analogy here is an aircraft flight. For almost every aircraft flight the pilot is required to file a flight plan that he or she has developed. This flight plan specifies all information, including course headings, distances, air and ground speed, fuel, time en route, emergency airfields, and other factors, for the specific destination the pilot has decided on. Using the flight plan, the pilot can compare actual course and progress in the air with the course and progress planned before the flight. The pilot can analyze this information rapidly to make the best decisions in minimum time. So important is this aspect of management control in flight planning that for some military flights an air crew spends as much time planning the flight on the ground as it spends flying in the air.

Plans do not go exactly as anticipated. The great German strategic thinker Clausewitz termed the difference between plans and reality, "battle friction." But when you have a good plan, you are ready for anything. So a decision that must be made under emergency conditions while flying, or under fire in battle, can be made surely and quickly.

The same is true in business. With a good marketing plan, you have already thought through potential problems ahead of time. And you have already come up with solutions. Then, despite battle friction, you know what do under the pressure of time and competition, and can take immediate action.

The marketing plan will give you management control over your project. It will help you to succeed while others, without a plan, will fail.

Briefing New Employees and Other Personnel

Many times you will wish to inform other people about progress toward project goals and objectives, and the way you intend on reaching them. Such individuals may be new employees whom you have recently hired for the project. Having a ready reference does more than simply allow for easy briefing. It enables you to document and show the objectives that you have set and how and when the plan envisions reaching them. It will show them where they fit into the "big picture" and not only will motivate them but will help them to do a better job for you and for implementation of the plan. In addition, once you organize and document the material in a marketing plan, you have it for all time. You will not need to run around to assemble the information every time you wish to discuss it or tell someone new about it.

Obtaining Money

No organization has unlimited resources. Therefore, projects must receive allocated resources according to the overall benefit to the organization. When you develop a marketing plan, you will be able to demonstrate exactly how the money and resources will be used to reach the goals and objectives established. The marketing plan in itself is documented proof that every aspect of the situation has been thought through.

For this reason, many businesspersons prepare a business or marketing plan to help them obtain investment capital for their business. Sources of this capital frequently say that, without question, the success in obtaining capital is primarily due to the quality of the business plan prepared. Business plans and marketing plans are really identical if the business concerns a single project, product line, or group of products considered at the same time. Success in obtaining money and the green light to go ahead with the plan are frequently primarily dependent on the marketing plan prepared. Sources of capital are approached by hundreds of entrepreneurs who seek capital every month. The only differentiating factors are the entrepreneurs themselves and what they want to do with the money. This is expressed in the marketing plan.

Seeing Problems and Opportunities

Sitting down to think through a marketing plan will help you see all the problems and opportunities in any business situation. Every business situation has problems; these problems can be anticipated, and solutions worked out ahead of time. In this way you can develop your plans to take advantage of the opportunities, to solve the problems that arise, and to avoid potential threats or obstacles to achieving your objectives.

THE STRUCTURE OF THE BUSINESS/MARKETING PLAN

A good marketing plan will contain a number of different sections. Marketing plans are situational, and additional sections can be added to those listed below or can be included as appendixes. But almost all marketing plans contain the following:

1. Executive summary
2. Table of contents
3. Project background and description
4. Project organization
5. Situation analysis
6. Problems and opportunities
7. Objectives
8. Marketing strategy
9. Marketing tactics
10. Budget
11. Financial plans
12. Strategy implementation time schedule

Let's look at each in turn.

Executive Summary

The executive summary is an overall view of your project and its potential, including what you want to do, how much money is needed for the project, how much money the project will make, and such financial measurements as return on investment. The executive summary is extremely important and should not be overlooked. As implied by its title, it is an overview or abstract of the entire plan. The target audience is the top-management executive, such as the individual making the decision as to whether to loan you money or not. As this individual goes through your marketing plan, he or she will frequently skip over parts of the plan which are not of interest. Only certain sections will be read; most will only be scanned. However, the executive summary will always be read. Therefore, it is important that you present the essence of your plan as clearly and succinctly as possible. In a maximum of two to three pages, describe the thrust of what the plan purports to do, the objectives and goals to be achieved, and the overall strategy so that any reader can instantly understand what you are trying to do and how you propose to do it.

Table of Contents

You may wonder about the inclusion of something as mundane as a table of contents under a subject as important as a marketing plan. However, you will find that the table of contents is extremely important. As indicated previously, most executives at the top levels of management will not read the entire plan in detail but, rather, will read only the executive summary and areas that are of particular interest to them. For example, a finance executive will surely read the finance section, while she or he may skip over sections pertaining to product development, sales, or marketing. However, an executive oriented toward marketing will certainly take particular note of what you have to say in these sections. It is not enough to ensure that every subject area pertaining to the project is covered in your plan. You have to make it as easy as possible for the executive who is looking for his or her topics of interest to find them quickly. Unless you do this in your table of contents, many executives will make a cursory attempt to locate the information they want. If they cannot do so, they will assume it is not there. Thus what might otherwise be a brilliant marketing plan will create a negative impact. Therefore, do not neglect to include a thorough table of contents as part of your plan.

Project Background and Description

In this paragraph you give the details of your project, including what it is, how it is going to be run, and, most important, why it will be successful. What differential advantage does it have over other similar projects either in your own company or the companies of your competition? This differential advantage is crucial. Without it there is no reason to invest in this project, since without a competitive advantage over your competition, you cannot win. Unless the project has advantages over other projects, they and not yours, should be funded. The differential advantage should be clearly spelled out, be it a unique product, lower cost, better service, closer location to markets, unique expertise, and so forth.

Project Organization

In this section you should detail exactly how the project will be organized, including who will report to whom in collateral organizations if it is a large project. Include a résumé of the principal project leaders in an appendix. These should zero in on experience, education, or background that specifically supports assigned positions in your plan.

Situation Analysis

The situation analysis has several subsections, all of which are important and should be included and discussed as a part of your marketing plan. These should include demand for your product or service, target market, competition, unique advantages, legal restrictions if any, and any and all other situational variables that you feel are important to successful completion of the project.

Demand includes both the need for your project or service and the extent of this need. This need may be very basic if your product is a food staple. On the other hand, products or services may satisfy psychological needs that are not necessarily obvious. A brass case for business cards has been on the market for several years and is sometimes advertised in the *Wall Street Journal*. The brass case has sold for as much as $20 or more, although in recent years the price has been reduced as it has gone through its product life cycle. The initials of the purchaser are frequently engraved free of charge. Now the question is, Is a brass case for business cards purchased primarily to protect business cards or to promote the status of the owner? Inasmuch as inexpensive plastic cases to protect business cards are frequently used as sales promotion giveaways and card cases are also frequently supplied free with the cards, chances are this product is purchased primarily to satisfy status needs. Whatever the needs satisfied by your product or service, they should be carefully considered and documented under this section. Indicate whether the product is a repeat product which will be purchased again and again by your customers, such as typewriter ribbon, or whether the product or service is a one-time need which is unlikely to be repeated, such as the purchase of a home. Also note whether the product or service is likely to continue to be sold over a long period of time or whether it is more likely to be a fad. Finally, what are the trends here? Is the demand for the product growing, leveling off, or declining?

The target market is the market that you intend to seek for your product or your service. Naturally, the larger the potential market, the better. But there are several different strategies you may follow. It might be advantageous to offer your product only to a certain segment of the total potential market. This is called a "strategy of market segmentation," and it offers a major advantage in certain situations, for you can concentrate all your resources on satisfying the specific needs of a certain segment of the market and can gear your promotional campaign to this segment. You will be stronger against this market segment than your competition will be if it spreads itself, its resources, and its promotional campaign across the total potential mass market. Because of this strategy and other possible strategies, you should note very carefully the market segments that make up the target market you intend to pursue, including the size of each market segment.

The importance of competition should never be underestimated. It is the only noncontrollable variable in your situation that will competitively react to your activities. Regardless of what product or service you offer, you will always have competition, even if the competition does not offer the exact same product or service. For example, home swimming pools may be indirect competition for health studios; however, they must be considered competition because the product or service fulfills the same need in your potential customers that your product or service fulfills. Perhaps you sell burglar alarms. Is your competition only other other firms selling burglar alarms? The answer is no. Other firms that fulfill the need for security must be considered competition. Such firms may offer iron bars to be installed over the windows, security guards, or watch-dogs. All are indirect competition. Therefore, when you begin to analyze the competition for your product or service, be sure that you include all potential competitors, not just the direct competition of firms producing the identical product or service.

When you analyze your competition, you should also consider the fact that your competition will never remain static and will react to your marketing strategy if it proves effective. If you introduce a new product into the marketplace that competes with some other firm already there, you can be assured that if your product is successful, you will not be ignored. Your competition will then initiate an action in response in order to try to overcome your success. You might expect your competition to do something with the price of the product, to change the product, or to change its advertising. Therefore, you must, when you analyze your competition, think ahead as to what actions your competition might take, just as you would if you were in a chess game, only more thoroughly—not only because the stakes are higher but also because you will usually have more than one business opponent.

Your firm is unique. So is your project. As pointed out earlier, you must sell this differential, or competitive, advantage. If you have no differential advantage, there is no reason to buy from you and you cannot win. In this section, emphasize the differential advantage from the point of view of your potential buyer. Some of these advantages have already been discussed, including specialized knowledge, lower prices, a totally unique product, additional services, and so forth. It is important to think through and write down these advantages in your marketing plan, so you will be certain not to overlook any and so you can exploit them to the fullest extent with the strategies you decide on. Remember, also, that although every organization for any product or service has its advantages over competitors, if they are not identified in the marketing plan, they will probably not be exploited. And if they are not exploited, it is as if they did not exist.

Legal restrictions should always be noted in your marketing plan if they are applicable. They don't always exist, but if they do, you must consider them and note them down, not only so that they will not be overlooked but also so that others will know what they are and what their impact will be on other projects within the company. Every applicable restriction should be noted carefully, along with licenses and other legal obligations necessary for you to do business. You should do the research necessary to be absolutely certain that you meet your legal obligations. There is an additional advantage in documenting everything here: Sometimes someone going over your marketing plan will note something that you have forgotten and that in itself can save you a great deal of time, money, and allocation of important company resources, as well as your reputation as a corporate strategist.

Some years ago an entrepreneur invested thousands of dollars in marketing to mix wine and fruit juice to produce a canned drink, not realizing that government tax made the cost of such a drink prohibitive unless the company itself manufactured the wine. The entrepreneur who eventually made this product an incredible success researched and documented this crucial legal restriction and developed a strategy that allowed for it.

Other important situation variables should also be noted. These may be anything that you consider important to your business situation and to the success of your marketing plan. Let us say your product is seasonal and sold only in the summer or during Christmas holidays or during the football season. In such a case, there are special problems, including expensive overhead during the off-season, peak periods of sale, and so forth. Thus seasonality, in this case, would be an important situational variable.

Problems and Opportunities

Problems and opportunities are really opposite sides of the same coin. Many people make millions of dollars because when they note a problem they also note within this problem a unique opportunity for success. Listerine is a mouthwash with a rather harsh taste. In the words of the advertisement of the competition, it tastes "mediciny." However, Listerine managed to make this problem an opportunity. The company realized that many consumers feel that if a mouthwash has a harsh taste, it must be harsher on germs, whereas if a mouthwash tastes sweet or, in the words of a Listerine ad, tastes like "soda pop," it may not be killing terms nearly as well. Look for the opportunity in every problem that you find. And in this section specify both problems you have found and their solutions and any opportunities inherent in them that your company can take advantage of.

Objectives

Objectives should be stated explicitly. They may be defined by stating the volume to be sold in dollars or units, and they may also include financial measurements, such as return on investment or some other profitability measure. If more than one objective is stated, be certain that the objectives do not conflict. For example, sometimes if a market share is specified as your objective, this can be reached only through a negative impact on short-term profitability. So if you specify more than one objective, check to be sure that one objective can be achieved only at the expense of another.

Marketing Strategy

Strategy for marketing your product should be stated as developed in previous chapters. What exactly are you going to do to reach your objectives?

Marketing Tactics

Marketing tactics refer to how you will carry out the strategy, that is, the different tasks involved, including who will do them, what they will cost, and when they will be done. Marketing tactics can be described in the budget and the financial plans. See also the section, Strategy Implementation Time Schedule.

Budget

As indicated previously, every strategy costs resources. Because it is very important to indicate exactly what these resources are in hard dollar amounts, establish a budget for your total marketing plan for the project, including exactly how much each task will cost and when these funds will be required. The Strategy Implementation Time Schedule section shows one way of describing the budget.

Financial plans

The financial plan should include not only the budget for the strategies and tactics required but also the projected income statement, as shown in Figure 7.1; a cash-flow projection as shown in Figure 7.2; and a balance sheet, as shown in Figure 7.3. Use of these forms is mandatory for most marketing plans. Financial plans give the entire financial picture for your project and will assist you not only with management control but also in allowing individuals who decide on the allocation of resources to your project or to other projects to h.ve the complete financial picture.

Using a Break-Even Analysis.   Sometimes it is also useful to put in a break-even analysis—a method for evaluating relationships between sales revenues, fixed costs, and variable costs. The break-even point is the point at which the number of units sold covers all costs of developing, producing, and selling the product. Above this point you will make money, and below it you will lose money. It is one excellent

	Month 1	Month 2	Month 3	Month 4	Month 5	Month 6	Month 7	Month 8	Month 9	Month 10	Month 11	Month 12
Total net sales												
Cost of sales												
Gross Profit												
Controllable expenses												
Salaries												
Payroll taxes												
Security												
Advertising												
Automobile												
Dues and subscriptions												
Legal and accounting												
Office supplies												
Telephone												
Utilities												
Miscellaneous												
Total controllable expenses												
Fixed expenses												
Depreciation												
Insurance												
Rent												
Taxes and licenses												
Loan Payments												
Total fixed expenses												
Total Expenses												
Net Profit (Loss) **(before taxes)**												

Figure 7.1. Income statement for marketing plan.

169

MONTHS AFTER START-UP

	Month 1	Month 2	Month 3	Month 4	Month 5	Month 6	Month 7	Month 8	Month 9	Month 10	Month 11	Month 12	Total
Cash (beginning of month)													
Cash on hand													
Cash in bank													
Cash in investments													
Total cash													
Income (during month)													
Cash sales													
Credit sales payments													
Investment income													
Loans													
Other cash income													
Total income													
Total Cash and Income													
Expenses (during month)													
Inventory or new material													
Wages													
Taxes													
Equipment expense													
Overhead													
Selling expense													
Transportation													
Loan repayment													
Other cash expenses													
Total Expenses													
Cash-Flow Excess (end of month)													
Cash-Flow Cumulative (monthly)													

Figure 7.2. Cash-flow projection for marketing plan.

_____ __ 19 __

	Year I	Year II
Current Assets		
Cash	$ _____	$ _____
Accounts receivable	_____	_____
Inventory	_____	_____
Fixed Assets		
Real estate	_____	_____
Fixtures and equipment	_____	_____
Vehicles	_____	_____
Other Assets		
License	_____	_____
Goodwill	_____	_____
Total Assets	$ _____	$ _____
Current Liabilities		
Notes payable (due within 1 year)	$ _____	$ _____
Accounts payable	_____	_____
Accrued expenses	_____	_____
Taxes owed	_____	_____
Long-Term Liabilities		
Notes payable (due after 1 year)	_____	_____
Other	_____	_____
Total Liabilities	$ _____	$ _____
Net Worth (Assets *minus* Liabilities)	$ _____	$ _____

Total Liabilities *plus* Net Worth should *equal* Assets

Figure 7.3. Balance sheet for marketing plan.

measurement for determining the ultimate success of the project before you begin. In sum, the break-even analysis will tell you the following:

1. How many units you must sell in order to start making money
2. How much profit you will make at any given level of sales
3. How changing your price will affect profitability
4. How expense reductions at different levels of sales will affect profitability

To accomplish a break-even analysis, you must first separate the costs associated with your project into two categories: fixed costs and variable costs.

"Fixed costs" are those expenses associated with the project that you would have to pay whether you sold 1 unit or 10,000 units or, for that matter, whether you sold any units at all. For example, if you rented a building for use in your project and the owner charged you a thousand dollars for the period of the project, then this would be a fixed cost for that period. You would have to pay the thousand dollars whether or not you sold any products or many products. Research and development costs for a project or a product would also be considered a fixed cost, and this money would have to be paid whether or not you sold any product.

"Variable costs" vary directly with the number of units that you sell. If it costs you $1.80 to manufacture a unit, then that $1.80 is considered a variable cost. If postage for mailing your product to a customer is $1, then $1 is a variable cost. If you sell 10 units, then your postage cost is 10 times $1, or $10. If you sell 100 units, your total variable cost for postage would be 100 times $1, or $100.

It is difficult to decide whether to consider some costs fixed or variable, and very frequently there is no single right answer. You must make this decision either by yourself or with the help of corporate financial experts. As a general guide, if there is a direct relationship between cost and number of units sold, consider the cost variable. If you cannot find such a relationship, consider the cost fixed.

The total cost of your project will always equal the sum of the fixed costs plus the variable costs. Consider the following example for an item you are going to sell for $10. How much profit would you make if you sold 1,000 units?

Fixed Costs

Utility expense at $300 per month for 12 months	=	$3600
Telephone at $50 per month for 1 year	=	600
Product development cost	=	1000
Rental expense	=	2500
Total fixed costs	=	$7700

Variable Costs

Cost of product	=	$1.00/unit
Cost of postage and packaging	=	0.50/unit
Cost of advertising	=	3.00/unit
Total variable costs	=	$4.50/unit

To calculate break-even, we start with an equation for profit. Total profit *equals* the number of units sold *multiplied* by the price at which we are selling them *less* the number of units sold *multiplied* by the total variable cost and that answer *minus* the total fixed cost. If P equals profit, p equals price, U equals the number of units sold, V equals variable costs, and F equals fixed costs, then our equation becomes:

$$P = (U \times p) - (U \times V) - F$$

Or we can simplify this to:

$$P = U(p - V) - F$$

Substituting the values given in our example, we have:

$$P = 1000(\$10.00 - \$4.50) - \$7700 = \$5500 - \$7700 = -\$2200$$

What is the significance of a minus number? This means that instead of making a profit, we have lost money—$2200 to be exact. Now, we may want to know how many units we must sell in order to make money, or at what point we will stop losing money—the break even point, beginning from which we will show a profit. In order to calculate this, we use the break-even equation: using the same variables from above, $P = U(p - V) - F$. At break-even, profit by definition $= 0$. Thus, if we transpose terms and let $P = 0$, break-even $=$

$$\frac{F}{p - V}$$

Since we know that F equals $7700, p equals $10, and V equals $4.50, break-even equals:

$$\frac{\$7700}{\$10 - \$4.50} = 1400 \text{ units}$$

This means if we don't change price or reduce expenses in any way, we need to sell 1,400 units of this product before we can start making any money. However, there is an easier way to calculate this. We can use the break-even chart shown in Figure 7.4. A break-even chart is a major advantage over the break-even and profit equation. It shows us graphically the relationship between profits and sales volume.

There are some limitations to break-even analysis:

1. Break-even analysis shows profit at various levels of sales but does not show profitability. Since there are always alternative uses for your firm's financial resources, it is impossible to compare products for profitability solely on the basis of break-even, yet profitability should be one of the major points of consideration. For a profitability comparison, you must use one of the financial ratio analyses.

2. Break-even analyses do not allow you to examine cash flow. It is generally accepted that one appropriate way to compare investment or capital budgeting alternatives is to consider the value of cash flows over a period of time and to

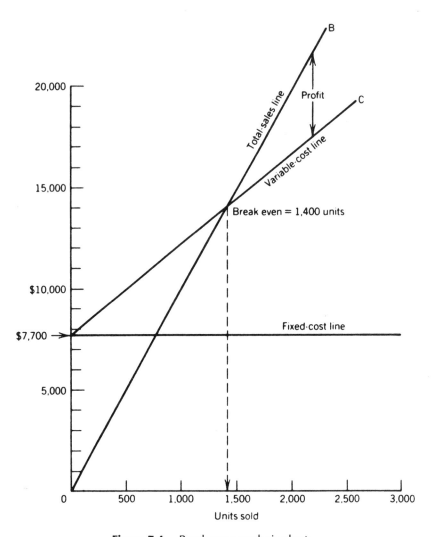

Figure 7.4. Break-even analysis chart.

discount the cost of capital by an appropriate percentage. This cannot be done with break-even analyses either.

The Strategy Implementation Time Schedule

The final section in your marketing plan should be a time schedule showing an overview of your strategy implementation and the time when each task will be completed. This is shown in Figure 7.5. The strategy implementation time schedule

Weeks after Project Initiation

Task	1	2	3	4	5	6	7	8	9	10	11	Total
Development and placement ads	$5,000	$5,000	$5,000	$5,000	$5,000	$5,000	$10,000	$10,000	$10,000	$10,000	$10,000	$80,000
Product manufacture, model I		$5,000	$7,500	$10,000	$10,000	$10,000						$42,500
Product manufacture, model II					$5,000	$5,000	$7,500	$10,000	$10,000	$10,000	$10,000	$57,500
Schedule promotional model II							$3,000	$3,000	$3,000	$3,000		$12,000
Running new contribution channel								$5,000	$5,000			$10,000
Phase-out promotion model I										$2,000	$2,000	$4,000
Monthly totals	$5,000	$10,000	$12,500	$15,000	$20,000	$20,000	$20,500	$28,000	$28,000	$25,000	$22,000	$206,000

Total for project strategy

Figure 7.5. Strategy implementation time schedule.

175

is extremely important, letting you know when you are supposed to do what, and it will greatly assist you in management control, as well as showing any reader of your marketing plan that you really know what you are doing.

HINTS FOR WRITING YOUR MARKETING PLAN

Some tips for writing an effective marketing plan follow:

1. *Establish your credibility.* Remember that your firm and this project have unique advantages (if they do not, you should not proceed with the project). State these advantages clearly.

2. *Document supporting facts about new concepts or ideas.* Remember that not everyone reading your marketing plan has your knowledge or experience. Therefore, new concepts or ideas should be carefully documented and described from established sources.

3. *Be optimistic, but be truthful.* There are always disadvantages or problems, but if you can anticipate them and indicate how you will overcome them, it will not only help in implementing the marketing plan at the appropriate time but will assist in convincing readers that your marketing plan can be implemented.

4. *Emphasize your uniqueness.* You have something that is different in some way from what everyone else has. Play up this difference

5. *Make sure your marketing plan is workable.* A marketing plan is useless if it is not workable. After you've gone through and completed the plan, be sure that each part of the plan fits together and is reasonable. Be especially critical of the cash-flow and financial aspects, as well as the anticipated sales. One of the biggest problems of marketing plans is sales realism; that is, the strategist sometimes anticipates much higher sales than can realistically be expected. Analyze your plan by asking yourself what would happen if sales were 20, 30, 40, or even 50% less than you have forecast. Analyze your costs to make sure they are also realistic. Just as sales are frequently inflated during marketing planning, costs are sometimes deflated.

6. *Update your plan.* No marketing plan is good forever. Further, the planning is never perfect, as you cannot foresee all circumstances that you will encounter at the start. Therefore, as the plan is implemented, it will have to be revised to be kept up to date. This is not to say that your plan has to be changed daily; however, you should be on top of conditions that are changing, and the plan should be adjusted accordingly. To do this, you should first be alert to the changes that come about in your industry, market, customers, competition, technology, and so forth. Second, check your plan against these changes to make sure that the plan is still workable and to determine what revisions are necessary in your plan.

MARKETING PLAN DEVELOPMENT FORM

A special marketing plan development form has been developed to assist you and is shown in Figure 7.6. It begins by listing required information for your plan,

Product _____

Required Information for Plan	How/Where Information Is to Be Obtained	Individual Responsible
Market Characteristics		
Customer identification and location		
Segments of market		
Growth trends		
Consumer attitudes and buying habits		
Size of market in dollars and numbers		
Needs of market		
Industry pricing		
Technological trends, threats, and opportunities		

Figure 7.6. Marketing plan development form. (Copyright © 1983 by William A. Cohen.)

(Figure continues on p. 178.)

Product _____

Required Information for Plan	How/Where Information Is to Be Obtained	Individual Responsible
Distribution factors and structure		
Key success factors		
Competition Identification of competing companies		
Size, trend, and share of market of each competitor		

Customers' perception of competition

Comparison of competitive products, pricing, and features

Comparison of competitive products, promotion and distribution

Competitor strengths and weaknesses

Competitors' strategies

Manufacturing and Engineering Factors
Processes and materials

Environmental Climate
Business, economic conditions

Figure 7.6. (Continued)

Product ____

Required Information for Plan	How/Where Information Is to Be Obtained	Individual Responsible
Social factors		
Political factors		
Governmental factors		
Legal constraints		
Internal Resources		
Marketing		
Engineering		
Financial resources		

Figure 7.6. (Continued)

including characteristics of customer identification; location; segments of market; growth trends; consumer attitudes and buying habits; size of market in dollars and numbers; needs of market; industry pricing; technological trends; threats and opportunities; distribution factors and structure; key success factors; identification of competing companies; size, trend, and share of market of each competitor; customers' perception of competition; comparison of competitive features; pricing in features; comparison of promotional distribution of competitor products; competitor strengths and weaknesses; competitor strategies; processes and materials; business and economic conditions; social factors; political factors; government factors; legal constraints; and internal resources for marketing, engineering, and financial resources. The form also has additional spaces for other information required to put your marketing plan together. Spaces are also allowed for listing how and where information is to be obtained and the name of an individual responsible for obtaining this information.

	Description of Strategy	Cost ($)
Product		
Price		
Distribution		
Promotion		

Figure 7.7. Strategy development form (functional approach). (Copyright © 1983 by William A. Cohen.)

To assist you in strategy development, the strategy development form using the functional approach (Figure 7.7) includes price promotion and distribution promotion aspects and asks you to write a description of the strategy and then to indicate an overall cost allocation for implementing it.

The marketing plan is one of the most powerful tools of the corporate strategist for planning. Literally billions of dollars have been made or lost through its use, misuse, or nonuse. Correctly put together, the marketing plan will guide your project from start-up to successful realization of your goals and objectives. It is totally worthy of your best efforts.

SOURCES OF ADDITIONAL INFORMATION

Basics of Successful Business Planning, by William R. Osgood, published by the American Management Association, 135 West 50th Street, New York, NY 10020.

Building Your Business Plan, by Harold J. McLaughlin, published by John Wiley & Sons, Inc., 605 Third Avenue, New York, NY 10158.

Developing a Winning Marketing Plan, by William A. Cohen, published by John Wiley & Sons, Inc., 605 Third Avenue, New York, NY 10158.

The Executive Guide to Operational Planning, by George L. Morrisey, Patrick J. Below, and Betty L. Acomb, published by Jossey-Bass Publishers, 433 California Street, San Francisco, CA 94104.

How to Prepare and Present a Business Plan, by Joseph R. Mancuso, published by Prentice-Hall, Inc., Englewood Cliffs, NJ 07632.

The Marketing Plan, by William M. Luther, published by AMACOM, a division of the American Management Association, 135 West 50th Street, New York, NY 10020.

Planning for Nonplanners, by Darryl J. Ellis and Peter P. Pekar, Jr., published by AMACOM, a division of the American Management Association, 135 West 50th Street, New York, NY 10020.

The Practice of Marketing Management, by William A. Cohen, published by Macmillan Publishing Co., 866 Third Avenue, New York, NY 10022.

Winning on the Marketing Front, by William A. Cohen, published by John Wiley & Sons, Inc., 605 Third Avenue, New York, NY 10158.

CHAPTER 8

MAIL ORDER MARKETING

MAIL ORDER SUCCESSES

In the latter part of the 19th century, Richard Sears and Julius Rosenwald got together to build Sears, Roebuck and Company into what would eventually become a $10 billion corporation. Meanwhile, Aaron Montgomery Ward started his own company, which would become a multimillion dollar operation. These three entrepreneurs became the world's first mail order millionaires.

Since that time, countless part-time and full-time entrepreneurs have been attracted to the mail order business. Many have failed. However, a surprising number of businesses have succeeded in both good times and bad. Today, you can buy everything from clothes to insurance to live lobsters from Maine, all through the mail.

What Qualities Are Required

For marketing wizards, mail orders can be highly profitable. Melvin Powers, a famous mail order publisher, started with a single book. Today, he has more than 400 books in print and has sold millions of copies. Another marketing genius, Richard Thalheimer, built a multimillion dollar company, The Sharper Image, starting with a chronograph watch and an advertisement in *Runner's World*. He now sells not only by mail but also through major retail outlets across the country. Although not everyone can expect to achieve the same level of success as these exceptional entrepreneurs, your chances for building a profitable mail order business are excellent if you possess the following essential qualities: imagination, persistence, honesty, and knowledge, and experience.

Imagination.   Imagination is needed to visualize the special appeal that will compel a potential customer to buy your product. Joe Cossman, in his book *How I Made*

$1 Million in Mail Order, describes how someone once brought an unsuccessful mail order product to him with an offer to sell the rights. The product consisted of earrings with little bells attached. Cossman managed to turn this mail order loser into a mail order winner simply by renaming the product "mother-in-law earrings" and selling them to newlyweds.

Persistence.   Success is rarely instantaneous—there are always obstacles and set-backs. Cossman struggled for over a year before making his first success. While holding down a full-time job, he worked at his kitchen table, tackling false leads, problems, and failures. He did nothing but lose money. Less persistent entrepreneurs would have quit much sooner. But when he finally was successful, his first product made him $30,000 in less than one month.

Honesty.   A successful mail order business is built on trust, satisfied customers, and repeat sales. Cheat your customers even a little and you've lost them forever. Without repeat customers, you might just as well invest your money in a dry oil well. The potential for successful enterprise is gone.

In addition, federal, state, and local government agencies as well as the Better Business Bureaus and consumer groups constantly watch advertising and are quick to take action against unsubstantiated claims or infractions of any laws. One of the most well-known laws you must be concerned with is the Federal Trade Commission's (FTC) Thirty Day Delay Delivery Rule. Basically, if you don't mention a date or period of time in your advertisement, you have thirty days after receipt of your customers' order to ship it. What if you can't make shipment within 30 days or the date you stated in your advertisement? Then you must send a notice of the new shipment date to the buyer before expiration of the original period. You also must enclose a self-addressed, stamped envelope and give your buyer a chance to cancel the deal. This rule is nothing to fool around with. A well-known, reputable mail order firm in Chicago was forced to pay a fine of several hundred thousand dollars when a snowstorm caused delays in mailing and it failed to use the required method of giving customers a chance to cancel their orders. The fine wasn't meant to reflect on the firm's integrity but rather to show that no company is exempt from the rules.

Knowledge.   Without knowledge—the how-to's and the why's—your chances for success are minimal. Success stories like those of Ward, Sears, and Cossman are built around those individuals' constant search for knowledge that answers two critically important questions: What works? What doesn't?

Experience.   Learning must never stop. You can increase your knowledge through both reading and experience. Experience is valuable, but it is also the most expensive way to learn. Because you can save time and money through the experiences of others, extensive reading is highly recommended. Joe Cossman says that he spends at least one full day a month at the public library.

You can also learn from successful competitors. Make a thorough study of magazines and newspapers, review the advertisements appearing over a period of time. Note advertisements that run consistently month after month or several times a year. Answer advertisements that are particularly interesting. Carefully study the catalogs, sales letters, brochures, and sales literature received. Particularly study all follow-up mailings. Know what your competitors are doing.

SELECTING A PRODUCT

Though it may appear that you can sell almost anything through the mail, this just isn't true. To develop ideas for products, you may want to study trade publications, attend product shows, contact manufacturers, and answer advertisements. To increase your chances of picking a winner, look for a product that is:

— Lightweight
— Nearly unbreakable
— Has a broad appeal to a large, specific segment of the population
— Has a large margin for profit

This last requirement means you have to be able to buy low and sell high. You should select a product that allows you to sell it for three to four times the cost. This is a much higher margin than for goods sold by retail merchants, who usually sell at about twice their cost. But you need this margin to make a profit because of the high cost of advertising. Although you can't get this kind of mark-up with all products, you can charge even more for many products. If customers won't pay the price that you need to make a profit, find a different product to sell. However, many mail order advertisers are willing to lose money on initial sales to obtain the customer's name. They hope that they will make up for the loss by selling additional products to future customers. Without the high cost of advertising, direct mail repeat sales can be made at much higher margins. Again, this is one of the reasons why honesty and efficiency in mail order operations are so important.

EVALUATING YOUR PRODUCTS

If you have many products to promote, you will have to decide which are the best; you probably cannot afford to promote all of them. To evaluate your products, list all factors that describe your product. Assign importance percentages to each factor. If lightweight is twice as important as breakability, assign lightness 10% importance, and breakability 5%. All the percentages for each factor must add up to 100%.

Next list all your products. Rate each product on a point basis:

4 Points—excellent
3 Points—very good
2 Points—good
1 Point—fair
0 Points—poor

Let's say you decide four factors are important. After some consideration about their relative importance, weight the factors as follows:

Broad Appeal	30%
Large Profit Margin	30%
Lightweight	20%
Breakability	20%
	100%

Let's say you have two candidate products. One product is a beautiful vase imported from Japan. The second product is a gold-plated "lucky" coin manufactured in your city.

We'll look at the vase first. Let's assume that the appeal is reasonably broad to a segment of the population interested in art. So you assign 3 points for that factor. However, because of the cost of the product, import duties, and shipping, the product has only a fair profit margin. You give it only 1 point for profit margin. The case is moderately light, so you give it 2 points for weight. Finally, no matter how carefully you package it, you're going to have some breakage. So it gets 0 points on that factor.

Use the same method to evaluate the lucky coin. Let's assume that you decide to assign 1 point, 1 point, 3 points, and 4 points for the same factors, respectively.

Now you can build a comparison matrix:

Product Importance Weighting × Evaluation Points = Value Rating

Vase			
Appeal	30%	3	.9
Margin	30%	1	.3
Weight	20%	2	.4
Breakability	20%	0	.0
			1.6

Coin			
Appeal	30%	1	.3
Margin	30%	1	.3
Weight	20%	3	.6
Breakability	20%	4	.8
			2.0

Since 2.0 is greater than 1.6, this tells you that the coin is a better product at this time. If any of the factors changed, you would need to do another analysis.

Of course, in real life there are many other factors you may want to include in your analysis. This might include the total market potential, the need for the product, whether the product is available in a store, whether the product lends itself to creating repeat business, the investment required, and so on.

PRICING STRUCTURE

How you structure your offer is also important. You may have the right product and the right price but still lose simply by the way you present it.

For example, you want to sell a product called a widget at two for $1.00. You could advertise your offer just like that, or you could advertise one widget for $1.00 and a second widget free. Or you could sell one widget for 99¢ and offer a second one for 1¢. All of these offers are exactly the same. However, they are perceived differently by your customers. Tests have shown that there can be a 600 percent difference in response depending on the way you present an offer. Unfortunately, because every situation is different, no one can tell you which is the best offer without knowing the product and project intimately—and without doing extensive testing.

FORECASTING SALES

Always be cautious when forecasting sales. Your break-even point should be set very low at least while you are testing your probable level of response. For example, if your break-even point is 5 percent of the names on a mailing list, up to 5 percent of the people can respond to your offer and you are still not making a profit. Keep your expectations reasonable. For many businesses, .25 percent is an excellent response.

The same idea applies to forecasting orders from magazine advertisements. One famous advertiser is happy if he gets 1.25 times the cost of his advertisement in sales. This means that if the advertisement cost $100, he is delighted if the resulting sales amount to $125. For one publication, this means .10 percent of the readership responded. However, many advertisements don't even bring in .01 percent of their readership.

TESTING—MAIL ORDER'S SECRET WEAPON

Testing is a scientific approach to mail order selling. It is an effective secret weapon that permits a mail order entrepreneur to fail with four out of five products and still walk away with big profits on the fifth product.

Successful mail order operators test almost everything. They measure the response to an advertisement or mailing by testing all advertising variables, such as:

— Offers
— Headlines
— Mailing lists
— Formats
— Prices
— Advertising media

How is it done? Spend a small amount of money for a test advertisement or mailing list. A complete failure tells you to drop the whole project. Marginal results tell you to experiment and rework some aspect of the project. A major success gives you the green light for a larger investment. In this way, you can afford to lose money on several dismal failures. But when your testing indicates a clear success, you can move immediately to capitalize on what you know to be a winner. The idea is not to risk a lot of money until you are more certain of success.

Basic Test Procedures and Decisions

Testing is never done haphazardly, and there are certain procedures and decisions that you must take into account as you enter into the process. When you start out, you must decide how confident you want to be in the results—how much risk you are prepared to assume in believing the results. If you want no risk whatsoever, then, of course, you must mail to the entire list of perhaps millions of names— not a very wise or practical approach. More realistically, a 95% confidence factor is usually acceptable. We will use the table shown in Figure 8.1 for doing the calculations associated with our testing. You must also decide how much error you are willing to accept as chance and what is unacceptable. If you are doing testing concerning direct mail, you must decide what your expected return will be before deciding on sample size. A different sample size is required, depending on your expected return. In fact, one basic procedure here that is hard for many beginners to understand is that sample size is dependent upon expected return, not on the total size of your list.

After these basic decisions are made, you will use the table shown in Figure 8.1 to pick the correct sample size, which is most important. There used to be an old rule in mail order: Check 10% of any list. Even today, many mail order or direct mail operators do very rough testing by simply testing lists by equal numbers, say 5,000 of one list, 5,000 of another list, and 5,000 of yet another. The problems with this approach are several. One obvious drawback is that the numbers you are testing may be larger than necessary. In that case, you are wasting money. On the other hand, this number may represent too few names, in which case your results

Percent Response	Limits of Error														
	.02	.04	.06	.08	.10	.12	.14	.16	.18	.20	.30	.40	.50	.60	.70
.1	95944.	23986.	10660.	5996.	3838.	2665.	1958.	1499.	1184.	959.	426.	240.	154.	107.	78.
.2	191696.	47924.	21300.	11981.	7668.	5325.	3912.	2995.	2367.	1917.	852.	479.	307.	213.	156.
.3	287256.	71814.	31917.	17953.	11490.	7979.	5862.	4488.	3546.	2873.	1277.	718.	460.	319.	234.
.4	382623.	95656.	42514.	23914.	15305.	10628.	7809.	5978.	4724.	3826.	1701.	957.	612.	425.	312.
.5	477799.	119450.	53089.	29862.	19112.	13272.	9751.	7466.	5899.	4778.	2124.	1194.	764.	531.	390.
.6	572783.	143196.	63643.	35799.	22911.	15911.	11689.	8950.	7071.	5728.	2546.	1432.	916.	636.	468.
.7	667574.	166894.	74175.	41723.	26703.	18544.	13624.	10431.	8242.	6676.	2967.	1669.	1068.	742.	545.
.8	762173.	190543.	84686.	47636.	30487.	21171.	15555.	11909.	9410.	7622.	3387.	1905.	1219.	847.	622.
.9	856581.	214145.	95176.	53536.	34263.	23794.	17481.	13384.	10575.	8566.	3807.	2141.	1371.	952.	699.
1.0	950796.	237699.	105644.	59425.	38032.	26411.	19404.	14856.	11738.	9508.	4226.	2377.	1521.	1056.	776.
1.1	1044819.	261205.	116091.	65301.	41793.	29023.	21323.	16325.	12899.	10448.	4644.	2612.	1672.	1161.	853.
1.2	1138650.	284663.	126517.	71166.	45546.	31629.	23238.	17791.	14057.	11387.	5061.	2847.	1822.	1265.	930.
1.3	1232289.	308072.	136921.	77018.	49292.	34230.	25149.	19255.	15213.	12323.	5477.	3081.	1972.	1369.	1006.
1.4	1325736.	331434.	147304.	82859.	53029.	36826.	27056.	20715.	16367.	13257.	5892.	3314.	2121.	1473.	1082.
1.5	1418991.	354748.	157666.	88687.	56760.	39416.	28959.	22172.	17518.	14190.	6307.	3547.	2270.	1577.	1158.
1.6	1512054.	378013.	168006.	94503.	60482.	42001.	30858.	23626.	18667.	15121.	6720.	3780.	2419.	1680.	1234.
1.7	1604924.	401231.	178325.	100308.	64197.	44581.	32754.	25077.	19814.	16049.	7133.	4012.	2568.	1783.	1310.
1.8	1697603.	424401.	188623.	106100.	67904.	47156.	34645.	26525.	20958.	16976.	7545.	4244.	2716.	1886.	1388.
1.9	1790090.	447522.	198899.	111881.	71604.	49725.	36532.	27970.	22100.	17901.	7956.	4475.	2864.	1989.	1461.
2.0	1882384.	470596.	209154.	117649.	75295.	52288.	38416.	29412.	23239.	18824.	8366.	4706.	3012.	2092.	1537.
2.1	1974486.	493622.	219887.	123405.	78979.	54847.	40296.	30851.	24376.	19745.	8775.	4936.	3159.	2194.	1612.
2.2	2066397.	516599.	229600.	129150.	82656.	57400.	42171.	32287.	25511.	20664.	9184.	5166.	3306.	2296.	1687.
2.3	2158115.	539529.	239791.	134882.	86325.	59948.	44043.	33721.	26643.	21581.	9592.	5395.	3453.	2398.	1762.
2.4	2249641.	562410.	249960.	140603.	89986.	62490.	45911.	35151.	27773.	22496.	9998.	5624.	3599.	2500.	1836.
2.5	2340975.	585244.	260108.	146311.	93639.	65027.	47775.	36578.	28901.	23410.	10404.	5852.	3746.	2601.	1911.
2.6	2432117.	608029.	270235.	152007.	97285.	67559.	49635.	38002.	30026.	24321.	10809.	6080.	3891.	2702.	1985.
2.7	2523067.	630767.	280341.	157692.	100923.	70085.	51491.	39423.	31149.	25231.	11214.	6303.	4037.	2803.	2060.
2.8	2623825.	653456.	290425.	163364.	104553.	72606.	53343.	40841.	32269.	26138.	11617.	6535.	4182.	2904.	2134.
2.9	2704390.	676098.	300488.	169024.	108176.	75122.	55192.	42256.	33388.	27044.	12020.	6761.	4327.	3005.	2208.
3.0	2794764.	698691.	310529.	174673.	111791.	77632.	57036.	43668.	34503.	27948.	12421.	6987.	4472.	3105.	2281.
3.1	2884946.	721236.	320550.	180309.	115398.	80137.	58876.	45077.	35617.	28849.	12822.	7212.	4616.	3205.	2355.
3.2	2974935.	743734.	330548.	185933.	118997.	82637.	60713.	46433.	36728.	29749.	13222.	7437.	4760.	3305.	2429.

Figure 8.1. Test sample table for mailing response levels and a 95% confidence level.

(Figure continues on p. 190.)

Percent Response	.02	.04	.06	.08	.10	.12	.14	Limits of Error .16	.18	.20	.30	.40	.50	.60	.70
3.3	3064732.	766183.	340526.	191546.	122589.	85131.	62546.	47886.	37836.	30647.	13621.	7662.	4904.	3405.	2502.
3.4	3154338.	788584.	350482.	197146.	126174.	87620.	64374.	49287.	38942.	31543.	14019.	7886.	5047.	3505.	2575.
3.5	3243751.	810938.	360417.	202734.	129750.	90104.	66199.	50684.	40046.	32438.	14417.	8109.	5190.	3604.	2648.
3.6	3332972.	833243.	370330.	208311.	133319.	92583.	68020.	52078.	41148.	33330.	14813.	8332.	5333.	3703.	2721.
3.7	3422001.	855500.	380222.	213875.	136880.	95056.	69837.	53469.	42247.	34220.	15209.	8555.	5475.	3802.	2793.
3.8	3510838.	877710.	390093.	219427.	140434.	97523.	71650.	54857.	43344.	35108.	15604.	8777.	5617.	3901.	2866.
3.9	3599483.	899871.	399943.	224968.	143979.	99986.	73459.	56242.	44438.	35995.	15998.	8999.	5759.	3999.	2938.
4.0	3687936.	921984.	409771.	230496.	147517.	102443.	75264.	57624.	45530.	36879.	16391.	9220.	5901.	4098.	3011.
4.1	3776197.	944049.	419577.	236012.	151048.	104894.	77065.	59003.	46620.	37762.	16783.	9440.	6042.	4196.	3083.
4.2	3864265.	966066.	429363.	241517.	154571.	107341.	78863.	60379.	47707.	38643.	17175.	9661.	6183.	4294.	3155.
4.3	3952142.	988036.	439127.	247009.	158086.	109782.	80656.	61752.	48792.	39521.	17565.	9880.	6323.	4391.	3226.
4.4	4039827.	1009957.	448870.	252489.	161593.	112217.	82445.	63122.	49874.	40398.	17955.	10100.	6464.	4489.	3298.
4.5	4127319.	1031830.	458591.	257957.	165093.	114648.	84231.	64489.	50955.	41273.	18344.	10318.	6604.	4586.	3369.
4.6	4214619.	1053655.	468291.	263414.	168585.	117073.	86013.	65853.	52032.	42146.	18732.	10537.	6743.	4683.	3441.
4.7	4301728.	1075432.	477970.	268858.	172069.	119492.	87790.	67214.	53108.	43017.	19119.	10754.	6883.	4780.	3512.
4.8	4388644.	1097161.	487627.	274290.	175546.	121907.	89564.	68573.	54181.	43886.	19505.	10972.	7022.	4876.	3583.
4.9	4475368.	1118842.	497263.	279710.	179015.	124316.	91334.	69928.	55251.	44754.	19891.	11188.	7161.	4973.	3658.
5.0	4561900.	1140475.	506878.	285119.	182476.	126719.	93100.	71280.	56320.	45619.	20275.	11405.	7299.	5069.	3724.
5.1	4648240.	1162060.	516471.	290515.	185930.	129118.	94862.	72629.	57386.	46482.	20659.	11621.	7437.	5165.	3794.
5.2	4734388.	1183597.	526043.	295899.	189376.	131511.	96620.	73975.	58449.	47344.	21042.	11836.	7575.	5260.	3865.
5.3	4820344.	1205086.	535594.	301271.	192314.	133898.	98374.	75318.	59510.	48203.	21424.	12051.	7713.	5356.	3935.
5.4	4906107.	1226527.	545123.	306632.	196244.	136281.	100125.	76658.	60569.	49061.	21805.	12265.	7850.	5451.	4005.
5.5	4991679.	1247920.	554631.	311980.	199667.	138658.	101871.	77995.	61626.	49917.	22185.	12479.	7987.	5546.	4075.
5.6	5077059.	1269265.	564118.	317316.	203082.	141029.	103613.	79329.	62680.	50771.	22565.	12693.	8123.	5641.	4145.
5.7	5162246.	1290562.	573583.	322640.	206490.	143396.	105352.	80660.	63731.	51622.	22943.	12906.	8260.	5736.	4214.
5.8	5247241.	1311810.	583027.	327953.	209890.	145757.	107087.	81988.	64781.	52472.	23321.	13118.	8396.	5830.	4283.
5.9	5332045.	1333011.	592449.	333253.	213282.	148112.	108817.	83313.	65828.	53320.	23698.	13330.	8531.	5924.	4353.
6.0	5416656.	1354164.	601851.	338541.	216666.	150463.	110544.	84635.	66872.	54167.	24074.	13542.	8667.	6019.	4422.

Figure 8.1. (Continued)

may be totally misleading. You may get good results with your test and then spend large amounts of money in mailing to what you thought was a successful list, only to lose a lot of money when you roll out and mail to the other names on the list. Or you could drop a list that would really pay off in general mailing if the test results were poor on numbers too small to be truly representative of the rest of the list.

After you have decided on the sample size, you mail to the sample size or, in the case of an ad campaign, you place your ads. When the results come in, you can use the table in Figure 8.1 to analyze your results. With this test, you're trying to answer two questions. First, you want to know if the results show a significant difference if you are testing one thing against another. In some cases, even though there is some difference in numbers of responses, the difference is not statistically significant. It could have happened by accident and have no real meaning. We'll talk about that in a minute. The second thing you want to know is how much error or deviation from the results you can possibly expect if you go ahead and mail to the remainder of the list—in other words, your confidence level, and the reason for your continuing to mail to the list.

Using the Tables for Testing

Let's look at several different cases for each of the reasons you might use the tables. The first is determining sample size. Here, you want to know how many names you need to mail to in order to have a statistically representative sample of the list you are testing.

The first step is to decide on a confidence level. I have chosen the 95% confidence level table in Figure 8.1, which means that you can be 95% confident that the results you get are repeatable on subsequent similar samples. Some people in mail order use a 99% table. However, with a 99% table, you would need a much larger sample size than with a 95% table. Other mail order operators use a 90% table, meaning much greater risk, even though the sample size required is lower. I feel that a 95% confidence level is about the right one and I recommend that you use it.

The next step, if you are testing sample size for a list, is to calculate your expected return. Now, it is important that when you calculate your expected return or expected response it is not wishful thinking. Of course, you should always "wish" big. You could wish that every single recipient of your direct mail package would respond. Then you would get a 100% response. But, of course, that's totally unrealistic. Some people have very profitable businesses at less than a 1% response. If you don't have prior records to go on, start with assuming a 1% response. Or you could calculate the response you need to break even and add a minimum profit and use that. Let's assume in our example that we expect to get a 1% return.

Our next step is to decide by how much we can miss our expected return and still have an acceptable lower response limit. For example, we assumed that we would get a 1% return. How low can we get and still be okay? Some people would say break-even. Some people would say something else. In this case, let's assume that we can live with a .2% difference. An .8% return will still be all right—we will still make money. We now refer to Figure 8.1. First, look at the response column all the way to the left and read down until you see the figure 1.0, which stands for 1% response. Go horizontally to the right and look under the .20 limits of error column. This means the .2% difference we decided we could live with in this particular situation. Read right across from the 1% response at the left, and under .20, we read the figure 9,508. This is the minimum sample size we should use, rounded off to 9,500 or 10,000.

How to Analyze the Results

Let's assume that we mailed 10,000 packages each to two different lists. In one list we got a 1% response. In the second we got a 1.5% response. Now, if we look at these percentages by themselves, we would say the second list is better. But is it? Is this difference statistically significant? If it is not, we should treat the lists equally. One may really not be better than the other, even though from the percentage of responses received, one list appears to be. To find this out we again enter with a 1% response. Move horizontally to the right until you find the number nearest 10,000. In this case we find the number we had before, 9,508. Then read up to .20. This means that if the difference is within .20, the number is not statistically significant. In this case the number is 1.0–1% we got on one list, minus 1.5% we got on the other, or a .5% difference. Because .5% is greater than the .2% we just calculated, this number is statistically significant and list 2 is greater than list 1. However, if the two lists had been 1% and 1.2%, respectively, there would have been no actual difference in quality between the two lists. They would have been considered the same in responsiveness and we would have treated them the same in our future operations—unless subsequent retestings proved the difference to be significant.

Now let's see how we test for permissible error in future mailings. Let's say that we mailed 30,000 pieces and got a 3% response. We enter our table again with 3% and read right across to the number closest to 30,000. This is 27,948. Again we read right up to .20. This means that the results we actually received were 3%, plus or minus .2%. Furthermore, in returns you can expect in the future from this mailing, the percentage can vary from 2.8, which is 3.0 minus .2%, to 3.2%, which is 3.0 plus .2%.

How to Test Ads

Testing ads requires somewhat special techniques because of certain inherent problems. It doesn't make sense to test one ad in one issue and a different ad in another issue of the same magazine. Why not? In the first place, one issue may attract buyers or pull better than others. Perhaps one issue contains an exposé and is therefore read by more potential customers. If you advertise in different issues, the position of the ad in the magazine may well be different unless a special position is purchased. Some national, local, or even international event that occurs at the time of publication of one issue can affect results. When a really hot news item, such as the tremendous changes in Eastern Europe and the Soviet Union, takes place, certain magazines will be much more closely read and bought by many more people than is the norm. At certain times the event itself may affect mail order purchase, such as when President Kennedy was assassinated. Products identified with President Kennedy were purchased at much higher levels than normally even though most mail order offers in the mail at that time suffered grievously. Also, in certain issues of the magazine, competition may be evident or not, or may be more severe than in others. For all these reasons, it seems that the obvious approach to testing different ads in different issues of the same magazine isn't a very good solution. Then what is?

One way to do this type of test is to use different geographical areas of distribution of the same magazine, so that in the same month you can have a different ad in each geographical area. However, there are some problems here as well. Circulation levels are different in different geographical areas of the country. Also, certain types of offers may not pull the same in different areas of the country, depending upon the climate, attitude of the people, and many other factors. You may be able to sell a heavy wool coat through a direct mail ad along the eastern seaboard in the middle of winter. In California or Florida or Hawaii, it would be highly unlikely.

A better solution is a so-called split run. A split run means that you run two different ads in a single issue of the magazine, but every other magazine leaving the production plant has one ad, while the other issue has the other ad. These two different ads are keyed differently so that you can measure the results easily. Also, in every geographical area, both ads appear in equal numbers. Now, there are some drawbacks with this approach too. You can expect to pay additional costs for a split run. Not all magazines offer the split-run feature. If you want to advertise with a split run, you should see the appropriate volume of SRDS or the rate card. Either will tell you whether the split run is available and the cost.

Telescopic testing is a variation of the split run. With the use of telescopic testing, you can test many more than two ads at the same time. In fact, the name comes from actually telescoping a year's work into a single test. Let's say that you have ads A, B, C, and D, and you want to test them simultaneously. In one geographical region of the magazine you test A versus B. In the second region you test A versus C. In the third, A versus D, and so forth. Regardless of the results achieved with ad A, we assign it a numerical weighting of 100. We then compare the results of each ad against ad A and assign them proportional numerical values. Then we rank the ads accordingly. Let us say in region 1 ad A pulled 3,000 inquiries and ad B got 2,000. In region 2, ad A pulled 3,200 and ad C, 5,000. In region 3, ad A pulled 500 inquiries and ad D, 1,000. From looking at these raw data, all we can see is that in region 1, ad A was better than ad B; in region 2, ad C was better than ad A; and in region 3, ad D was better than ad A. But which of these ads is best and how do they rank? Well, we let the results of ad A equal 100. To calculate B, we divide B's returns by A's and multiply times 100, so the results for ad B are 67. In the same way, C equals 156 and D, 200. Therefore, the best ad is ad D, the second best is ad C, the third, ad A, and the worst, ad B. Of course, telescopic testing also costs more and a split-run capability is necessary.

Another technique that is effective and doesn't cost quite as much as split runs or telescopic testing is called crisscross testing. If you are testing two different ads, do the crisscross by testing two different magazines or newspapers. The first month you test one ad in, say, *Hunting and Fishing* magazine and the second ad in *Outdoor Life*. Then, the second month, you crisscross: The second ad goes in *Hunting and Fishing* and the first ad in *Outdoor Life*. You then compare the results to see which ad is better.

Another technique along the same lines is to alternate your ads in the same magazine every other month. This technique takes a long time to work, up to six months or more. To guard against the competition coming in and copying a successful campaign, you certainly wouldn't want to expose yourself by testing in this way right at the start. However, at some point after you are established in the marketplace, it can be a fully acceptable way of testing two good ads against one another.

What do the results mean when you're testing one ad against the other, or one ad in three different magazines? Let's say you're running one ad in three different magazines. In one month, magazine A brings you 500 orders, magazine B brings 300 orders, and magazine C results in 100 orders. In their raw form, these figures mean very little. However, when combined with the cost of advertising, they will tell you not only whether you are profitable, but also what your profitability is. If advertisement A costs $3000, you are paying $6 per order. If advertisement B costs $1500, this ad cost you $5 per order. And if advertisement C costs you $300, it costs $3 per order. If the combined cost of fulfillment, overhead, advertising, and so forth was $4, then you lost $2 per order in advertising in magazine A, you made $1 advertising in B, and you made $2 per order in advertising in C. So we eliminate magazine A because you are losing money. In magazine B, at $1 per order you made $300, whereas in magazine C, even though we made $2 per order, we made only $200 total. Therefore, profit margin was greater in magazine C, but magazine B was more profitable. Of course, as always, we must consider back-end profits and profitability to get the true picture. If we consider everything together, perhaps even magazine A is worth advertising in.

Direct Mail Testing

You must be extremely careful in testing direct mail lists in that you must be sure that you have a fair sample in terms of sample size. It has been the practice for some time to request an Nth name list. "N" stands for a number. If the number selected was nine, a test list of every ninth number would be generated. However, even the Nth name is not completely statistically correct because Nth names are not random names. Many mail order experts today are recommending geographical selections as being more correct statistically and netting better results for the test versus the results received later when the full list is used. A geographical name split can be done fairly easily using several zip code numbers. A method that provides a more representative selection of names can be worked out with your list broker, manager, or compiler. Frequently you can arrive at a better sampling methodology than the older "Nth name" selection, and today random name selection is available.

You should also test your largest good list first. If one list has a total of 500,000 names and another has only 20,000, it's far better to start testing the larger list first, because if it is successful, it allows you a much better population base to mail to than would the smaller list. However, you should use the largest "good" list. "Goodness" is a measure of quality, and you must remember that the most recent mail order buyers' names are much better than those whose purchases were made at an earlier date. It has been calculated that lists lose their effectiveness at the rate of as high as 20% a year; thus even a few months can make big differences in results.

ADVERTISING

Nothing determines the success of a mail order enterprise so much as its advertising, whether it be magazine, newspaper, radio, TV, direct mail, or some other form of promotion. Writing advertising copy, preparing art, selecting media, determining price, and other factors usually require expert skills. If you decide to work with an advertising agency, select one primarily on the basis of its successful experience in producing profitable mail order advertising.

Whether you decide to use an agency or go at it alone, there are some important concepts to remember.

Where to Advertise

It is important to recognize that not everyone is a good prospect for your product or service. Concentrate your efforts on the segments of the market that are more likely to buy than others. For example, if you have a new type of cooking pot, you may think everybody would be a prospect because everybody cooks. But many individuals are uninterested in cooking or feel no need to try something new. Some people may think your price is too high (or too low), and some won't buy anything through the mail.

A good strategy is to advertise where similar items are advertised. This is true whether the medium you are considering is a magazine or a list of names for a direct mail campaign.

When to Advertise

The month in which you advertise a product or service can have a great effect on the results. Although most products can be advertised all year, some should be advertised and sold only during certain seasons. For example, you should not try to sell garden hoses during the winter.

Major events can affect the results of your promotion. For example, November is usually a good month for most products; however, depending on what you are selling, November sales may be better or worse in an election year. Similarly, a war, the death of an important person, or other major events will affect the results of a mail order promotion.

Whatever your product, some months are better for sales than others. You can find out the best months for your product only by testing. Generally, the best to worst months for mail order sales are ranked: January, February, October, November, March, September, August, April, December, July, May, and June.

When starting off a new product or service, advertise during the logical months, considering your product and the season of the year. Then analyze your response. If you test in a good month, the results may be much better than you can expect in an average or poor mail order sales month. In the same way, if your test ad appears in a bad month and the results are only marginal, you may get better sales in other months.

Depending on the strength of the response, you can estimate the most effective frequency for advertising. For example, if the response was strong, you may decide to advertise your product frequently. If the response was only moderate, you should probably advertise less frequently—perhaps every other month or once a quarter or only during certain peak months. Finally, if the response was profitable but weak during a good mail order month, possibly you should advertise this particular product infrequently.

SPECIAL CONSIDERATIONS

Use of Post Office Box Numbers

Some states require you to state a business (or home) address in your advertisement, even if you want orders to come to a post office box number. If you have the choice as to whether to use a post office box number or your home address, here are the trade-offs:

1. A classified advertisement will probably cost more with a home address since you pay by the word.
2. Use of a post office box will allow you to pick up mail seven days a week.
3. A prospect generally associates lower risk in ordering from a business or home address. Thus, you are likely to have increased returns with a full address over a post office box number.
4. A post office box number protects your personal privacy if you don't want to be bothered at home by customers.

In my experience, use or nonuse of a post office box will *not* mean the difference between success and failure. It is more a decision having to do with personal preference.

Credit Card Sales

Credit card sales will increase your returns. This is because prospects who aren't familiar with your company do know the names Visa and Mastercard. Use of credit cards also means that your customers can easily order higher priced items on credit, but the bank grants the credit, not you. Since some mail order companies find that they are only able to collect from about 60 percent of their credit sales, this may be no small thing.

However, the bank will charge you several percent on each order for allowing people to charge your products against their credit cards. If you are new to business, you may also have a problem convincing a bank to let you use their credit card service. You should also know that some individuals who have become mail order millionaires did so dealing on a strictly cash basis.

If you sell expensive items, or inexpensive items likely to total a fair amount for each order, credit card sales may be worthwhile investigating. It definitely makes sense to enable your customers to order through a toll-free 800 line (see below).

Toll-Free 800 Numbers

Toll-free 800 numbers allow your customers to order more easily. Anything that does will increase your sales. The question is, will it increase your profits? Remember that toll-free means that the caller doesn't pay—but you do. Some mail order operators have found that, for their product, use of a toll-free 800 number is not profitable. Others have found that a toll-free 800 service is exactly what makes their businesses profitable.

As for other important business decisions, one way to find out whether you should use a toll-free 800 number or not is to test. Installation and toll costs vary; you can find out more about toll-free numbers for your business in your area by locating companies in the Yellow Pages of your telephone book.

Direct Mail

Direct mail involves sending your sales material directly to your prospective customer. You can either mail to your own established list of customers, a list of names obtained from inquiries to some other type of advertisement of yours, or rent lists from others. Direct mail allows you to be more selective in reaching a precise target market, personalize your advertising by the inclusion of the prospect's name, and to send much more advertising copy than you could supply in a medium such as a classified or display advertisement.

In fact, a typical direct mail piece will include:

— an outer envelope with a "teaser" to encourage your prospect to open the envelope
— a hard-hitting sales letter that explains your offer in detail
— a separate brochure or flyer that resells your offer and may include some sort of graphics, such as a photograph or drawing
— a self-addressed envelope to make it easy to respond (sometimes this envelope may carry a special indicia available from the post office so your prospect doesn't even need to pay postage)
— an order form, sometimes combined with a money-back guarantee
— a folded "publisher's letter" (on the outside it says "open this only if you have decided *not* to order"; inside it again attempts to make a sale)

You can rent lists from list brokers, compilers, or list managers. Some can be found in the Yellow Pages under Mailing Lists. You should also check *Standard Rate and Data Service* (SRDS), which your library may subscribe to. SRDS is published several times a year and covers magazines, radio, and television media in huge telephone book–size volumes. Here are a few sources from which you can obtain free catalogs of mailing lists:

Ed Burnett Consultants
99 W. Sheffield Ave.
Englewood, NJ 07631
(201) 871-1100
(800) 223-7777

Dunhill International List
1100 Park Central Blvd. South
Pompano Beach, FL 33064
(305) 974-7800
(800) 445-5386

Ziff-Davis Publishing
One Park Ave.
New York, NY 10016
(212) 503-5394
(800) 999-5478

Lists may rent for $60 or more per thousand names depending on a number of factors including how specialized the list is. Usually the best lists are response lists. These are lists of people who actually responded to a similar item by mail. However, lists compiled of likely candidates for a particular product or service (such as doctors, gardeners, small business owners, etc.) may also be successful.

As with any other type of advertising, you should test a small portion of a list before attempting to mail to the whole list, or even most of it. That way you won't waste money on a list that won't work for your product or service.

What to Put in Your Advertisements

An advertisement's words—the "copy"—are critical, and require more than casual consideration. In his book *Tested Advertising Methods*, John Caples described two advertisements that were the same size, used the same illustrations, and were in identical publications; only the copy differed. One ad sold 19½ times as many goods as the other. This could signal the difference between failure and a small fortune.

There are many different formulas for developing copy. Initially you should write your advertisement according to a definite copy structure. Once you know that you can write good mail order copy, you can experiment with less structured forms of communicating. The Copywriting Checklist (see p. 201) lists several important considerations. One good basic structure to begin with is described below:

— Get attention/Develop interest
— Demonstrate benefits
— Build credibility
— Encourage orders

Get Attention/Develop Interest

The most important element of your ad and copy is the headline. This is how you gain attention. Yet many copywriters, who spend hours writing the body of the ad, will spend just a few minutes on the headline. The weekly magazine *Advertising Age* once related that Maxwell Sackheim sold 500,000 copies of a book by changing the title, and therefore the headline, from *Five Acres* to *Five Acres and Independence*.

All good headlines have certain things in common. First, they appeal to the reader's self-interest and stress the most important benefit of the product or service. A powerful headline arouses the curiosity of the reader, presents startling news, or suggests a quick and easy way to obtain benefits.

Second, good headlines use key words that are psychologically powerful in attracting potential readers. In *Confessions of an Advertising Man*, David Ogilvy cites as the most important of these key words "free" and "new," but there are many other powerful words. Here is a list[1] of some words psychologists have discovered to be powerful in stopping readers and getting their attention:

amazing	announcing	at last
bargain	challenge	easy
how to	hurry	important
just arrived	last chance	miracle
power	remarkable	revolutionary
secret	sensational	success
wanted	who else	why

Demonstrate Benefits

Once you have gained the reader's attention, demonstrate the benefits of buying. The benefits must override the cost of the product and the trouble involved in finding a stamp and envelope, writing a check, and mailing the order. Don't sell product descriptions. Sell benefits. A customer at a restaurant buys the taste, smell, and sizzle, not a piece of meat. It is your job to describe your product in terms of taste, smell, and sizzle.

Build Credibility

Credibility is very important in making your copy effective. Regardless of what you say about the benefits or advantages of a product, if your potential customer does not believe what you say, he or she will not place an order. Testimonials can be very helpful, particularly if you have permission to use the name of an individual whose testimonial is on file. An alternative is to omit the name or use only initials.

Another means of achieving credibility is to identify a bank, accountant, or attorney who is willing to be a reference. Even showing a picture of the building that houses your business can add credibility, especially if it is an imposing structure.

Encourage Orders

A basic law of sales is that a face-to-face salesperson must ask for an order. As a salesperson selling through an advertisement, you should also call your customer to immediate action. You don't want your customers to cut out the coupon and put it away for another day. You want your customers to order immediately. Research has demonstrated that regardless of initial intent, in most instances if your prospects

---

[1] For a comprehensive list, see *Building a Mail Order Business*, 3rd edition, William A. Cohen (New York: John Wiley & Sons, Inc., 1991).

don't order immediately they don't order at all. Include incentives, such as a statement on limited quantities or a limited time offer.

COPYWRITING CHECKLIST

Headline

— Does the headline appeal to self-interest, offer exciting news, or arouse interest?
— Is the headline positive, rather than negative?
— Does the headline suggest that the reader can obtain something easily and quickly?
— Does the headline make use of the powerful words of mail order advertising?
— Does the headline stress the most important benefit to the product?
— Does the headline stop the reader and cause him or her to read further?
— Is the headline believable?
— Does the headline tie in with the copy?

The Offer

Are all the elements of the offer present in the copy?

— Product   — Price
— Terms   — Guarantee
— Options   — Additional reasons to buy
— Dates   — Places

Is your offer irresistible?

— Do you gain interest at once by use of a story, a startling or unusual statement, a quote, or news item?
— Do you show benefits and advantages that appeal to emotional needs so that your offer is irresistible?
— Do you establish credibility with your reader through the use of testimonials, statements by your accountant, or some other means?
— Do you encourage immediate action by listing a reason to order now, i.e., limited quantities, time limit on offer, etc.?

Copy Quality

— Is the copy written in a conversational tone?
— Does your copy move right along?

— Do you use short words, short sentences, and short paragraphs?
— Do you use several subheadings throughout your copy?

What Cost?

Top quality advertising costs more, but it usually brings the best results. However, don't overspend on advertising, direct mail, and other promotions. Don't invest in full-color printing when one or two colors will do the job. There is no need to use the costliest papers and elaborate art, or other extravagances, to sell profitably.

KEEP GOOD RECORDS

A word of caution: To succeed in mail order, pay close attention to details—but don't get bogged down in them. Keep accurate records of all figures that are important to the success of your business, for example:

— Results of advertisements
— Advertising costs
— Printing costs
— Postage costs
— Cost-per-order

However, do it in the simplest, easiest, least time-consuming way possible.

Use a Computer

Although you can still start a mail order business without a computer, it is hard to imagine anyone operating this way for very long. More than any other tool, a computer will help you keep accurate records, raise your productivity, and stay competitive. Wait until your business is established and you have a profitable product; once you have established good credit, a computer should be one of your first important investments.

A computer can help you to perform most of the key functions of running a mail order business. Below is an outline of how various types of software systems can help you.

Database

— Maintain an updated list of customers
— Find new customers
— Research media

— Track most popular products
— Record ordering information: how frequent, average size, fulfillment dates

Spreadsheet

— Maintain income tax records
— Make "what if" forecasts and plans
— Record price information
— Maintain cash flow information and projections

Word Processor

— Write and maintain a file of your business letters
— Personalize your direct mail

Desktop Publishing

— Write advertisements
— Do your own layout
— Do your own typesetting for advertisements

The computer has revolutionized the mail order business. When you are ready to get a computer, go to your local business software store to learn about programs available and a lot more. If no store in your town sells software, get a copy of one of the many computer magazines that are now being published. You will not only see programs advertised and described but you can obtain catalogs from companies that publish hundreds of other programs that can help you run and build your business.

REPEAT BUSINESS—KEY TO MAXIMUM PROFITS

Continuous profits come from continuous sales. As already suggested, rarely is a profitable mail order business established on a one-time sale. Paul Muchnick, president of Paul Muchnick Company in Los Angeles, offers the following methods to stimulate repeat orders at minimal cost.

Never Forget the Customer.   Your list of customers is your most valuable asset. Use it to send offers of merchandise at frequent intervals.

Use Package Stuffers.   Include a regular catalog or special offer in outgoing orders. Package enclosures can bring in new sales and will ride free since postage and packing costs already are being paid to ship the merchandise.

Offer Quantity Discounts.   Everyone loves a bargain. A discount price or a similar incentive for an order over a given amount will stimulate larger orders. Gift certificates are another way to spark sales, especially during Christmas and other holiday seasons.

Advertise on Envelopes.   If you are enclosing advertising in the envelope, consider using the envelope itself to feature one or more special offers. The additional printing cost may prove insignificant compared to the extra sales produced.

Mail order can be a profitable and interesting full- or part-time business. But remember, you will probably lose money before you start making it. So don't make major investments until you have gained experience and found the right product at the right price and the best means of communicating it to the most receptive market.

SOURCES OF ADDITIONAL INFORMATION

Building a Mail Order Business, 3rd ed., by William A. Cohen, published by John Wiley and Sons, Inc., 605 Third Ave., New York, NY 10158.

Direct Mail and Mail Order Handbook, 3rd ed., by Richard S. Hodgson, published by the Dartnell Corporation, 660 Ravenswood Ave., Chicago, IL 60640.

Direct Marketing Success, by Freeman Gosden, Jr., published by John Wiley and Sons, Inc., 605 Third Ave., New York, NY 10158.

How I Made $1 Million in Mail Order, by E. Joseph Cossman, published by Prentice-Hall, Englewood Cliffs, NJ 07632.

How to Get Rich in Mail Order, by Melvin Powers, published by the Wilshire Book Co., 12015 Sherman Road, North Hollywood, CA 91605.

How to Start and Operate a Mail Order Business, 4th ed., by Julian Simon, published by McGraw-Hill Book Co., 1221 Avenue of the Americas, New York, NY 10020.

Mail Order Know-How, by Cecil Hoge, Sr., published by Ten Speed Press, P.O. Box 7123, Berkeley, CA 94707.

Mail Order Magic, by Herman Holtz, published by McGraw-Hill Book Co., 1221 Avenue of the Americas, New York, NY 10020.

More Than You Ever Wanted to Know About Mail Order Advertising, by Herschell Lewis, published by Prentice-Hall, Inc., Englewood Cliffs, NJ 07632.

Successful Direct Marketing Methods, 3rd ed., by Bob Stone, published by Crain Books, 740 Rush St., Chicago, IL 60611.

Tested Advertising Methods, 4th ed., by John Caples, published by Prentice-Hall, Inc., Englewood Cliffs, NJ 07632.

The Do-It-Yourself Direct Mail Handbook, by Murray Raphel and Ken Erdman, published by the Marketers Bookshelf, 402 Bethlehem Pike, Philadelphia, PA 19118.

The Complete Direct Mail List Handbook, by Ed Burnett, published by Prentice-Hall, Englewood Cliffs, NJ 07632.

CHAPTER 9

HOW TO SELL TO THE GOVERNMENT

The United States government represents a huge market for the small business. Even in this era of cutbacks, it exceeds $100 billion. However, the government also demands special marketing techniques and methodologies. If you know how to apply these techniques, you can make millions. If you do not, you can spend thousands of dollars in resources and end up without a single government contract.

The process of selling to the government marketplace and the government customer is far from automatic. You must market and sell just as you do in any other marketplace. Although the regulations state that you merely need to get on a bidder's list and wait for the bid to come in, or that you only need to pick up a copy of the *Commerce Business Daily* and bid according to the specifications contained therein, this is not enough. You cannot do only this and expect to be successful, any more than you could in supplying a similar product (or perhaps the same one) to an industrial buyer who doesn't know you and hasn't done business with you previously. You cannot be a total unknown and expect to win.

The government buyer, no matter who he is, doesn't want to risk his career on someone he doesn't know: You will have to plan to expend some resources in the right way to overcome this initial hurdle. Just as in other markets, once you have your first contract, other contracts will be much easier to get and at much less cost to you.

There is a process for winning government contracts that will make you successful. It will ensure that your win rate for Sole Source Requests for Proposals (RFPs)— the "look-see" process of Uncle Sam—is high and will enable you to make millions of dollars. Briefly, this process involves five phases: locating your customer; contacting the customer; planning your marketing presentation; submitting your proposal; and, finally, contract negotiation and post-contract follow-up.

Let's look at each phase individually.

HOW TO LOCATE YOUR CUSTOMER

Regardless of what product or service you have, you will find that there are many government customers, both in the United States and abroad, who are interested in buying your product or service. These customers, who are found in every government agency and department, buy almost every product or service you can imagine. For a complete list of products and government customers, order a copy of the *U.S. Government Purchasing and Sales Directory* from the Superintendent of Documents, Government Printing Office, Washington, DC 20402. It is worth the cost of a few dollars.

Another way to locate specific customers for your product or service is through the *Commerce Business Daily*. It comes out five days a week and lists all contract awards above a certain minimum amount. In addition, it has all requirements by various government agencies above certain dollar amounts listed. Remember that the value of the *Commerce Business Daily* is not that you will bid on the advertisements contained in it. In fact, you should not bid, no matter how closely you feel you can meet the bid requirements. Perhaps 98 percent of the awards made as bids advertised in the *Commerce Business Daily* are made to firms that have already made the preproposal contact and done the marketing necessary to win.

You could end up bidding approximately 100 times against advertised bids in the *Commerce Business Daily* and only win two, if any, contracts. But, the list of awards made and the advertisements of products and services needed is a tremendous source of potential government customers; these are the people who actually want to buy your kind of product and service. You can order the *Commerce Business Daily* from the same address as that for the *U.S. Government Purchasing and Sales Directory*.

A third way of finding government customers is to seek help from the Small Business Administration. The SBA is eager to help you find new customers in the government. Contact your local office and explain your product or service and that you are interested in dealing with the government. They will make an appointment for you to talk with one of their management-assistance specialists. You will find a list of SBA field offices in the appendix.

Still another source is the government's purchasing agent, the General Services Administration, or GSA. The GSA buys thousands of products and services for government agencies and other organizations. The GSA has also established business service centers throughout the country that exist primarily to serve the entrepreneur in search of government contracts. Look under "U.S. Government" in the phone book to contact the center nearest you.

CONTACTING YOUR CUSTOMER

Once you have located a customer by government agency or other organization, the next step is to contact that agency or organization and get the name of the individual who is responsible for and interested in your goods or services. Sometimes you will have to go through several telephone numbers before you get the right one. Your general class of product or service is probably handled by several people, and you must find the one who handles your specific item. Your first contact may be at the managerial level rather than the actual government customer, at the working level, that you are looking for.

When you have the right customer, explain your product or service and ask for a general idea of some of the items in which he or she is interested. This is especially true with research and development products or services, where general information about the customer's requirements is insufficient to enable you to understand what he is actually buying. Try to get as much information as you can from the customer over the phone. The main object of talking to this person is not to sell at this point, but merely to establish interest and to determine that this is truly the correct place for you to expend time and financial resources in making your first sale. Frequently you will find that, despite considerable screening by yourself and others in the government who have helped you, this is not really a customer for your product or service at all. This is the main point of the telephone call—to establish the fact that this is a bona fide customer who will be interested in buying from you.

During this initial telephone call you should arrange to meet the customer, if possible. This may be difficult if you are on one coast and your potential customer is on the other, but, with few exceptions, face-to-face contact and a presentation of your capabilities are essential. This is absolutely true for research and development programs, and probably 90 percent true for all other programs.

If you cannot set up an immediate visit, arrange to send a brochure describing your capabilities and request all information your potential customer can supply about his interests and the way his particular government agency is organized and does business. Indicate that you would like to get together with him to make a full presentation of your interests and capabilities in the near future and would like to call him the following week to set up an appointment.

PREPARING A PRESENTATION

Preparing a special presentation for each customer, at each potential customer visit, can be tremendously effective for obtaining future government orders. Decide on the basic message you want to get across to your potential customer, make an outline, and prepare a few graphs, slides, or reproduction copies. Collect any samples you wish to show. Before you leave for the meeting, practice your presentation in front of someone who can give you constructive criticism.

Deciding on a Basic Message

The first point is to document the basic message that you want your customer to receive. This message may be "My widget is better than any other widget in the world" or "my widget is just as good as any other widget, but cheaper than any other in the world." Document your basic sales pitch to insure that everything you say supports that one message and that nothing you say is contradictory or irrelevant to the main point.

Outlining Your Presentation

Start by noting the overall time you are allowed for your presentation. Your outline and your presentation will differ depending on whether you have one hour, three hours, or the entire day. Make sure that every point supports the basic contention that you have documented. Do not write the entire presentation as if it were a speech. A speech has to be memorized and does not allow for questions by the customer. Do not memorize your presentation. Work from an outline to ensure that all points will be covered.

Preparing Viewgraphs, Slides, or Reproduction Copies of Your Outline

Once you have the basic points documented and have completed the outline, the next step is to transcribe this outline either into viewgraphs, slides, or other formats that can be processed into printed copy. Which method or methods you use depends on the size of your audience and which method you are most comfortable with. If you are making a presentation to only a few people, it is easiest to reproduce your presentation and give each person a copy to follow. If you have 15 customers receiving your presentation at once, it is probably better to put your outline on viewgraphs or slides. (You may wish to give each a reproduced copy as well.) Availability of the projector for viewgraphs or slides is also a factor. If the government has no projector available (and you should check into this prior to your trip) you may not have any choice. In any case, if you leave a copy with your customers, they will be able to refer back to your presentation without having to depend on their memories or notes.

Tracking a Program to Win

One of your main tasks at the first meeting with your potential customer is to identify what future procurement programs are being planned. Once you have determined that these programs exist and the money is available for them, you should begin to track them. Tracking is done not only through contacts with this particular government customer, but also with other government customers who are knowledgeable about these programs. For example, your customer may be an engineer who is a candidate for the project's program manager, product engineer, or so-called program monitor. You can certainly track the program through him. You will also want to discuss this program with contracting personnel, the individual's supervisor, and, if possible, other commands or units associated with this program that are not at the same location.

HOW TO WRITE A PROPOSAL

There are actually three main types of government requests for bidding. With the IFB (invitation for bid), you need only bid the price; the winner is simply the low price bid. This type of request requires no proposal. An RFP (request for proposal) requires a formal proposal as well as a bid price, and the decision is made not only on the price bid, but also on your technical proposal. In addition, there is a type of proposal that government regulations allow you to submit, known as the unsolicited proposal—a proposal that has not been formally solicited by the government.

The first thing you should know about an unsolicited proposal is that it really isn't unsolicited. If you have a great new idea that you think the government should buy, the most useless thing you can do is submit a truly unsolicited proposal. All you will do is waste your time and money; contrary to law, you could even find that outstanding features of your proposal have been borrowed and used in competitive solutions.

Consider the environment into which a true unsolicited proposal is introduced. First, there is no money to buy your proposal because the government organization's budget was prepared a year or more prior to your submission. Planning, which of course excluded your proposal, was done even earlier. Like a proposal in response to an RFP, you have only so many pages in which to make the sale. In fact, you can't make a sale in your proposal—you can only confirm it. Therefore, you cannot submit a true unsolicited proposal and expect to win, at least not often enough to make it worthwhile.

The key to winning with an unsolicited proposal—as in any proposal you submit to the government—is preproposal marketing. Use the principles of marketing so that your unsolicited proposal is actually invited and fully sold to your government customer before you ever sit down to write it.

Let's say that you have been sent an RFP and given 30 days to respond. You should already know, through your contacts with the government and your marketing activities, that the proposal was on its way and more or less what it would contain. Further, you should have already sold your main ideas to the government. The first principle of winning is to lay a groundwork for the proposal before you receive it. The government customer should have a pretty good idea of what you are going to submit and should not be surprised by anything in your proposal.

This raises a question: What if you have a brilliant idea after your last meeting with the government? Do you include this brilliant idea in the proposal or not? My strong recommendation is that you do not. There should be no surprises in your proposal. If something occurs to you that is so vital that you feel you must include it in a proposal in a response to an RFP, make up two proposals, one of which contains the new idea as an alternative. The chances of winning with a proposal that includes significant surprises is very low. Even if you are overwhelmed with your new idea, present it only as an alternate proposal. Your main proposal should contain the ideas that you have already discussed with the customer.

Why is this so important? For one thing, a proposal is a limited resource document. This means that it has a limited number of pages in which you can sell your ideas. You don't have enough space to sell any but the very simplest of your ideas. It is also more difficult to convince a government customer by the printed word when you are not there to answer questions he might have about a new idea. Even if this new idea is really great, and the government customer evaluating the proposal immediately recognizes it, he or she needs time to sell this idea to the boss. There is not enough time to do this during a proposal evaluation, when a proposal evaluator has very little chance to talk to his superiors about new ideas.

What do you put in the proposal? The first section should be an executive summary of the whole idea of the proposal and how you intend to solve the government's problem. Next comes your technical proposal, in which you cover all areas in your customer's statement of work (a part of his RFP) and tell him exactly what you intend to do, in detail. Other important sections are the management proposal, which tells him how you are going to manage the contract; a biographical section containing short biographies of the major contributors to the project from your company; a facilities brochure or report, which discusses the facilities you have for performing the contract; and a review of your past performance, showing contracts you have successfully performed for various agencies of the government in the past, if you have done any. Finally, your proposal contains a summary in which all the salient points of your proposal are reviewed and emphasized.

It is a wise move to use as many graphs and charts as necessary to illustrate each point. The cost proposal (or price proposal) is usually contained in a separate section. The government likes it this way so that their technical evaluation can be done separately from an evaluation of the relative prices of the different competitors. Let's look at each of these sections in turn.

The Management Summary

This brief statement is designed to be read by management personnel rather than the technical personnel, who will go much deeper into the technical portions of your proposal. Therefore, while you should use appropriate technical language, you should write the management summary in such a way that it can be understood by individuals who are not working on the technical end of the project.

The Technical Portion

Your technical proposal must be organized around the requirements in the government's RFP. Make a checklist of the government requirements and follow it exactly, organizing your technical proposal in the same way as the government has organized its request for proposal. The government evaluators will be going through your proposal, as well as your competitors' proposals, in a point-by-point attempt to ensure that every requirement of their RFP is met. The solution to a particular problem in the RFP may lose points with one of the government evaluators because he doesn't like it or isn't fully sold on it, but if you fail to include any solution at all, you will lose all the points. If the evaluator can't find your solution in that area, he may think you have not included it—and you will lose all the points. Make it as easy as possible for him to locate every requirement listed in the RFP. Many successful government contractors find that a special table of contents, in which the government requirements are set against your solutions and the page numbers given, is very useful in helping them to win government contracts. An example of such a table of contents is shown in Figure 9.1.

Your outline for a technical proposal has actually been provided by the government. But do you merely claim that you will fill all requirements? The answer is no. Go down the line, requirement by requirement. Against every major requirement, list your solution and why it is the best one. If one of the requirements for a fire extinguisher is that it should shoot a stream of water 20 feet, it is not enough merely

Proposal Paragraph	RFP Requirement	Description	Page
1.0	1.0	Introduction	1
2.0	2.0	Design approach	2
2.1	2.1	Facepiece/Hardshell	2
2.2	2.2	Inhalation/Exhalation valve	3
2.3	2.3	Web-type suspension	4
3.0	2.4	Mask development	5
3.1	2.4.1	Faceseal development	5
3.2	2.4.2	Hardshell design	6
3.3	2.5	Mock-up	7
3.4	2.6	Prototype models	7
3.5	2.7	Final development models	8
3.6	3.0	Government-furnished property	9
4.0	4.0	Quality assurance	9
4.1	4.1	Quality assurance organization	10
4.2	4.2	Quality assurance program	10
4.3	4.3	Quality assurance test and evaluation plan	10
4.4	4.4	Acceptance test procedure	11
4.5	4.5	Systems safety	11
4.6	4.6	Maintainability demonstration plan	12
5.0	5.0	Corporate experience	12
6.0	6.0	Project personnel	24
7.0	7.0	Facilities and capabilities	25
8.0	10.0	Development schedule	35
9.0	—	Conclusion	37

Figure 9.1. Table of contents for a proposal, with RFP requirements.

to state that you propose a fire extinguisher that will shoot 20 feet; you must state how you propose to do this. Furthermore, you should mention other methods of achieving the same requirement that you have considered but rejected, and tell why you reject these alternatives. Simply stating that you will meet a requirement does not convince government officials that you will do so; it doesn't give them any understanding of how you intend to do this, nor any basis for judgment between you and your competitors. You must state how you will actually meet the requirement of squirting the water 20 feet.

Why should you talk about alternative methods? Letting the evaluator know that you have considered alternatives shows that you have put considerable thought into your solution and have not merely proposed the easiest way or the first idea that came to mind. Since you have given reasons for rejecting these alternative solutions, any competitor who might offer one or more of your rejected solutions will suffer accordingly.

Wherever you can, illustrate your point by a chart or some other graphic means. Caption this so that it demonstrates and sells your point to the government. In the case of a fire extinguisher, you might want to show a comparison of your method and three other methods you have considered. Perhaps you have rejected the other methods because they are all costly. In that case, you might use this caption for your graph: "XYZ Company's Proposed Valving for Achieving 20 Feet of Water Is Far Cheaper Than All Other Methods."

Evaluators, being human, sometimes tend to skip through the wording in the various paragraphs, but people look at graphs. A properly titled chart will get the point across to your customer even if he missed it when he read the paragraph containing it.

Always include a schedule that shows the tasks needed to complete all requirements and when each will be done. An example of this is given in Figure 9.2. A development schedule is useful in demonstrating to your customer that you have really thought the entire project through, including all the steps necessary to do what he wants done within the required time frame. This gives you a tremendous advantage over competitors who do not include development schedules and who expect the evaluator to take it on faith that they will complete the program within the desired time period. If you include a development schedule, he knows that you will complete the schedule as required because you have a firm plan for doing so.

The Management Proposal

A management proposal tells how you will handle the contract. It is necessary for all but the very simplest proposals. Any program that requires developmental work as well as production drawings, prototypes, or purchasing from outside the company requires good coordination and management. Even if you are technically qualified, the government wants to satisfy itself that you are capable of completing and managing a complex program. Again, some sort of picture or graph showing how

Months after Award of Contract

TASK	1	2	3	4	5	6	7	8	9	10	11	12
Development of Research Tool	→											
Secondary Data Collection	→											
Interviewing							→					
Data Recording							→					
Data Analysis and Computations								→				
Follow-up Interviews										→		
Development of Conclusion and Recommendation											→	
Preparation of Final Report												→

Figure 9.2.   Research schedule.

you are going to manage the project can be very useful. An organization chart is also valuable here. Even if you are a small company of one or two people, you can draw an organization chart that shows the reporting relationship within your company as well as how outside organizations will be supporting you for various aspects of your program.

Show your management plan to other knowledgeable individuals who have not participated directly in writing the program to ensure the clarity of what you have written. Any questions about your chart or your method of management should be answered in your management proposal in anticipation of the evaluators' similar questions. For example, if certain raw materials are in short supply and you are proposing to deal with a source at the other end of the country, what will you do if there is a strike and you cannot immediately receive these raw materials?

Perhaps you are developing a project, but someone else must construct a set of tooling for you; he is located in Chicago and you are in San Francisco. You should indicate your solutions to potential problems, maybe in a weekly or even daily telephone conversation, or by sending an engineer to Chicago for several days or weeks while the tooling is constructed. In any case, make your management plan clear. Show that you have considered all the possibilities and contingencies and have developed alternative plans and alternative solutions.

The Biographical Section

Include short biographies of all major personnel concerned with this program. If yours is a small company, this should include the president, whether he is directly involved in working on the program or not, other executives, and the program manager. One common mistake that many small companies make is to use a standard résumé for every type of contract bid, regardless of to whom it is bid or what type of service or product is being bid. Instead of doing this, keep a basic résumé of everyone on file, but tailor every biography included in your biographical section specifically for the contract you are bidding. You should keep a file of these biographies, should similar RFPs be received on which you desire to bid in the future.

The Facilities Section

List in detail all your facilities and capital equipment that have an impact on accomplishing the specific job under consideration. Do not take anything for granted here or assume that the customer knows what you have. Much of the equipment you consider commonplace or even obsolete should be explained and listed if it is useful for the job you are proposing. The more you can help convince the customer that you have the equipment and facilities to do a good job, the better your chances of winning.

Prior Contracts

If you have had prior government contracts you should list them along with the name of a customer who is likely to give a favorable evaluation of the job you did (or are doing) for his government organization. Give his or her address and telephone number, too. Don't leave anything to chance. Even if you know that you have done a good job, someone who is unfamiliar with the program and the job may be contacted and may give a false or negative impression based on insufficient information or things he has heard from secondhand sources. If you have had no prior government contracts, list civilian contracts, again including name, address, and telephone number of someone who is aware of the program, knows it in some detail, and is likely to give a fair and favorable evaluation of your performance.

The Price Proposal

Not only should you learn how much money the government plans to spend on your project long before the RFP comes out, but you should also learn what amount the customer considers reasonable for the scope of work he anticipates. In any case, you must fully justify the price you bid to the government in your cost proposal, so that the customer not only knows why everything costs what it does, but also is convinced of the reasonableness of these costs. Remember that government pricing of contracts is just like the pricing of any other goods or services sold by a small business; it depends not only on the cost to you, but also and primarily upon what the government customer is willing to pay.

There are certain rules and regulations for dealing with the government which limit the amount of profit you are allowed to take. However, costing figures are almost invariably open to judgment and interpretation. The first and primary rule should be: What is the customer willing to pay? Then work back and see if this price is profitable to you, either for this contract or in future anticipated business. If the government is not willing to pay a price at which you can sell your product or service, either because of immediate business or other business on other contracts, then you should know this long before receipt of the RFP. At that point you should have made this known to the customer and either changed the scope of the work he wanted done in order to reduce the cost or made him aware of the fact that what he wants will cost more. If you know that the price necessary for you to make a profit cannot be borne by the government, that there is no possibility of making this loss up on future contracts or on goodwill, and that you are unable to convince him to alter his price before receipt of the RFP, don't bid. Any bid on a government contract costs money, time, and personnel resources. Don't use up these commodities unless you are going to win. If the government is unwilling to pay a price that is profitable to you, you will end up as a loser even if you are awarded the contract.

HOW TO NEGOTIATE A GOVERNMENT CONTRACT

Once you have submitted your proposal, you wait for the government to evaluate it. If you are successful, your customer will contact you, usually for additional negotiations. To cover every aspect of negotiating with the government is beyond the scope of this book. There are many books devoted entirely to this subject. I recommend three of them: *The Negotiating Game*, by Chester L. Karrass (Thomas Y. Crowell Co., New York); *Negotiation of Contracts*, by Paul R. McDonald (Procurement Association, Inc., Covina, CA); and *Fundamentals of Negotiating*, by Gerard I. Nierenberg (Hawthorne Books, Inc., New York).

There are certain things about government negotiating that you should know before you start. For one thing, negotiations with the government are like negotiations with anyone else. The government customer will frequently assume that your price can be reduced by 10 to 15 percent or more. Sometimes he will intentionally enter into negotiation with several contractors at once in order to bid the price down, even though this is contrary to procurement regulations. This is done by asking you for a "best and final offer. There have been contracts awarded by the government when no less than five separate "best and final" offers have been requested. I was once involved in a bid in which the government succeeded in getting me to reduce my price by 10% through a requirement for a "best and final" offer and the implied threat of competition. I learned at a later date that I had no competition! Though this tactic is supposed to be illegal, it has been used.

You should think of imaginative ways to change the price or the costing of the program. I once negotiated to retain the tooling (worth over $10,000) in return for lowering the price by $2,000. Another technique used is not to price out the required set of reprocurement drawings on a research development contract, but to offer the government a free set of drawings coincident with an order for a certain number of units in any one year. This lowers price by several thousand dollars, maybe as much as $10,000 or $20,000 as compared with that of competitors, and at the same time encourages the government to issue a contract at some future date in order to get the free drawings. This is a "win" for both sides, because should the government decide not to go into production, it has saved the cost of the drawings. If winning the present contract will lead to a future contract with big profits later on, you can afford to break even or lose a little money on this contract in order to make more money later.

You should also consider the fact that if you are going after a certain type of development contract for a new product, you are going to go through an improvement in the learning process; you will learn how to make the product faster and better than your competitors can, allowing you lower costs than your competition in the future.

The government market is huge. Once you learn how to locate potential customers in it and how to win government contracts, you are on your way to large sales volumes and big profits. The government market presents special problems, but also special opportunities. If you decide to market your product or service to the government, and if you follow the procedures outlined, you can make a fortune at the same time that you help our government to obtain good products and services.

SOURCES OF ADDITIONAL INFORMATION

Arming America, by J. Ronald Fox, published by Harvard University Press, 79 Garden Street, Cambridge, MA 02138.

The Consultant's Guide to Proposal Writing, by Herman Holtz, published by John Wiley and Sons, Inc., 605 Third Ave., New York, NY 10158.

Government Contracts, by Herman Holtz, published by Plenum Publishing Corp., 227 West 17th Street, New York, NY 10011.

How to Sell to the Government, by William A. Cohen, published by John Wiley and Sons, Inc., 605 Third Ave., New York, NY 10158.

Marketing High Technology, by William L. Shanklin and John K. Ryans, Jr., published by Lexington Books, D.C. Heath and Company, 125 Spring Street, Lexington, MA 02173.

The One Hundred Billion Dollar Market, by Herman Holtz, published by AMACOM, 135 West 50th Street, New York, NY 10020.

Selling to the Military, by the Department of Defense, published by the U.S. Government Printing Office, Washington DC 20402.

Selling to the Federal Government, by Jack W. Robertson, published by McGraw-Hill Book Company, 1221 Avenue of the Americas, New York, NY 10020.

U.S. Government Purchasing and Sales Directory, published by the U.S. Government Printing Office, Washington, DC 20402.

SMALL BUSINESS ADMINISTRATION FIELD OFFICES

REGION	TYPE	CITY	STATE	ZIP CODE	ADDRESS		PHONE
01	RO	BOSTON	MA	02110	60 BATTERYMARCH STREET	10TH FLOOR	(617) 223-3204
01	DO	AUGUSTA	ME	04330	40 WESTERN AVENUE	ROOM 512	(207) 622-8378
01	DO	BOSTON	MA	02114	10 CAUSEWAY STREET	ROOM 265	(617) 565-5590
01	DO	CONCORD	NH	03301	55 PLEASANT STREET	ROOM 210	(603) 225-1400
01	DO	HARTFORD	CT	06106	330 MAIN STREET	2ND FLOOR	(203) 240-4700
01	DO	MONTPELIER	VT	05602	87 STATE STREET	ROOM 205	(802) 828-4474
01	DO	PROVIDENCE	RI	02903	380 WESTMINISTER MALL	5TH FLOOR	(401) 528-4586
01	BO	SPRINGFIELD	MA	01103	1550 MAIN STREET	ROOM 212	(413) 785-0268
02	RO	NEW YORK	NY	10278	26 FEDERAL PLAZA	ROOM 29-118	(212) 264-7772
02	POD	ALBANY	NY	12207	445 BROADWAY	ROOM 242	(518) 472-6300
02	POD	CAMDEN	NJ	08104	2600 MT. EPHRAIM AVE.		(609) 757-5183
02	POD	ROCHESTER	NY	14614	100 STATE STREET	ROOM 601	(716) 263-6700
02	POD	ST. CROIX	VI	00820	4C & 4D ESTE SION FRM	ROOM 7	(809) 773-3480
02	POD	ST. THOMAS	VI	00801	VETERANS DRIVE	ROOM 210	(809) 774-8530
02	DO	HATO REY	PR	00918	CARLOS CHARDON AVE.	ROOM 691	(809) 753-4002
02	DO	NEW YORK	NY	10278	26 FEDERAL PLAZA	ROOM 3100	(212) 264-4355
02	DO	NEWARK	NJ	07102	60 PARK PLACE	4TH FLOOR	(201) 645-2434
02	DO	SYRACUSE	NY	13260	100 S. CLINTON STREET	ROOM 1071	(315) 423-5383
02	BO	BUFFALO	NY	14202	111 W. HURON STREET	ROOM 1311	(716) 846-4301
02	BO	ELMIRA	NY	14901	333 E. WATER STREET	4TH FLOOR	(607) 734-8130
02	BO	MELVILLE	NY	11747	35 PINELAWN ROAD	ROOM 102E	(516) 454-0750
03	RO	PHILADELPHIA	PA	19004	231 ST. ASAPHS ROAD	SUITE 640-W	(215) 596-5889
03	DO	BALTIMORE	MD	21202	10 N. CALVERT STREET	3RD FLOOR	(301) 962-4392
03	DO	CLARKSBURG	WV	26301	168 W. MAIN STREET	5TH FLOOR	(304) 623-5631
03	DO	PHILADELPHIA	PA	19004	231 ST. ASAPHS ROAD	SUITE 400-E	(215) 596-5889
03	DO	PITTSBURGH	PA	15222	960 PENN AVENUE	5TH FLOOR	(412) 644-2780
03	DO	RICHMOND	VA	23240	400 N. 8TH STREET	ROOM 3015	(804) 771-2617
03	DO	WASHINGTON	DC	20036	1111 18TH STREET, NW	6TH FLOOR	(202) 634-4950

RO = REGIONAL OFFICE   DO = DISTRICT OFFICE   BO = BRANCH OFFICE   POD = POST OF DUTY

DAO = DISASTER AREA OFFICE

REGION	TYPE	CITY	STATE	ZIP CODE	ADDRESS		PHONE
03	BO	CHARLESTON	WV	25301	550 EAGAN STREET	SUITE 309	(304) 347-5220
03	BO	HARRISBURG	PA	17101	100 CHESTNUT STREET	SUITE 309	(717) 782-3840
03	BO	WILKES-BARRE	PA	18701	20 N. PENNSYLVANIA AVE.	ROOM 2327	(717) 826-6497
03	BO	WILMINGTON	DE	19801	844 KING STREET	ROOM 5207	(302) 573-6294
04	RO	ATLANTA	GA	30367	1375 PEACHTREE ST., NE	5TH FLOOR	(404) 347-2797
04	POD	STATESBORO	GA	30458	52 N. MAIN STREET	ROOM 225	(912) 489-8719
04	POD	TAMPA	FL	33602	700 TWIGGS STREET	ROOM 607	(813) 228-2594
04	POD	W. PALM BEACH	FL	33407	3500 45TH STREET	SUITE 6	(305) 689-2223
04	DO	ATLANTA	GA	30309	1720 PEACHTREE RD, NW	6TH FLOOR	(404) 347-4749
04	DO	BIRMINGHAM	AL	35203-2398	2121 8TH AVE. N.	SUITE 200	(205) 731-1344
04	DO	CHARLOTTE	NC	28202	222 S. CHURCH STREET	ROOM 300	(704) 371-6563
04	DO	COLUMBIA	SC	29201	1835 ASSEMBLY STREET	ROOM 358	(803) 765-5376
04	DO	CORAL GABLES	FL	33146	1320 S. DIXIE HIGHWAY	SUITE 501	(305) 536-5521
04	DO	JACKSON	MS	39269	110 W. CAPITOL STREET	SUITE 322	(601) 965-0121
04	DO	JACKSONVILLE	FL	32202	400 W. BAY STREET	ROOM 261	(904) 791-3782
04	DO	LOUISVILLE	KY	40202	600 FEDERAL PLACE	ROOM 188	(502) 582-5976
04	DO	NASHVILLE	TN	37219	404 JAMES ROBERTSON PKWY	SUITE 1012	(615) 736-5881
04	BO	GULFPORT	MS	39501	ONE HANCOCK PLAZA	SUITE 1001	(601) 863-4449
05	RO	CHICAGO	IL	60604-1779	230 S. DEARBORN STREET	ROOM 510	(312) 353-0359
05	POD	EAU CLAIRE	WI	54701	500 S. BARSTOW COMMO	ROOM 17	(715) 834-9012
05	DO	CHICAGO	IL	60604-1779	219 S. DEARBORN STREET	ROOM 437	(312) 353-4528
05	DO	CLEVELAND	OH	44199	1240 E. 9TH STREET	ROOM 317	(216) 522-4180
05	DO	COLUMBUS	OH	43215	85 MARCONI BLVD.	ROOM 512	(614) 469-6860
05	DO	DETROIT	MI	48226	477 MICHIGAN AVE.	ROOM 515	(313) 226-6075
05	DO	INDIANAPOLIS	IN	46204	575 N. PENNSYLVANIA ST.	ROOM 578	(317) 269-7272
05	DO	MADISON	WI	53703	212 E. WASHINGTON AVE.	ROOM 213	(608) 264-5261
05	DO	MINNEAPOLIS	MN	55403	100 N. 6TH STREET	SUITE 610	(612) 349-3550
05	BO	CINCINNATI	OH	45202	550 MAIN STREET	ROOM 5028	(513) 684-2814
05	BO	MARQUETTE	MI	49885	300 S. FRONT ST.		(906) 225-1108
05	BO	MILWAUKEE	WI	53203	310 W. WISCONSIN AVE.	ROOM 400	(414) 291-3941
05	BO	SPRINGFIELD	IL	62701	4 N. OLD STATE CAP PLAZA	1ST FLOOR	(217) 492-4416

		City	State	ZIP	Address	Room	Phone
06	RO	DALLAS	TX	75235	8625 KING GEORGE DR.	BLDG. C	(214) 767-7643
06	POD	AUSTIN	TX	78701	300 E. 8TH STREET	ROOM 520	(512) 482-5288
06	POD	MARSHALL	TX	75670	505 E. TRAVIS	ROOM 103	(214) 935-5257
06	POD	SHREVEPORT	LA	71101	500 FANNIN STREET	ROOM 8A08	(318) 226-5196
06	DO	ALBUQUERQUE	NM	87100	5000 MARBLE AVE., NE	ROOM 320	(505) 262-6171
06	DO	DALLAS	TX	75242	1100 COMMERCE STREET	ROOM 3C36	(214) 767-0605
06	DO	EL PASO	TX	79935	10737 GATEWAY W.	SUITE 320	(915) 541-7586
06	DO	HARLINGEN	TX	78550	222 E. VAN BUREN ST.	ROOM 500	(512) 427-8533
06	DO	HOUSTON	TX	77054	2525 MURWORTH	SUITE 112	(713) 660-4401
06	DO	LITTLE ROCK	AR	72201	320 W. CAPITOL AVE.	ROOM 601	(501) 378-5871
06	DO	LUBBOCK	TX	79401	1611 TENTH STREET	SUITE 200	(806) 743-7462
06	DO	NEW ORLEANS	LA	70112	1661 CANAL STREET	SUITE 2000	(504) 589-6685
06	DO	OKLAHOMA CITY	OK	73102	200 N. W. 5TH STREET	SUITE 670	(405) 231-4301
06	DO	SAN ANTONIO	TX	78206	727 E. DURANGO STREET	ROOM A513	(512) 229-6250
06	BO	CORPUS CHRISTI	TX	78401	400 MAIN STREET	SUITE 403	(512) 888-3331
06	BO	FT. WORTH	TX	76102	819 TAYLOR STREET	ROOM 10A27	(817) 334-3613
07	RO	KANSAS CITY	MO	64106	911 WALNUT STREET	13TH FL	(816) 374-5288
07	DO	CEDAR RAPIDS	IA	52402-3118	373 COLLINS ROAD NE	ROOM 100	(319) 399-2571
07	DO	DES MOINES	IA	50309	210 WALNUT STREET	ROOM 749	(515) 284-4422
07	DO	KANSAS CITY	MO	64106	1103 GRAND AVE.	6TH FL	(816) 374-3419
07	DO	OMAHA	NB	68154	11145 MILL VALLEY RD.		(402) 221-4691
07	DO	ST LOUIS	MO	63101	815 OLIVE STREET	ROOM 242	(314) 425-6600
07	DO	WICHITA	KS	67202	110 E. WATERMAN ST.	1ST FLOOR	(316) 269-6571
07	BO	SPRINGFIELD	MO	65805	309 N. JEFFERSON ST.	ROOM 150	(417) 864-7670
08	RO	DENVER	CO	80202	999 18TH STREET	N. TOWER	(303) 294-7001
08	POD	BILLINGS	MT	59101	2601 FIRST AVE. N.	ROOM 216	(406) 657-6047
08	DO	CASPER	WY	82602	100 EAST B. STREET	ROOM 4001	(307) 261-5761
08	DO	DENVER	CO	80202	721 19TH STREET	ROOM 407	(303) 844-2607
08	DO	FARGO	ND	58102	657 2ND AVE. N	ROOM 218	(701) 237-5771
08	DO	HELENA	MT	59626	301 S. PARK	ROOM 528	(406) 449-5381
08	DO	SALT LAKE CITY	UT	84138	125 S. STATE STREET	ROOM 2237	(801) 524-5800
08	DO	SIOUX FALLS	SD	57102	101 S. MAIN AVE.	SUITE 101	(605) 336-2980

REGION	TYPE	CITY	STATE	ZIP CODE	ADDRESS		PHONE
09	RO	SAN FRANCISCO	CA	94102	450 GOLDEN GATE AVE.	ROOM 238	(415) 556-7487
09	POD	RENO	NV	89505	50 S. VIRGINIA ST.	BOX FB-33	(702) 784-5268
09	POD	TUCSON	AZ	85701	300 W. CONGRESS ST.	SUITE 108	(602) 629-6715
09	DO	FRESNO	CA	93721	2202 MONTEREY ST.	ROOM 2213	(209) 487-5189
09	DO	HONOLULU	HI	96850	300 ALA MOANA	ROOM 301	(808) 541-2990
09	DO	LAS VEGAS	NV	89125	301 E. STEWART ST.	6TH FLOOR	(702) 388-6611
09	DO	LOS ANGELES	CA	90071	350 S. FIGUEROA ST.	5TH FLOOR	(213) 894-2956
09	DO	PHOENIX	AZ	85004	2005 N. CENTRAL AVE.	ROOM 4S29	(602) 261-3732
09	DO	SAN DIEGO	CA	92188	880 FRONT STREET	4TH FLOOR	(619) 293-5440
09	DO	SAN FRANCISCO	CA	94105	211 MAIN STREET	ROOM 508	(415) 974-0642
09	BO	AGANA	GM	96910	PACIFIC DAILY NEWS BLD	ROOM 215	(671) 472-7277
09	BO	SACRAMENTO	CA	95814	660 J STREET	ROOM 400	(916) 551-1445
09	BO	SANTA ANA	CA	92701	2700 N. MAIN STREET		(714) 836-2494
10	RO	SEATTLE	WA	98121	2615 4TH AVENUE	ROOM 440	(206) 442-5676
10	DO	ANCHORAGE	AK	99513	8TH & C STREETS		(907) 271-4022
10	DO	BOISE	ID	83702	1020 MAIN STREET	SUITE 290	(208) 334-1696
10	DO	PORTLAND	OR	97204	1220 S. W. THIRD AVE.	ROOM 676	(503) 423-5221
10	DO	SEATTLE	WA	98174	915 SECOND AVE.	ROOM 1792	(206) 442-5534
10	DO	SPOKANE	WA	99201	W. 920 RIVERSIDE AVE.	ROOM 651	(509) 456-3783
CO	DAO1	FAIRLAWN	NJ	07410	15-01 BROADWAY	1ST FLOOR	(201) 794-8195
CO	DAO2	ATLANTA	GA	30308	120 RALPH McGILL ST.	14TH FLOOR	(404) 347-3771
CO	DAO3	GRAND PRAIRIE	TX	75051	2306 OAK LANE	SUITE 110	(214) 767-7571
CO	DAO4	SACRAMENTO	CA	95853	77 CADILLAC DRIVE	SUITE 158	(916) 978-4578

BETTER BUSINESS BUREAUS

National Headquarters

Council of Better Business Bureaus, Inc., 1515 Wilson Boulevard, Suite 300, Arlington, VA 22209; (703) 276-0100.

Local Bureaus

Alabama

1214 South 20th Street, **Birmingham**, AL 35205; (205) 933-2893.

P.O. Box 383, **Huntsville**, AL 35804; (205) 533-1640.

707 Van Antwerp Building, **Mobile**, AL 36602; (205) 433-5494, 5495.

Union Bank Building, Commerce Street, Suite 810, **Montgomery**, AL 36104; (205) 262-5606.

Alaska

3380 C Street, Suite 100, **Anchorage**, AK 99503; (907) 562-0704.

Arizona

4428 North 12th Street, **Phoenix**, AZ 85014; (602) 264-1721.

50 West Drachman Street, Suite 103, **Tuscon**, AZ 85705; (602) 622-7651 (inquiries), (602) 622-7654 (complaints).

Arkansas

1216 South University, **Little Rock**, AR 72204; (501) 664-7274.

California

705 Eighteenth Street, **Bakersfield**, CA 93301; (805) 322-2074.

290 North 10th Street, Suite 206, **Colton**, CA 92324; (714) 825-7280.

5070 North Sixth, Suite 176, **Fresno**, CA 93710; (209) 222-8111.

639 South New Hampshire Avenue, 3rd Floor, **Los Angeles**, CA 90005; (213) 383-0992.

508 16th Street, Room 1500, **Oakland**, CA 94612; (415) 839-5900.

400 S Street, **Sacramento**, CA 95814; (916) 443-6843.

Union Bank Building, Suite 301, 525 B Street, **San Diego**, CA 92101; (619) 234-0966.

2740 Van Ness Avenue, #210, **San Francisco**, CA 94109; (415) 775-3300.

P.O. Box 8110, **San Jose**, CA 95155; (408) 978-8700.

20 North San Mateo Drive, P.O. Box 294, **San Mateo**, CA 94401; (415) 347-1251.

P.O. Box 746, **Santa Barbara**, CA 93102; (805) 963-8657.

1111 North Center Street, **Stockton**, CA 95202; (209) 948-4880, 4881.

17662 Irvine Boulevard, Suite 15, **Tustin**, CA 92680; (714) 544-6942.

Colorado

P.O. Box 7970, **Colorado Springs**, CO 80933; (303) 636-1155.

1780 South Bellaire, Suite 700, **Denver**, CO 80222; (303) 758-8200.

140 West Oak Street, **Fort Collins**, CO 80524; (303) 484-1348.

113 West 4th Street, **Pueblo**, CO 81003; (303) 542-6464.

Connecticut

Fairfield Woods Plaza, 2345 Black Rock Turnpike, **Fairfield**, CT 06430; (203) 374-6161.

630 Oakwood Avenue, Suite 223, **West Hartford**, CT 06110; (203) 247-8700.

100 South Turnpike Road, **Wallingford**, CT 06492; (203) 269-2700 (inquiries), (203) 269-4457 (complaints).

Delaware

20 South Walnut Street, P.O. Box 300, **Milford**, DE 19963; (302) 856-6969 (Sussex), (302) 422-6300 (Kent).

2055 Limestone Road, Suite 200, **Wilmington**, DE 19808; (302) 652-3833.

District of Columbia

1012 14th Street, N.W., 14th Floor, **Washington**, DC 20005; (202) 393-8000.

Florida

13770 58th Street North, Suite 309, **Clearwater**, FL 34620; (813) 535-5522.

3089 Cleveland Avenue, **Fort Myers**, FL 33901; (813) 334-7331, (813) 597-1322 (Naples).

16291 North West 57th Avenue, **Miami**, FL 33014; (305) 625-1302 (complaints).

608 Gulf Drive West, Suite 3, **New Port Richey**, FL 33552; (813) 842-5459, (904) 683-6060 (Hernando), (813) 782-4151 (E. Pasco).

132 East Colonial Drive, Suite 213, **Orlando**, FL 32801; (305) 843-8873.

210 Intendencia Street, **Pensacola**, FL 32501; (904) 433-6111.

3015 Exchange Court, **West Palm Beach**, FL 33409; (305) 686-2200.

Georgia

100 Edgewood Avenue, Suite 1012, **Atlanta**, GA 30303; (404) 688-4910 (inquiries), (404) 688-2380 (complaints).

P.O. Box 2085, **Augusta**, GA 30903; (404) 722-1574.

8 13th Street, **Columbus**, GA 31901; (404) 324-0712, 0713.

P.O. Box 13956, **Savannah**, GA 31416; (912) 354-7521.

Hawaii

1600 Kapiolani Boulevard, Suite 714, **Honolulu**, HI 96813; (808) 942-2355.

Idaho

409 West Jefferson, **Boise**, ID 83702; (208) 342-4649.

Illinois

211 West Wacker Drive, **Chicago**, IL 60606; (312) 444-1188 (inquiries), (312) 346-3313 (complaints).

109 Southwest Jefferson Street, Suite 305, **Peoria**, IL 61602; (309) 673-5194.

Indiana

118 South Second Street, **Elkhart**, IN 46516; (219) 293-5731.

113 Southeast Fourth Street, **Evansville**, IN 47708; (812) 422-6879.

1203 Webster Street, **Fort Wayne**, IN 46802; (219) 423-4433.

4231 Cleveland Street, **Gary**, IN 46408; (219) 980-1511.

Victoria Centre, 22 East Washington Street, Suite 310, **Indianapolis**, IN 46204; (317) 637-0197.

204 Iroquois Building, **Marion**, IN 46952; (317) 668-8954.

Ball State University BBB, Whitinger Building, Room 160, **Muncie**, IN 47306; (317) 285-5668.

50985 U.S. #33, North, **South Bend**, IN 46637; (219) 277-9121.

Iowa

Alpine Centre, 2435 Kimberly Road, Suite 110 N, **Bettendorf**, IA 52722; (319) 355-6344.

1500 2nd Avenue, S.E., Suite 212, **Cedar Rapids**, IA 52403; (319) 366-5401.

615 Insurance Exchange Building, **Des Moines**, IA 50309; (515) 243-8137.

318 Badgerow Building, **Sioux City**, IA 51101; (712) 252-4501.

Kansas

501 Jefferson, Suite 24, **Topeka**, KS 66607; (913) 232-0455.

300 Kaufman Building, **Wichita**, KS 67202; (316) 263-3146.

Kentucky

629 North Broadway, **Lexington**, KY 40508; (606) 252-4492.

844 South Fourth Street, **Louisville**, KY 40203; (502) 583-6546.

Louisiana

1407 Murray Street, Suite 101, **Alexandria**, LA 71301; (318) 473-4494.

2055 Wooddale Boulevard, **Baton Rouge**, LA 70806; (504) 926-3010.

300 Bond Street, **Houma**, LA 70360; (504) 868-3456.

800 Jefferson Street, **Lafayette**, LA 70501; (318) 234-8341.

1413 Ryan Street, Suite C, P.O. Box 1681, **Lake Charles**, LA 70602; (318) 433-1633.

141 De Siard Street, Suite 114, **Monroe**, LA 71201; (318) 387-4600.

301 Camp Street, Suite 403, **New Orleans**, LA 70130; (504) 581-6222.

1401 North Market Street, **Shreveport**, LA 71107; (318) 221-8352.

Maine

812 Stevens Avenue, **Portland**, ME 04103; (207) 878-2715.

Maryland

401 North Howard Street, **Baltimore**, MD 21201; (301) 347-3990.

11426 Rockville Pike, Suite 301, **Rockville**, MD 20852; (301) 468-3405.

Massachusetts

8 Winter Street, 6th Floor, **Boston**, MA 02108; (617) 482-9151 (inquiries), (617) 482-9190 (complaints).

106 State Road, Suite 4, **Dartmouth**, MA 02747; (617) 999-6060.

1 Kendall Street, Suite 307, **Framingham**, MA 01701; (617) 872-5585.

The Federal Building, Suite 1, 78 North Street, **Hyannis**, MA 02601; (617) 771-3022.

316 Essex Street, **Lawrence**, MA 01840; (617) 687-7666.

293 Bridge Street, Suite 324, **Springfield**, MA 01103; (413) 734-3114.

32 Franklin Street, **Worcester**, MA 01608; (617) 755-2548.

Michigan

150 Michigan Avenue, **Detroit**, MI 48226; (313) 962-7566.

620 Trust Building, **Grand Rapids**, MI 49503; (616) 774-8236.

Minnesota

1745 University Avenue, **St. Paul**, MN 55104; (612) 646-7700 (inquiries), (612) 646-4631 (complaints).

Mississippi

2917 West Beach Boulevard, Suite 103, **Biloxi**, MS 39531; (601) 374-2222.

105 Fifth Avenue, **Columbus**, MS 39701; (601) 327-8594.

1201 West Pine Street #4, **Hattiesburg**, MS 39401; (601) 582-0116.

P.O. Box 2090, **Jackson**, MS 39225; (601) 948-8222.

601 22nd Avenue, Suite 313, **Meridian**, MS 39301; (601) 482-8752.

Missouri

306 East 12th Street, Suite 1024, **Kansas City**, MO 64106; (816) 421-7800.

5100 Oakland, Suite 200, **St. Louis**, MO 63110; (314) 531-3300 (inquiries).

205 Park Central East, Room 312, **Springfield**, MO 65806; (417) 862-9231.

Montana

Does not have a local Better Business Bureau.

Nebraska

719 North 48th Street, **Lincoln**, NE 68504; (402) 467-5261.

417 Farnam Building, 1613 Farnam Street, **Omaha**, NE 68102; (402) 346-3033.

Nevada

1829 East Charleston Boulevard, Suite 103, **Las Vegas**, NV 89104; (702) 382-7141.

372-A Casazza Drive, **Reno**, NV 89502; (702) 322-0657.

New Hampshire

One Pillsbury Street, **Concord**, NH 03301; (603) 224-1991.

New Jersey

690 Whitehead Road, **Lawrenceville**, NJ 08648; (609) 396-1199 (Mercer County); (201) 536-6306 (Monmouth County); (201) 329-6855 (Middlesex, Somerset and Hunderton counties).

34 Park Place, **Newark**, NJ 07102; (201) 643-3025.

2 Forest Avenue, **Paramus**, NJ 07652; (201) 845-4044.

1721 Route 37 East, **Toms River**, NJ 08753; (201) 270-5577.

16 Maple Avenue, Box 303, **Westmont**, NJ 08108; (609) 854-8467.

New Mexico

4600-A Montgomery, N.E., Suite 200, **Albuquerque**, NM 87109; (505) 884-0500.

308 North Locke, **Farmington**, NM 87401; (505) 326-6501.

1210 Luisa Street, Suite 5, **Santa Fe**, NM 87502; (505) 988-3648.

New York

775 Main Street, Suite 401, **Buffalo**, NY 14203; (716) 856-7180.

266 Main Street, **Farmingdale**, NY 11735; (516) 420-0500.

257 Park Avenue, South, **New York**, NY 10010; (212) 533-6200.

1122 Sibley Tower, **Rochester**, NY 14604; (716) 546-6776.

200 University Building, **Syracuse**, NY 13202; (315) 479-6635.

258 Genesee Street, **Utica**, NY 13502; (315) 724-3129.

120 East Main, **Wappinger Falls**, NY 12590; (914) 297-6550.

One Brockway Place, **White Plains**, NY 10601; (914) 428-1230.

North Carolina

29½ Page Avenue, **Asheville**, NC 28801; (704) 253-2392.

1130 East 3rd Street, Suite 400, **Charlotte**, NC 28204; (704) 332-7151.

3608 West Friendly Avenue, **Greensboro**, NC 27410; (919) 852-4240, (919) 889-4297 (High Point).

P.O. Box 425, **Newton**, NC 28658; (704) 464-0372.

3120 Poplarwood Drive, Suite G-1, **Raleigh**, NC 27604; (919) 872-9240.

2110 Cloverdale Avenue, Suite 2-B, **Winston-Salem**, NC 27103; (919) 725-8348.

Ohio

P.O. Box 596, **Akron**, OH 44308; (216) 253-4590.

1434 Cleveland Avenue, North, **Canton**, OH 44703; (216) 454-9401.

898 Walnut Street, **Cincinnati**, OH 45202; (513) 421-3015.

2217 East 9th Street, **Cleveland**, OH 44115; (216) 241-7678.

527 South High Street, **Columbus**, OH 43215; (614) 221-6336.

40 West Fourth Street, Suite 280, **Dayton**, OH 45402; (513) 222-5825.

P.O. Box 1706, **Mansfield**, OH 44901; (419) 522-1700.

425 Jefferson Avenue, Suite 909, **Toledo**, OH 43604; (419) 241-6276.

311 Mahoning Bank Building, P.O. Box 1495, **Youngstown**, OH 44501; (216) 744-3111.

Oklahoma

17 South Dewey, **Oklahoma City**, OK 73102; (405) 239-6081, (405) 239-6083 (complaints).

4833 South Sheridan, Suite 412, **Tulsa**, OK 74145; (918) 664-1266.

Oregon

520 South West 6th Avenue, Suite 600, **Portland**, OR 97204; (503) 226-3981.

Pennsylvania

528 North New Street, **Bethlehem**, PA 18018; (215) 866-8780.

53 North Duke Street, **Lancaster**, PA 17602; (717) 291-1151, (717) 232-2800 (Harrisburg), (717) 846-2700 (York County).

511 North Broad Street, **Philadelphia**, PA 19123; (215) 574-3600.

610 Smithfield Street, **Pittsburgh**, PA 15222; (412) 456-2700.

601 Connell Building, 6th Floor, **Scranton**, PA 18503; (717) 342-9129.

Puerto Rico

GPO Box 70212, **San Juan**, PR 00936; (809) 756-5400.

Rhode Island

270 Weybosset Street, **Providence**, RI 02903; (401) 272-9800 (inquiries), (401) 272-9802 (complaints).

South Carolina

1338 Main Street, Suite 500, **Columbia**, SC 29201; (803) 254-2525.

311 Pettigru Street, **Greenville**, SC 29601; (803) 242-5052.

Tennessee

1010 Market Street, Suite 200, **Chattanooga**, TN 37402; (615) 266-6144.

P.O. 3608, **Knoxville**, TN 37927; (615) 522-1300.

1835 Union, Suite 312, **Memphis**, TN 38104; (901) 272-9641.

506 Nashville City, Bank Building, **Nashville**, TN 37201; (615) 254-5872.

Texas

Bank of Commerce Building, Suite 320, **Abilene**, TX 79605; (915) 691-1533.

1008 West 10th, **Amarillo**, TX 79101; (806) 374-3735.

1005 M Bank Plaza, **Austin**, TX 78701; (512) 476-6943.

P.O. Box 2988, **Beaumont**, TX 77704; (409) 835-5348.

202 Varisco Building, **Bryan**, TX 77803; (409) 823-8148, 8149.

109 North Chapparal, Suite 101, **Corpus Christi**, TX 78401; (512) 888-5555.

2001 Bryan Street, Suite 850, **Dallas**, TX 75201; (214) 220-2000.

6024 Gateway East, Suite 1-C, **El Paso**, TX 79905; (915) 778-7000.

709 Sinclair Building, 106 West 5th Street, **Fort Worth**, TX 76102; (817) 332-7585.

2707 North Loop West, Suite 900, **Houston**, TX 77008; (713) 868-9500.

1015 15th Street, **Lubbock**, TX 97408; (806) 763-0459.

Airport 20 Road, P.O. Box 6006, **Midland**, TX 79711; (915) 563-1880, (915) 563-1881 (complaints).

115 South Randolph, **San Angelo**, TX 76903; (915) 653-2318.

1800 Northeast Loop 410, Suite 400, **San Antonio**, TX 78217; (512) 828-9441.

6801 Sanger, Suite 125, **Waco**, TX 76710; (817) 772-7530.

P.O. Box 69, **Weslaco**, TX 78596; (512) 968-3678.

1106 Brook Avenue, **Wichita Falls**, TX 76301; (817) 723-5526.

Utah

385 24th Street, Suite 717, **Ogden**, UT 84401; (801) 399-4701.

1588 South Main Street, **Salt Lake City**, UT 84115; (801) 487-4656.

Virginia

105 East Annandale Road, Suite 210, **Falls Church**, VA 22046; (703) 533-1900.

2019 Llewellyn Avenue, P.O. Box 11133, **Norfolk**, VA 23517; (804) 627-5651, (804) 851-9101 (Peninsula area).

701 East Franklin Street, Suite 712, **Richmond**, VA 23219; (804) 648-0016.

151 W. Campbell Avenue, S.W., **Roanoke**, VA 24011; (703) 342-3455.

Washington

127 West Canal Drive, **Kennewick**, WA 99336; (509) 582-0222.

2200 Sixth Avenue, **Seattle**, WA 98121; (206) 448-8888.

South 176 Stevens, **Spokane**, WA 99204; (509) 747-1155.

1101 Fawcett Avenue, #222, **Tacoma**, WA 98402; (206) 383-5561.

P.O. Box 1584, **Yakima**, WA 98907; (509) 248-1326.

Wisconsin

740 North Plankinton Avenue, **Milwaukee**, WI 53203; (414) 273-1600.

Wyoming

Does not have a local Better Business Bureau.

TRADE ASSOCIATIONS

Ms. Suzanne Comer, Public Relations, **American Ambulance Association**, 1800 K Street N.W., Suite 1105, Washington, DC 20006; (202) 887-5144. Membership: Private providers of pre-hospital medical care and medical transportation.

Ms. Ann Lawrence, Director, Education and Conventions, **American Apparel Manufacturers Association**, 2500 Wilson Boulevard, Suite 301, Arlington, VA 22201; (703) 524-1864. Membership: Manufacturers of wearing apparel.

Public Relations Director, **American Arbitration Association**, 140 West 51st Street, New York, NY 10020; (212) 484-4006. Membership: Arbitrators.

American Automobile Association, 8111 Gatehouse Road, Room 535, Falls Church, VA 22047; (703) 222-6446. Membership: Federation of automobile clubs.

Mr. David Peterson, Director of Public Relations, **American Collectors Association**, 4040 West 70th Street, P.O. Box 35106, Minneapolis, MN 55435; (612) 926-6547. Membership: Collection services handling overdue accounts for retail, professional, and commercial credit grantors.

Information Department, **American Council of Life Insurance/Health Insurance Association of America**, 1001 Pennsylvania Avenue, N.W., Washington, DC 20004 (written inquiries only). Membership: Life, accident, and health insurance companies authorized to do business in the United States.

Ms. Jane Marden, Director, Consumer Affairs, Ms. Lisa Hill Williams, Director, Community Affairs, **American Gas Association**, 1515 Wilson Boulevard, Arlington, VA 22209; (703) 841-8583. Membership: Distributors and transporters of natural, manufactured, and liquified gas.

American Health Care Association, 1200 15th Street, N.W., Washington, DC 20005; (202) 833-2050. Membership: Federation of state associations of long-term health care facilities.

American Hotel and Motel Association, 888 Seventh Avenue, New York, NY 10106 (written inquiries only). Membership: Federation of state and regional hotel associations.

Mr. Herb Finkston, Director, Professional Ethics, **American Institute of Certified Public Accountants**, 1211 Avenue of the Americas, New York, NY 10036; (212) 575-6209. Membership: Professional society of accountants certified by the states and territories.

Mr. Ray Greenly, Director, Consumer Affairs, **American Society of Travel Agents, Inc.**, P.O. Box 23992, Washington, DC 20026; (703) 739-2782. Membership: Travel agents.

Mr. James A. Morrissey, Director, Communications Division, **American Textile Manufacturers Institute**, 1101 Connecticut Avenue, N.W., Suite 300, Washington, DC 20036; (202) 862-0552. Membership: Textile mills operating machinery for the manufacturing and processing of cotton, man-made, wool, and silk textile products.

National Administrator, **Automotive Consumer Action Program (AUTOCAP)**, 8400 Westpark Drive, McLean, VA 22102; (703) 821-7000. Third-party dispute resolution program administered through the National Automotive Dealers Association.

BBB Auto Line, Council of Better Business Bureaus, 1515 Wilson Boulevard, Arlington, VA 22209; (703) 276-0100. Third-party dispute resolution program for AMC, Audi, General Motors and its divisions, Honda, Jeep, Nissan, Peugeot, Porsche, Renault, SAAB, and Volkswagen.

BBB National Consumer Arbitration Program, Council of Better Business Bureaus, 1515 Wilson Boulevard, Arlington, VA 22209; (703) 276-0100. Third-party dispute resolution.

Better Hearing Institute, P.O. Box 1840, Washington, DC 20013; (703) 642-0580, (800) EAR-WELL. Membership: Professionals and others dedicated to helping persons with impaired hearing.

Consumer Affairs, **Blue Cross and Blue Shield Association**, 1709 New York Avenue, N.W., Suite 303, Washington, DC 20006; (202) 783-6222. Membership: Local Blue Cross and Blue Shield plans in the United States, Canada, and Jamaica.

Mr. Richard N. Hopper, Director of Governmental Affairs, **Carpet and Rug Institute**, 1100 17th Street, N.W., Washington, DC 20036 (written inquiries only). Membership: Manufacturers of carpets, rugs, bath mats, and bedspreads; suppliers of raw materials and services to the industry.

Mr. Robert M. Fells, Assistant Secretary, **Cemetery Consumer Service Council**, P.O. Box 3574, Washington, DC 20007; (703) 379-6426. Council members: The American Cemetery Association, Cremation Association of North America, and the Pre-Arrangement of Interment Association of America.

Chrysler Customer Arbitration Board, P.O. Box 1718, Detroit, MI 48288; (313) 956-5970.

Ms. Lorna Christie, Director, Ethics and Consumer Affairs, **Direct Marketing Association**, 6 East 43rd Street, New York, NY 10017 (written complaints only). Membership: Members who market goods and services directly to consumers using direct mail, catalogs, telemarketing, magazine and newspaper ads, and broadcast advertising.

Mr. William Rogal, Code Administrator, **Direct Selling Association**, 1776 K Street, N.W., Suite 600, Washington, DC 20006; (202) 293-5760. Membership: Manufacturers and distributors selling consumer products door-to-door and through home-party plans.

Ms. Mary Ann Bernald, Manager, Consumer Affairs, **Edison Electric Institute**, 1111 19th Street, N.W., Washington, DC 20036; (202) 778-6560. Membership: Investor-owned electric utility companies operating in the United States.

Ms. Sally Browne, Executive Director, Consumer Affairs, **Electronic Industries Association**, Consumer Electronics Group, 2001 Eye Street, N.W., Washington, DC 20006; (202) 457-4977. Membership: Manufacturers of electronic parts, tubes, and solid state components; radio, television and video systems; audio equipment; and communications electronic products.

Ford Consumer Appeals Board, P.O. Box 1805, Dearborn, MI 48126; (313) 337-6950, (800) 241-8450 (toll free outside Michigan).

Funeral Service Consumer Action Program (ThanaCAP), 11121 West Oklahoma Avenue, Milwaukee, WI 53227; (414) 541-2500. Third-party dispute resolution program sponsored by the National Funeral Directors Association.

Ms. Nancy High, Executive Director, **Furniture Industry Consumer Action Panel (FICAP)**, HP-7, High Point, NC 27261 (written inquiries only). Third-party dispute resolution program affiliated with the American Furniture Manufacturers Association.

Ms. Carole M. Rogin, Director, Market Development, **Hearing Industries Association**, 1255 23rd Street, N.W., Washington, DC 20037; (202) 833-1411. Membership: Companies engaged in the manufacture and/or sale of electronic hearing aids, their components, parts, and related products and services on a national basis.

Home Owners Warranty Program (HOW), 2000 L Street, N.W., Washington, DC 20036, (800) 241-9260 (Eastern zone), (800) 433-7657 (Western zone). Third-party dispute resolution program for new homes built by HOW-member home builders.

Director, Consumer Affairs, **Insurance Information Institute**, 110 William Street, New York, NY 10038; (212) 669-9200 (call collect in New York), (800) 221-4954 (toll free outside New York). Membership: Property and liability insurance companies.

Consumer Affairs Department, **International Airline Passengers Association**, P.O. Box 660074, Dallas, TX 75266; (214) 520-1070. Membership: Persons who are frequent users of airlines.

National Headquarters, **International Association for Financial Planning**, 2 Concourse Parkway, Suite 800, Atlanta, GA 30328; (800) 241-2148. Membership: Individuals involved in financial planning.

Mr. Jack C. Thompson, Director, Subscription Inquiry Service, **Magazine Publishers Association**, 575 Lexington Avenue, New York, NY 10022; (212) 752-0055 (written complaints only). Membership: Publishers of 1,000 consumer and other magazines issued not less than 4 times a year.

Major Appliance Consumer Action Panel (MACAP), 20 North Wacker Drive, Chicago, IL 60606; (312) 984-5858, (800) 621-0477 (toll free outside Illinois). Third-party dispute resolution program of the major appliance industry.

Mr. John E. Dianis, Executive Vice President, **Monument Builders of North America**, 1612 Central Street, Evanston, IL 60201; (312) 869-2031. Membership: Monument retailers, manufacturers, and wholesalers; bronze manufacturers and suppliers.

Mr. Scott H. McCleary, Consumer Affairs Coordinator, **Mortgage Bankers Association of America**, 1125 15th Street, N.W., 7th Floor, Washington, DC 20005; (202) 861-6583. Membership: Principal lending and investor interests in the mortgage finance field, including mortgage banking firms, commercial banks, life insurance companies, title companies, and savings and loan associations.

Multi-Door Dispute Resolution Program, District of Columbia Courthouse, Room C-500, 500 Indiana Avenue, N.W., Washington, DC 20001; (202) 879-1549 (DC residents only).

National Advertising Division (NAD), Council of Better Business Bureaus, 845 Third Avenue, New York, NY 10022; (212) 754-1320. Program: Handles complaints about fraudulent and deceptive advertising.

Mr. William Young, Director, Consumer Affairs/Public Liaison, **National Association of Home Builders**, 15th and M Streets, N.W., Washington, DC 20005; (202) 822-0409, 1 (800) 368-5242 (toll free outside District of Columbia). Membership: Single and multi-family home builders, commercial builders, and others associated with the building industry.

National Association of Personnel Consultants, 1432 Duke Street, Alexandria, VA 22314; (703) 684-0180. Membership: Private employment agencies.

Consumer Arbitration Center, **National Association of Securities Dealers, Inc.**, Two World Trade Center South Tower, 98th Floor, New York City, NY 10048; (212) 839-6251. Third-party dispute resolution for complaints about over-the-counter stocks and corporate bonds.

Accrediting Commission, **National Association of Trade & Technical Schools**, 2251 Wisconsin Avenue, N.W., Washington, DC 20007; (202) 333-1021 (written inquiries only). Membership: Private schools providing occupational training.

Mr. Lawrence Graham, Consumer Affairs, **National Food Processors Association**, 1401 New York Avenue, N.W., Washington, DC 20005; (202) 639-5939. Membership: Commercial packers of food products, such as fruit, vegetables, meats, seafood, and canned, frozen, dehydrated, pickled, and other preserved food items.

Ms. Deb Deutsch, Manager, Compliance, **National Futures Association**, 200 West Madison Street, Chicago, IL 60606; (312) 781-1410, (800) 621-3570 (toll free outside Illinois). Membership: Futures commission merchants; commodity trading advisors; commodity pool operators; brokers and associated individuals.

Ms. Paula Smith, Assistant to Executive Director, **National Home Study Council**, 1601 18th Street, N.W., Washington, DC 20009 (written inquiries only). Membership: Home study (correspondence) schools.

National Tire Dealers and Retreaders Association, 1250 Eye Street, N.W., Suite 400, Washington, DC 20005; (202) 789-2300. Membership: Independent tire dealers and retreaders.

Department of Consumer Affairs, **National Turkey Federation**, 11319 Sunset Hills Road, Reston, VA 22090 (written inquiries only). Membership: Turkey growers, turkey hatcheries, turkey breeders, processors, marketers, and allied industry firms and poultry distributors.

Mr. Craig Halverson, Assistant Executive Director of Industry, Services and Communications, **Photo Marketing Association**, 3000 Picture Place, Jackson, MI 42901 (written complaints only). Membership: Retailers of photo equipment, film, and supplies; firms developing and printing film.

Ms. Mildred Gallik, Director of Consumer Affairs, **The Soap and Detergent Association**, 475 Park Avenue South, New York, NY 10016; (212) 725-1262. Membership: Manufacturers of soap, detergents, fatty acids, and glycerine; raw materials suppliers.

Ms. Diane Cardinale, Assistant Communications Director, **Toy Manufacturers of America**, 200 Fifth Avenue, Room 740, New York, NY 10010; (212) 675-1141. Membership: American toy manufacturers.

Mr. Robert E. Whitley, President, **U.S. Tour Operators Association (USTOA)**, 211 East 51st Street, Suite 12-B, New York, NY 10022; (212) 944-5727. Membership: Wholesale tour operators, common carriers, suppliers, and purveyors of travel services.

UPSTART COMPUTERS: A SAMPLE MARKETING PLAN

Developed by:
Carl Barbata
Jimmy Blanco
Bang Dam
Maria Hynes
Frank Miller
Used with permission of the authors.

TABLE OF CONTENTS

EXECUTIVE SUMMARY

A. Background

The computer revolution has finally arrived at home. No longer used just to play games, small and powerful computers are now being utilized at home for other purposes. Advanced technical knowledge is no longer a requirement. Instead, affordable and powerful combinations of hardware and software allow individuals to access applications at home previously reserved for mainframe computers.

The widespread use of personal computers at home can be attributed to their increased employment in the business world. The use of these machines in the business world has dramatically increased in the last six years, taking away from the mainframe dominance. As a result, personal computer knowledge is now required of existing and potential employees. Graduating students are expected to have computer knowledge when they enter the work force. Undergraduate students are also required to use personal computers for the completion of school assignments.

Hectic business deadlines sometimes force employees to take home unfinished work, many times borrowing a portable computer from the office. Employees quickly find out that with the use of the proper hardware/software combination their productivity increases.

These and other factors have created a need for individuals to want to have their own computers at home. As with other consumer products, an increase in demand has led to a dramatic drop in prices. As prices decrease, more individuals can afford to own a personal computer.

Once individuals make the commitment to purchase their own systems, misconceptions abound. Many think of these machines as magical tools, with high expectations of what they can do. Reality presents a different picture. While it is true that to run many software packages one does not need to be technically proficient, it is also true that these machines are far away from the myth of "plug them and run them." First-time users are often discouraged to find out that starting to use a personal computer is not as intuitive and easy as expected. Furthermore, choosing the most appropriate type of software to purchase is just as hard a task as installing the package and using it. Add to these the lack of technical knowledge of many of the dealers that sell this equipment and/or a poor attitude toward novice users, and we can easily see why the number of home computer users has not increased as dramatically as that of users of other products, such as VCRs, after a few years of availability.

B. Objective

It is the objective of this company to market the Upstart® system, a product that will provide first time computer buyers with the best combination of hardware, software, and technical support to make their first purchase a pleasant experience. This will allow us to:

- Gain a **23.5%** share of the market
- Earn **18.54%** return on initial investment
- Achieve **$6.24** million on sales the first year
- Achieve thereafter **28.5%** growth through sales and good service

C. Scope and Limitations

The purpose of this marketing plan is to act as a road map to Upstart® Computers in their quest for the marketing of a new personal computing solution.

Research was limited to secondary research sources and the personal experience of the team members in the industry.

Because of time constraints, the implementation of this plan is initially limited to five cities in the San Gabriel Valley and it contains only a three-year projection. Computer technology is undergoing rapid and constant changes, thus making a long-term plan unrealistic to attain. After three years, all findings will be evaluated and any necessary adjustments made. A long-term marketing plan for other areas in Southern California will then be developed.

SITUATIONAL ANALYSIS

A. Situational Environment

The market for personal computers is continuously growing. Of the $72.7 billion spent on personal computers in 1987, $10.5 billion was spent for home use (*Statistical Abstract*, 1989). It is estimated that by 1992 personal computers will account for over 80% of all computers in use (McCrossen, 1989), with over $250 billion in sales (See Figures 1–3).

According to 1984 U.S. Census Bureau statistics, "Ownership of a home computer was most likely (22.9 percent) in households with yearly incomes of $50,000 or more." Households with school-age children were three times as likely as those without children to own a computer. The average age of ownership was in the range of 35 to 44 years. This is due in part to the fact that "Persons in the 35–44 age group are among the more likely to have children" (U.S. Census, 1984). The *Los Angeles Times* (1984) reported that people with personal computers in Los Angeles County had a household income of $35,000 or more.

Recent demographic studies (REZIDE, CACI, U.S. Census) have shown that personal computer use was highest among white, male, and single individuals. In addition to these characteristics, it was determined that persons working full-time

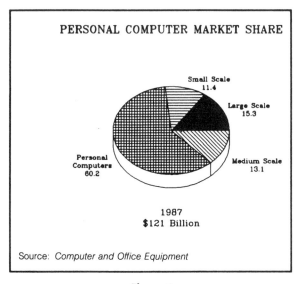

Figure 1

in managerial/professional and technical/sales occupations as well as in the finance, insurance, and real estate industries were more likely to own a personal computer (U.S. Census, 1984). Furthermore, of the personal computer owners in Los Angeles County, 61.1 percent were employed as professionals/managers (*L.A. Times*, 1984), and 50.3 percent of the household heads had a college degree.

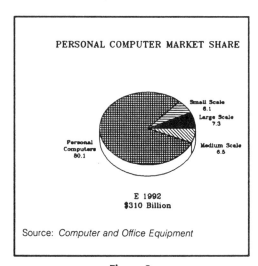

Figure 2

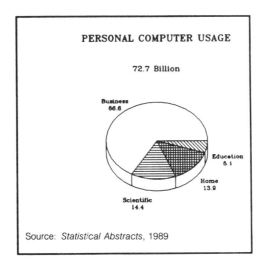

Figure 3

From statistics published by the U.S. Census (1984), of individuals using home computers, the following categories provided these percentages of various uses (see Figure 4);

■ Games	45.0%
■ Learning to use this technology	59.0%
■ Household record keeping	40.2%
■ Job related activities	36.6%
■ Word processing	32.9%

B. The Neutral Environment

The personal computer business is a relatively new business dominated by American, Japanese, and Chinese companies. Because it is still considered a new business, the financial institutions, government, media, and special interest groups are constantly changing their views toward it.

1. Financial Environment

Despite climbing interest rates and fears of inflation, the economy remains strong enough to resist recession. Consumers continue to spend because of higher wages and benefits. The increase in wages is largely seen in the service sector, where all new jobs are created (Cooper and Madigan, 1989). This trend is clearly apparent in the San Gabriel Valley, where small

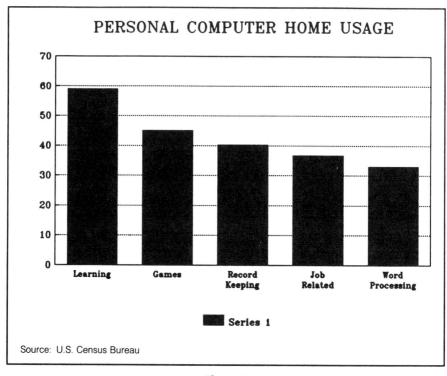

Figure 4

businesses continue to grow and the sales of homes to flourish, factors that provide for constantly changing demographics.

In addition to this growth, easier credit policies and lower interest rates make more money available to borrowers. The prime rate is down from 10.50 percent a year ago to ten percent. According to Kahan (1989), inflation will "remain relatively stable in the neighborhood of 4 percent" and the slowing pace of economic activity and favorable price behavior will push interest rates lower, therefore attracting borrowers.

2. Government Environment

Because of the intensive research nature of this industry, protecting intellectual property rights, through the use of patents, trademarks, and copyrights, is critical. Many application software and microcomputer systems are easily copied and counterfeited. As a result, several laws have been enacted to protect the developers of hardware and software. Until these laws are fully enforced, the lack of effective protection may reduce sales revenues.

Proposed changes to the tax law, requiring mail order companies to "charge sales tax and return it to the customer's state, would put a lot of mail order firms out of business" (Foremski, 1989). These tax changes would allow local vendors, such as us, to compete more effectively with mail order firms.

3. Media Environment

A positive trend toward personal computers has emerged lately. Reputable magazines and newspapers continue to emphasize the importance of the personal computers in our lives. An increasing number of articles have been published that provide first-time buyers with detailed advice on how to purchase personal computers and related software (*U.S. News, PC Magazine, PC Computing*).

4. Special Interest Groups

Special interest groups, such as Compuserve® and Prodigy®, may provide us with a potential segmentation of our target market. According to Michael Miller (chief consultant for Compu-Ade), nearly 25% of his sales to first-time buyers are attributable to multiapplication modem services, such as Compuserve® and Prodigy®.

A second special interest environment actually has nothing to do with personal computers alone. In the metropolitan areas of Southern California, transportation gridlock and work-to-home commutes are major topics on the minds of people today. A recent *Los Angeles Times* study (1989), in conjunction with KNX 1070 AM radio, reported that in-home computer use is a viable alternative to the transportation problem. Many government and corporate firms are now allowing employees to work out of the home, with many more companies to follow in the future. These changes in employers' attitudes provide us with a great opportunity to sell systems to individuals who want to work at home.

C. The Company Environment

Because technology is changing so rapidly, customer dissatisfaction is a common problem for most first-time buyers. Therefore, we plan to market a product that will provide a combination of hardware components and applications software, plus toll-free customer support and training, that will accommodate the current and future needs of most first-time buyers.

Various types of personal computer architectures are currently in use. Apple®, and IBM and its clones, are the computers most widely used in schools, businesses, and homes. IBM and its compatible totally dominate the business world, while

Apple® computers are usually found at schools. For this reason, we shall concentrate on IBM compatible computers only. For a detailed breakdown of our product, please refer to the section on Product Tactics.

We feel that the strength of our company lies in our ability to provide the technical support required by our customers. We base this on the following facts:

- We have a combined 30 man-years of experience in data processing.
- We possess the technical expertise necessary to support our customers' needs, in our knowledge of both hardware and software.
- We have the financial background necessary to acquire and provide the financing required by our customers.
- We have a combined 20 man/years of experience in teaching and training in software packages.
- We have been using personal computers since 1977.

D. The Competitor Environment

Sales of personal computers is evolving from a highly centralized corporate environment, such as Businessland, Computerland, Radio Shack, etc., to a more competitive, neighborhood-oriented store and mail order companies. The sales of software has been left almost completely to mail order services and a few big software retailers, such as Egghead.

Late last year, Headstart® computers started marketing the same concept as the one we plan. They sell a complete system, bundled with software and telephone support, and provide their own service facility. Other companies, such as Radio Shack, have also marketed systems bundled with some software, but in a package not as complete as Headstart's.

According to the *Consumer Buying Guide Report* (1989), Headstart's primary product is based on the obsolete 8088 microchip. It includes a monochrome monitor, two 5¼ floppy, 512K memory, multi I/O card, and a regular keyboard. The software included with the system is made up basically of the same packages that we have selected (minus the last three options). The retail price for this package is $995. In our opinion, one of Headstart's weaknesses is that instead of known brand names, they include their own unknown versions of these products.

Mail order companies provide a multitude of hardware combinations and brand name software packages. Their prices are usually lower than in local stores, because of lower overhead factors, no sales tax, no need for technical support, and because the customer pays for the freight charges (Foremski, 1989). A major drawback is the lack of customer support. Merchandise is sometimes delivered damaged and returns and exchanges are not processed as quickly as the orders. Technical advice is not readily available and the consumer is expected to know already exactly what he/she is buying before making the phone call; no advice is provided over the phone.

Retailers, such as Egghead, dominate the software part of the business. By providing lower-than-average prices and excellent customer support, they have become the largest retailer of personal computer software. By concentrating on sales to major companies, they are able to purchase large quantities, which in turn allow them to offer lower prices to the average consumer. The only potential drawback to their operation is that they do not sell any hardware components.

TARGET MARKET ANALYSIS

A. Characteristics

Although the market in 1984 (the last year when adequate data were readily available) was composed primarily of people in the $50,000 income range, with a high level of education, we believe that is no longer the case. It is important to note that prices of personal computers in 1984 were up to four times higher than they are today for comparable systems. This is a trend that we have observed not only personally, but by looking through advertisements in older issues of computer periodicals, such as *PC Magazine* and *PC Computing*.

For these reasons, we have determined that our target market will remain basically in the same age group, 35 to 44 years old, with children. However, as a result of lower prices of personal computers and related software, we can now focus on the $25,000 to $60,000 income range.

By lowering our target income level, we can market to those groups that have not been able to purchase a personal computer in the past. This, we believe, was due to the relationship of high prices and lower disposable income. As prices have dropped, income for most people has also increased.

B. Location Analysis

Once our target market was defined, the next step was to select our geographical location. For this purpose, we have selected, as a test site, five cities in the San Gabriel valley: Alhambra, Monterey Park, Temple City, Rosemead, and San Gabriel.

C. Demographics Analysis

The demographics supporting our decision were based on the REZIDE and CACI publications, from which the following numbers were derived:

- Total combined population   331,998
- Total households   124,493
- Households with incomes over $25,000   60.0%

- Households with children   27.1%
- Nonfamily households   29.44%
- Population in the 35–44 years range   13.18%
- Population under 18 years   26.8%
- Population with some college education   45.4%
- Population that already owns a PC   9.0%

These numbers ratify our marketing decision to focus on the 35 to 44 age group, which more than likely has children under the age of 18 living at home. It accounts for a combined 40% of the total population in this area. Furthermore, over 72,000 households have incomes greater than $25,000 and almost half, 45.4 percent, of the population have attended at least one year of college.

D. Media Analysis

An analysis of the four major forms of media was conducted to determine the media characteristics of our target market.

1. Television

Based on Arbitron's system of Areas of Dominant Influence, which measures each county's viewing patterns, households in the San Gabriel Valley ranked 91st among the nation's leading television viewers (*Sales and Mar-*

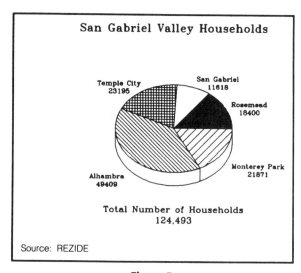

Figure 5

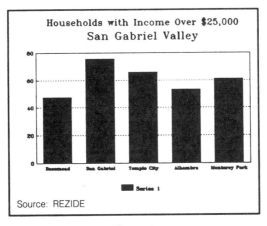

Figure 6

keting, 1987). According to a recent survey of television viewing habits, 90.1 percent of all college graduates view television on a regular basis.

2. Radio

AM radio has been losing audience share to the clean stereo sound of FM. The holdover AM fans are older and poorer than audiences advertisers prefer (*Newsweek*, 1988). Despite this downward trend, audiences are still

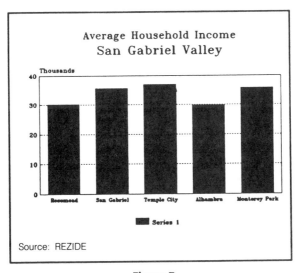

Figure 7

listening to radio. A recent survey reported that national expenditures for TV sets and radios has increased from $19.9 billion in 1980 to $41.2 billion in 1987. It is estimated that 93.7 percent of 23–39-year-olds listen to radio.

3. Newspapers

A recent study reports that for residents living in the San Gabriel Valley with a combined effective income of over $24 billion, over 50 percent of the households subscribe to newspapers (*Sales and Marketing*, 1988). According to a recent report, 89.1 percent of households with incomes of $35,000 to $44,000 read newspapers regularly (*Statistical Abstract*, 1989).

In the San Gabriel Valley, the *Tribune News* enjoys a paid circulation of 60,884 for the morning edition and 81,975 for the Sunday edition (*Information Please Almanac*, 1989).

4. Magazines

Based on a sample survey of 1,429 respondents, 24 percent with a college-level education read magazines. In the same survey, 39 percent of the households with incomes between $25,000 and $44,000 read magazines. At the national level, expenditures for magazines and newspapers have increased over 50 percent, from $10.4 billion in 1980 to $15.8 billion in 1987 (*Statistical Abstract*, 1989).

PROBLEMS AND OPPORTUNITIES

Poor Customer Support

"A large percentage of first-time computer buyers end up never using their systems because they made a poor choice or never receive training in computer use. This situation is caused by a widespread lack of technical support for inexperienced users" (Jenkin, 1989). The primary goal of our company will be to fill this void for first-time computer buyers. We believe that by emphasizing free customer support, and providing the proper combination of hardware and software at a reasonable and competitive price, we can successfully fill this void. An example of a company that has successfully tried this approach of unlimited toll-free support and has gained over 50% share of their market, is WordPerfect Corp. (*Wright*, 1988).

Gridlock and Working Out of the Home

We can segment the market further by providing an optional modem, and related software, to people who may eventually want to work out of the home. We can take advantage of this opportunity by offering this optimal package to our customer at cost.

Competitive Pricing

A major problem facing our company will be arriving at a competitive, yet profitable, pricing scheme, since "low prices entice U.S. consumers to buy microcomputers through the mail, now a major part of the computer market" (Foremski, 1989). Even though mail order companies do not provide the support needed for first-time buyers, they offer extremely low, tax-free prices that lure inexperienced users. We believe that the lack of support is such a major problem that, with the proper marketing, we can offset the low mail order prices by emphasizing our toll-free support.

MARKETING OBJECTIVES AND GOALS

Our primary objectives are to:

- gain a **23.5%** share of the market
- earn **18.54%** return on initial investment
- achieve **$6.24** million on sales the first year
- achieve thereafter **28.5%** growth through sales and good service

Our primary competition currently has a 58% share of the personal computer market (see Figure 8). Because of our concentration in the San Gabriel Valley area,

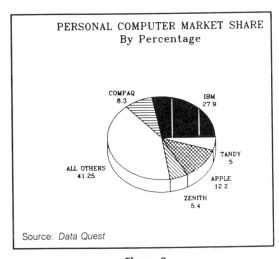

Figure 8

we expect to take away 40% from their share of the market in three years. This allows us to project a 23.5% share of the total potential target market.

Based on the results of our demographic analysis, we believe we will accomplish the following goals with a total expenditure of $1,200,000 for advertisement and promotion:

- Total households   124,493
- Households in our target market (42%)   52,287
- Potential sales (10% target households) $47,059
- Target unit sales (approximately 23.5 share) $11,059
  - First-year sales $2,500
  - Second-year sales $3,500
  - Third-year sales $4,900
- Return on investment (NI/Investment)   18.54%
  - Initial investment $125,000
  - Net income (first year) $148,170

MARKETING STRATEGY

A. Positioning

We feel we can maintain a strong position in the market because we have the technical expertise to provide our customers with total service and support. Because of our close proximity to the downtown Los Angeles area and the Inland Empire, we feel we can be in a competitive position to quickly expand our market in the near future.

Recommended activities designed to aggressively achieve the foregoing objectives are based on the following major points of marketing strategy:

- Differentiate our product from our competition
- Segment our target market
- Develop/exploit a niche market
- Establish ourselves both technically and geographically
- Competitor's position

1. Product Differentiation

The main part of our overall marketing strategy is to differentiate our product from our competitors'. To achieve this goal, we bundle brand name software with hardware and provide excellent customer support and training.

Headstart, our main competitor, bundles hardware and their own software as a complete package. We will distinguish our product by introducing a package that features well-known, popular brand name software. Additionally, we plan to publish a monthly newsletter, free of charge, to all of our customers. Combined with toll-free telephone support, this approach will allow us to develop an image, in the customers' minds, that they are buying a system that is a step above Headstart.

We know of no other competitor that offers such a comprehensive system at such an affordable price. We feel this approach will help us become a leader in the personal computer market.

2. Segmentation

Our primary target market is the first-time personal computer buyer. We plan to divide this group into two segments:

- First-time buyers with no prior personal computer knowledge
- First-time buyers with working knowledge of personal computers

3. Niche Markets

Although our current market is first-time buyers, we plan to expand horizontally by introducing our product to two growing segments of the population:

- Small home businesses
- Tele-commuters

B. Competitors' Reaction

It is our expectation that as our business becomes more successful, our competitors will attempt to provide the same services, or more, at the same or lower price.

While anticipating the competition's reaction to our success, we plan to expand vertically by:

- Changing our product mix, based on customer's feedback and technological advancements
- Lowering our price as a result of natural business efficiencies
- Increasing our promotional incentives

MARKETING TACTICS

The following tactics will help us to achieve our goals and implement our strategies:

A. Product

Based on projected sales of seven systems per day, we plan to maintain enough inventory to cover a six-week period, which is approximately 252 systems. Our main warehouse should maintain a minimum of 204 systems. To provide immediate delivery to in-store customers, each retail outlet will carry 48 systems in stock at all times. Each package that we sell will be made up of the following components:

1. Hardware

Various hardware components will be purchased from different manufacturers at high-volume discounts, and assembled at our sites. A basic configuration will look like this:

CPU	80286 based
Memory	640 kilobytes
Monitor	Monochrome, Hercules high resolution card Color, VGA adapter card (optional)
Storage	20 megabyte hard disk 40 megabyte hard disk (optional) 1.44 megabyte, 3½ high density drive 1.2 megabyte, 5¼ high density drive (optional)
Keyboard	101 key enhanced
Ports	1 parallel (for printer) 2 serial (mouse and modem) 2 game port
Modem	An internal 300/1200/2400 Baud rate (optional)

2. Software

The fact that a large number of users (61.1%) are in managerial and/or professional occupations has led us to decide that the software we include must be the same as or highly compatible with the software being used at work. According to *Duffy R* (1985), a survey of personal computer buyers indicated that "89% said that the price of the software package did not affect their buying decision." For these reasons the following packages will be purchased directly from the software developers:

- *MS DOS 3.31:* The operating system needed to execute programs.
- *Learning DOS:* An easy-to-use, step-by-step, on-line tutorial of the operating system.
- *Le Menu:* A menu-generator, multipurpose disk management utility. Extremely easy to use.
- *WordPerfect:* The most widely used word processor in the business (Wright, 1988). Easy enough for the novice user, yet extremely powerful for advanced users.
- *Quattro:* A spread sheet, 100% Lotus compatible. Easier to learn than Lotus and a lot cheaper.
- *Managing Your Money:* A popular package that allows you to maintain a budget, pay bills, keep track of one's financial status, stock portfolio and many more (optional).
- *Children Publishing Center:* A word processor designed specially for children ages 8–14, extremely easy to use, combines graphics and text.
- *Game:* A choice of two computer games, from a selected list of over 100 titles, or a banner/sign maker program, such as Banner Mania (optional).
- *Xtalk:* A telecommunications software package (optional for those purchasing a modem).

3. Product/Customer Support

In addition to the hardware and software configurations stated above, our standard package will also provide:

- Up to 20 hours of training, to be used at the customer's discretion
- Unlimited toll-free telephone customer support
- On-site repair services, for up to two years
- Free delivery and installation
- Free monthly newsletter, providing tips and advice

B. Distribution

Since Upstart is marketed as a powerful, complete computer system with basic functions for the first-time user, our strategy will be to use the "direct" approach. We will purchase our computer hardware and software products directly from the various manufacturers and distribute them through two retail outlets to our customers. In addition, we will provide intensive training and support right on the spot.

We plan to lease a central warehouse located in south El Monte. This low-income area was chosen because square footage is cheaper there than elsewhere and because it is geographically near our retail outlets.

We will lease two retail outlets, located in Temple City and Monterey Park. Both outlets will tap into our target cities and other areas not covered in this marketing plan.

C. Pricing

The regular retail price of our complete package will be $2,499. However, during the introductory period, a 10% coupon will bring this price down to $2,250. Based on the quality of the products being bundled, we feel our price is highly competitive. Even though our price is not high, considering the wide array of free support included and brand name software, we want to project an image of a high-quality product.

Based on the assumption that the personal computer industry operates on a 30% profit markup, we were able to derive our costs from published retail prices on the following products:

80286 CPU	$285
Power Supply	120
640K Memory	70
VGA Monitor	350
20 MB hard disk	190
1.44 MB 3½ drive	90
1.2 MB 5¼ drive	75
Keyboard	55
Multi I/O Ports	20
Modem	120
MS DOS 3.31	90
Learning DOS	40
Le Menu	40
WordPerfect	215
Quattro	100
Managing Your Money	200
Children Publishing Center	30
Game	40
Xtalk	100
Total Price	$2,230

Our cost is derived by the formula:

$$\text{Retail Price} \times .70 = \text{our cost}$$
$$\$2{,}230 \times .70 = \$1560$$

D. Sales Promotion

The primary objective of our sales promotion plan is to inform and convince first-time buyers of personal computers of the benefits of owning an Upstart personal computer system. Through the marketing tactics of advertising, personal selling, and sales promotion, we hope to achieve product awareness, product interest, and, ultimately, product adoption by the end of the first six months of our campaign.

1. Advertising

The advertising campaign will be launched throughout the first year. During the first six months of the product introductory stage, advertising will be extremely heavy promoting the Upstart system and its related support services. A competitive advertisement format will be used to point out how consumers will benefit from Upstart's features and advantages not available in other similar brands.

At the end of the six months, advertising will be reduced in order to evaluate its effectiveness on sales.

The media plan used to penetrate out target audiences includes San Gabriel Valley newspapers, local radio stations, direct mail, and specialty magazines. The following is an outline of the plan:

a. *Newspapers*

- Two local San Gabriel Valley editions (the *San Gabriel Valley Tribune* and the *Los Angeles Times*) are expected to cover the primary purchase group
- Print advertisement will be one full page, four times a month, in each edition (for six months)

The advantages of using newspapers are:

- Almost everyone reads them
- Geographically flexible
- Frequent publications

b. *Radio*
Radio spot time will be used primarily on the basis of:

- Three popular radio stations, KJOI, KOST, KNX, providing coverage of an estimated 100% of the targeted market segment
- Each radio copy will be in the form of 30-second commercials between 6:00 A.M. and 9:00 A.M. with emphasis on quality and simplicity
- Air time will be five days a week for the first six months; however, evaluation of its effectiveness on sales will be exercised at the end of each month

The advantages of using radio are:

- Low cost
- If necessary, message can be changed quickly
- A large part of the segmented market audiences can be reached quickly
- Geographically selective

c. *Direct Mail*

Direct mail will be used in the form of brochures, coupons, circulars, newsletters, and post cards. The mailings will include:

- A full color copy of the Upstart system and details about its features and qualities
- 50,000 solo mailings in each category will go out monthly for six months
- The brochures and circulars will be four-color card stock. Each mailing will include a business reply card and a coupon
- Monthly newsletter will provide information, tips, and upcoming proportional activity about Upstart
- Post cards will be mailed singularly and inserted in mailings

The advantages of direct mail are:

- A highly selective market
- Personal
- Stimulates action
- Measures performance
- Is hidden from competitors

d. *Specialty Magazines*

A monthly computer magazine geared for beginners will display a full-page, four-color print advertisement of Upstart®. The add will run for six months.

The advantages of using a specialty magazine are:

- Socioeconomic selectivity
- Geographic location
- Appeal to the targeted market

We believe our advertisement plan will be extremely cost-efficient because it will reach a large number of our segmented market at a low cost per person.

2. Personal Selling

Through personal selling we will be able to fully inform customers about our product and persuade them to purchase Upstart. The ability to use personal communication will enable sales personnel to highlight the advantages of our systems over the competition. Additionally, the advantage of immediate consumer feedback will allow us to adjust our promotional format accordingly. For example, improving communication techniques will ensure our message is getting across to the customer; or, awareness of our competition's offerings will assist us in developing and maintaining customer satisfaction. An outline of our sales promotion plan follows:

- Support personnel will facilitate the selling function by educating customers, building good will, and providing service after the sale.
- Technical salespersons will provide the technical expertise necessary to advise customers of the product's characteristics and applications.
- Sales personnel will be highly trained technicians with excellent communications skills.

3. Sales Promotion

Through sales promotion activities, we hope to stimulate primary demand in the first six months by reaching 60% of our potential target market and establishing sales of $3.75 million. This marketing tactic will produce quick short-term results. Our objectives are to:

- Introduce the product
- Educate our customers
- Bring new customers to the retail outlet

We can encourage potential consumers to patronize our retail outlets and purchase Upstart® by using the following sales promotions methods:

- Free samples of floppy diskettes will be handed out to walk-in customers.
- Coupons will be strategically placed in direct mail pamphlets, offering 10% off the purchase price. Coupons will stimulate sales volume quickly and attract purchasers. It is estimated that 80% of all households use coupons.

4. Promotional Allocations

Twenty percent of estimated sales for fiscal year 1990 will be appropriated for promotion costs as follows:

Advertising	$ 840,000	70%
20% Newspapers	$ 168,000	
20% Radio	$ 168,000	
30% Direct Mail	$ 252,000	
25% Magazines	$ 210,000	
5% Miscellaneous	$ 42,000	
Sales Promotion	$ 300,000	25%
45% Free samples	$ 135,000	
45% Coupons	$ 135,000	
5% Promotion Materials	$ 15,000	
5% Miscellaneous Expenses	$ 15,000	
General Reserves	$ 60,000	5%
TOTAL BUDGET	$1,200,000	100%

CONTROL AND IMPLEMENTATION

The following pages contain information that shows our break-even analysis, projected income statements for the first three years, projected balance sheet for the first three years, and projected cash flow for the first year, by month. Break-even point calculated by equation:

$$BE = \frac{FC}{P - VC}$$

SUMMARY

Changes to current environments in both the business and nonbusiness worlds have led to an explosion in the use of personal computers. This product is making a

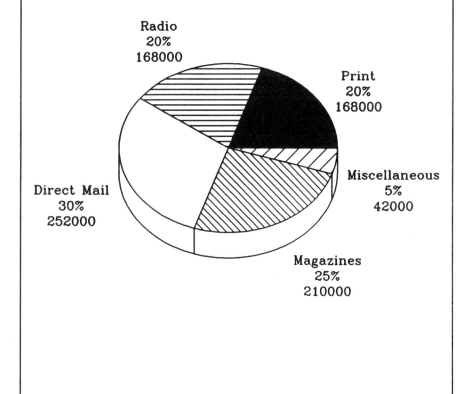

Figure 9

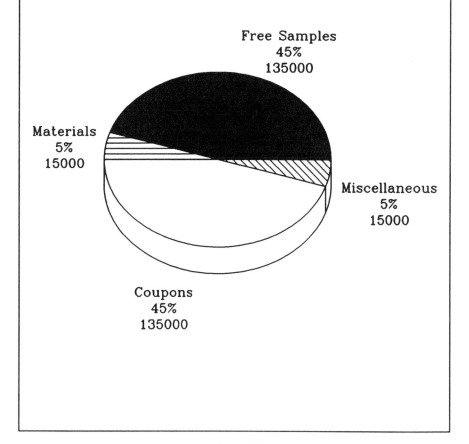

SALES PROMOTION ALLOCATION
In Dollars

Free Samples
45%
135000

Materials
5%
15000

Miscellaneous
5%
15000

Coupons
45%
135000

Figure 10

Breakeven Analysis		
Fixed Costs	180,500	FC
Variable Costs	1,560	VC
Price	2,500	P
Breakeven Point	192	Units

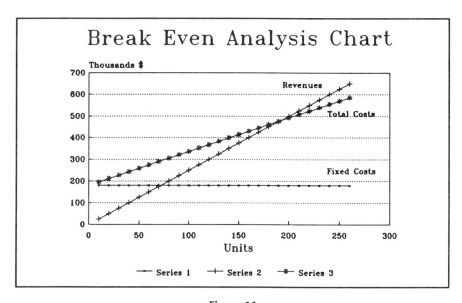

Figure 11

transition from being a piece of office equipment, to becoming a featured asset in the home.

Upstart computers is positioned to take full advantage of this evolution. More and more households will soon be purchasing computer systems. Upstart will be there to make the initial buy as easy as possible. We anticipate gaining a 23.5% share of the San Gabriel Valley market by providing a complete system of popular, brand name hardware and software. Our growth rate of 28.5% will be achieved through excellent services and follow-up, with training, personal contact, and toll-free telephone service. This one-on-one service, combined with reputable products, is the differential advantage of Upstart computers over our established or would-be competitors.

PROJECTED INCOME STATEMENTS			
	1990	1991	1992
Gross Sales	6,247,500	8,746,500	12,245,100
Cost of Goods Sold	3,900,000	5,460,000	7,644,000
Selling & Administrative	150,000	210,000	294,000
Total Cost of Goods	4,050,000	5,670,000	7,938,000
Gross Margin	2,197,500	3,076,500	4,307,100
Start-up Costs	50,000	0	0
Promotion Costs	1,200,000	1,680,000	2,352,000
Delivery	40,000	56,000	78,400
Salaries	400,000	560,000	784,000
Supplies	50,000	70,000	98,000
Rent	67,000	93,800	131,320
Utilities	66,000	92,400	129,360
Miscellaneous Expenses	100,000	140,000	196,000
Total Expenses	1,973,000	2,692,200	3,769,080
Net Income Before Taxes	224,500	384,300	538,020
Taxes (34%)	76,330	130,662	182,927
Net Income	148,170	253,638	355,093

Notes:

Year	Units	Price	Unit CGS
1991:	2,500	$2,499	$1,560
1992:	3,500	$2,499	$1,560
1993:	4,900	$2,499	$1,560

Taxes were calculated at 34%. No increases are expected in the next 3 years.

BALANCE SHEET			
	1990	1991	1992
Current Assets			
Cash	346,000	484,400	678,160
Accounts Receivable	147,000	205,800	288,120
Inventory	260,000	364,000	509,600
	753,000	1,054,200	1,475,880
Fixed Assets			
Real Estate	0	0	0
Fixtures and Equipment	230,000	230,000	230,000
Vehicles	40,000	52,000	64,000
	270,000	282,000	294,000
Total Assets	1,023,000	1,336,200	1,769,880
Current Liabilities			
Notes Payable	0	0	0
Accounts Payable	230,000	322,000	414,000
Accrued Expenses	122,000	128,100	134,200
Taxes Owed	228,000	319,200	410,400
	580,000	769,300	958,600
Long Term Liabilities			
Notes Payables	15,000	15,000	15,000
	15,000	15,000	15,000
Total Liabilities	595,000	784,300	973,600
Net Worth	428,000	551,900	796,280
Liabilities & Net Worth	1,023,000	1,336,200	1,769,880

First Year Cash-Flow Projections by Month

	Start	01	02	03	04	05	06	07	08	09	10	11	12	Total
Cash	5	5	5	5	5	5	5	5	5	5	5	5	5	
Deposits	120	20	20	20	20	20	20	20	20	20	20	20	20	
Total Cash	125	25	25	25	25	25	25	25	25	25	25	25	25	25
Cash Sales	0	240	240	240	240	240	240	240	240	240	240	240	240	2,880
Credit Sales	0	290	290	290	290	290	290	290	290	290	290	290	290	3,480
Total Income	0	530	530	530	530	530	530	530	530	530	530	530	530	6,360
Total sources	125	555	555	555	555	555	555	555	555	555	555	555	555	6,785
Inventory	262.1	424.2	149.8	149.8	149.8	149.	149.8	149.8	149.8	149.8	149.8	149.8	149.8	2,334
Wages	0	33.4	33.4	33.4	33.4	33.4	33.4	33.4	33.4	33.4	33.4	33.4	33.4	401
Taxes	0	20	20	20	20	20	20	20	20	20	20	20	20	240
Supplies	4.5	4.5	4.9	4.9	4.9	4.9	4.9	4.9	4.9	4.9	4.9	4.9	4.9	63
Overhead	0	5.5	5.5	5.5	5.5	5.5	5.5	5.5	5.5	5.5	5.5	5.5	5.5	66
Promotions	0	100	100	100	100	100	100	100	100	100	100	100	100	1,200
Deliveries	3.4	3.4	3.4	3.4	3.4	3.4	3.4	3.4	3.4	3.4	3.4	3.4	3.4	44
Lease	0	5.6	5.6	5.6	5.6	5.6	5.6	5.6	5.6	5.6	5.6	5.6	5.6	67
Miscellaneous	0	8.4	8.4	8.4	8.4	8.4	8.4	8.4	8.4	8.4	8.4	8.4	8.4	101
Total Uses	270	605	331	331	331	331	331	331	331	331	331	331	331	4,516
Excess	(145)	(50)	224	224	224	224	224	224	224	224	224	224	224	
Cumulative Flow	(145)	(195)	29	253	477	701	925	1,149	1,373	1,597	1,821	2,045	2,269	2,269

With sales provided at two convenient retail locations, an investor should expect an 18.54% return on initial investment. Upstart will be in the forefront of the first-time personal computer buyer market.

BIBLIOGRAPHY

CACI, California Profiles, pp. 25A–25D, 26A–26D.

Consumer Buying Guide Report (1989), pp. 203–205.

Cooper, James, & Madigan, Kathleen, "Inflation Won't Cool Off," *Business Week*, 5 February 1989, pp. 19–20.

Foremski, Tom, "Mail Order Alternative," *PC User*, 11 October 1989, p. 74.

Home Computer Systems, Consumer Trend Analysis, Los Angeles Times Marketing Research Department, June 1984.

Information Please Almanac (1989).

Jenkin, Dennis, "Insiders: Write Behind the Action," *PC User*, 2 August 1989, p. 97.

McCrossen, Stephanie, "The Industry Looks to Networking," *Computers and Office Equipment*, 1989, pp. C75–C78.

"Radio Audiences Speak Up," *Newsweek*, 19 December 1988, p. 47.

REZIDE (1984), *PC User*, pp. 39–47.

Sales and Marketing Management, "Guide to TV Marketing," 26 October 1987.

Sales and Marketing Management, "Survey of Newspapers Markets," 7 November 1988.

Simmons Market Research Bureau, 1987, "Personal Computers," pp. P8–0285, P8–0324.

Statistical Abstract of the United States, 1989, pp. 743–744.

U.S. Bureau of the Census, "Computer Use in the United States: 1984," 1984.

Wright, Carla, "What's So Special About WordPerfect?" *Personal Computing*, March 1988, pp. 100–116.

INDEX